POLICING COMPASSION

Do you give to someone begging? For centuries, the figure of the beggar has caused public fear, sympathy and confusion. In this book, criminologist Joe Hermer explores how the dilemma of giving to someone begging today has become an unusual site of regulation, public inquiry and law reform. This book investigates why handing pocket change to someone begging is now widely viewed as a gift crime, one that attempts to make the giving public complicit in the policing and control of visibly poor people.

Drawing on the historical insight that public feeling is a central problem of policing the vagrant beggar, the author examines how a quirky provincial experiment to stop people giving to beggars morphed into an unlikely movement across England. Hermer ranges widely in his analysis, with discussions of 'diverted giving' schemes, specialised police operations, activist efforts to repeal the Vagrancy Law, and begging-like activities such as busking, Big Issue vending and flag day collections. The author pays particular attention to the Vagrancy Act 1824 and the historic reforms enabled by gift crime regulation to this storied area of criminal law. The consequence, this book argues, is the continuing abandonment of some of the most vulnerable individuals in society through direct appeals to compassion and kindness.

Policing Compassion

Begging, Law and Power in Public Spaces

Joe Hermer

·HART·

OXFORD · LONDON · NEW YORK · NEW DELHI · SYDNEY

HART PUBLISHING

Bloomsbury Publishing Plc

Kemp House, Chawley Park, Cumnor Hill, Oxford, OX2 9PH, UK

1385 Broadway, New York, NY 10018, USA

29 Earlsfort Terrace, Dublin 2, Ireland

HART PUBLISHING, the Hart/Stag logo, BLOOMSBURY and the Diana logo are
trademarks of Bloomsbury Publishing Plc

First published in Great Britain 2019

First published in hardback, 2019
Paperback edition, 2021

A catalogue record for this book is available from the British Library.

Library of Congress Cataloging-in-Publication Data

Names: Hermer, Joe, 1967- author.

Title: Policing compassion : begging, law and power in public spaces / Joe Hermer.

Description: Oxford ; New York : Hart, 2019. | Includes bibliographical references and index.

Identifiers: LCCN 2019028799 (print) | LCCN 2019028800 (ebook) | ISBN 9781841132693 (HB) |
ISBN 9781509901197 (ePDF) | ISBN 9781509901203 (EPub)

Subjects: LCSH: Begging—Great Britain. | Begging—Law and
legislation—Great Britain. | Compassion—Great Britain.

Classification: LCC HV4545.A4 H47 2019 (print) | LCC HV4545.A4 (ebook) | DDC 364.1/4—dc23

LC record available at https://lccn.loc.gov/2019028799

LC ebook record available at https://lccn.loc.gov/2019028800

ISBN: HB: 978-1-84113-269-3
PB: 978-1-50995-272-4
ePDF: 978-1-50990-119-7
ePub: 978-1-50990-120-3

Typeset by Compuscript Ltd, Shannon

To find out more about our authors and books visit www.hartpublishing.co.uk. Here you will find
extracts, author information, details of forthcoming events and the option to sign up for our newsletters.

For my mother

How often in the overflowing Streets
Have I gone forward with the Crowd, and said
Unto myself, the face of everyone
That passes by me is a mystery …

William Wordsworth – *The Prelude*, 1888

Streets can nicely provide the ingredients for a character contest

Erving Goffman – *Relations in Public*, 1971

ACKNOWLEDGEMENTS

The foundation of this book was my doctoral thesis at the Centre for Socio-Legal Studies at the University of Oxford. A very real debt of gratitude remains to my supervisor Professor Keith Hawkins. Others who assisted me with that early work include Mavis Maclean, Doreen McBarnet, Richard Young, Michael Adler, David Downes and Lord William Bradshaw.

Many friends and colleagues provided assistance and encouragement at crucial times: Kim Stanford, Jonathan Simon, Julian Tanner, Alan Hunt, Janet Mosher, Mariana Valverde, Patricia Landolt, David Simmonds, Bruce Curtis, Jennifer Wood, Richard Hart and the late Richard Ericson. A special thanks to Deirdre McCann and David MacGregor, who diligently read parts of the manuscript at key points.

I thank the many officials who were extremely generous with their time and assistance in interviews or obtaining materials. Special thanks to 'Citizen B', who was crucial in providing materials on the ASA adjudication; to Matthias Kelly QC and Ruth Bush, who provided me access to the archives of End the Vagrancy Act (EVA); and to the Home Office, which allowed me access to the preserved papers of the 1976 Working Party on Vagrancy and Street Offences, before they were released into the public domain. I am grateful to Hartley Dean and Rowland Atkinson, who included early work on this project in workshops in Luton and Glasgow.

My research assistants Prashan Ranasinghe, Mriganka Saxena, Reem Radhi and Kimia Fardfini provided valuable field support and technical assistance at various stages of this project.

Many thanks to my Toronto editor, Gillian Watts, who tirelessly worked on the manuscript at crucial stages. Lastly, I am indebted to Sinead Moloney and Sasha Jawed at Hart Publishing, who exercised both great enthusiasm and unflagging patience. This book would not have been possible without their support.

CONTENTS

LIST OF ILLUSTRATIONS

LIST OF TABLES

Introduction

Q. Do you give money to beggars?

A. I don't, no. I do buy the *Big Issue* occasionally but I don't put that in the same category. I don't want to make a big thing of it, but I make certain donations to charities.

Tony Blair, 1997[1]

When we approach the vagrant in the spirit of charity, we are merely advertising ourselves in order to seduce him into our ideology; when we approach him juridically, we are trying to justify ourselves by means of his annihilation. He shows us our weakness, and he shows us the utter equivocation of our morality. We cannot in good faith say that he is as he is because he is wicked; because we know only too well the ethical poverty of our own successful practice.

Philip O'Connor[2]

I. Gift Crimes

During the historic 1997 election campaign, the question 'Do you give to beggars?' circulated in everyday conversation as a sort of moral litmus test about where one stood after almost two decades of radical Conservative reform. For some, people begging on the street stood as a kind of accusation to the public that something had gone badly wrong in how we collectively cared for one another. For others, however, the hands of people cadging change were evidence of the success of a reformed welfare state that had flushed out lazy and incorrigible scroungers who no longer had an easy ride on the public purse. With Tony Blair, the connotation was clear enough: if such a future prime minister can steel his heart and hold his pocket change within arm's reach of a poor person asking for money, then surely he would be just as tight-fisted about distributing welfare funds from the Treasury coffers. At a time when New Labour was anxious to prove that it could be both fiscally conservative and 'tough on crime and the causes of crime', Blair's passing by of the beggar performed a potent allegory: even if those people living and begging on the street were victims of Thatcherism, a Blair government was not going to be a soft touch and indulge in handouts.

---

[1] 'Tony Blair', *The Big Issue* 214 (6–12 January 1997).
[2] P O'Connor, *Britain in the Sixties: Vagrancy, Ethos and Actuality* (London, Penguin, 1963).

Figure 1 Thames Reach Bondway 'Money-man' diverted-giving poster, London 2003 (photo by author)

Twenty-two years later, the beggar continues to haunt the public conscience and provoke the most human of questions about what we owe strangers who ask our help. At a time of widespread austerity and divisive debates about inequality, when much of our political discourse is about giving and taking, the encounter between the beggar and the passer-by has become an extraordinary site of regulation and public inquiry. In cities across England, police services, city councils, town centre managers, high-street retailers, and even some homeless advocates are involved in widespread campaigns to stop the public from giving to those begging. Officials warn that to give to a beggar is to be tricked by a fraud who is pretending to be homeless, and who will use this cadged money to feed his drug addiction. The public is urged to 'hold that thought' of giving at the sight of a beggar, to 'think before you give', to 'focus' their pocket change, to 'make every penny count', by 'giving to the box not the beggar'. These prescriptions for modern-day alms are often accompanied by 'alternative' or 'diverted' giving opportunities that encourage donations to established homelessness services, often through specially designed charity boxes. Some cities have even urged the public to 'text' a charitable donation instead of dropping pocket change into the hands of a drug addict.

The most visible examples of these diverted-giving programmes are 'Your Kindness Can Kill' campaigns. As illustrated in the original campaign poster developed by Thames Reach in 2003 (see Figure 1), officials are explicit that giving to someone begging may even help to buy the drugs that kill them. Giving '20p for a cup of tea' to a beggar is really contributing '£10 for a bag of heroin' or '£12 for a rock of crack'. The result of giving to a beggar is the corpse of a 'money-man', his prostrate body made up of the pocket change of a gullible and unsuspecting public. The beggar on the street now represents the scene of a possible 'gift crime', where the kindness of someone giving to a beggar makes them directly complicit in the suffering and death of a drug addict. There are currently 31 Your Kindness Can Kill schemes in England, with at least 15 of them using the 'money-man' icon promoted by Thames Reach.[3]

If these 'diverted-giving' schemes consisted simply of scattered local projects, one might find them novel, but probably of limited importance to criminologists and social policy scholars. However, over the last 20 years, initiatives that have attempted to stop people from giving to beggars have morphed into a national gift-crime movement, one that has attempted to relocate begging from an aspect of rough sleeping to solely an expression of drug addiction and disorder. The most formal consequences of this movement have been new reforms to historic vagrancy law powers. In a series of largely unnoticed changes between 2003 and 2005, the archaic Vagrancy Act 1824 has been rearmed with a new offence of 'persistent begging', accompanied by increased policing powers and expanded forms of surveillance.

The now widely circulated representation of those begging as drug users who are not legitimately homeless – and thus deserving of new policing and crime control attention – stands in dramatic contrast with what is known about the lives and experience of those who beg and sleep rough in England. The great majority of people who beg and sleep rough are desperately poor, hungry, traumatised, and in dire need of medical and social services, including drug and alcohol treatment. The ongoing movement to label people begging as fake homeless who are a fraud on public kindness is a grotesque denial of the face of poverty in the early twenty-first century.

To understand this clearly, one must first observe the differences in how begging, rough sleeping and homelessness are officially organised as distinct populations that nonetheless overlap in complex ways. Homelessness in England is measured by the number of people to whom a housing duty is owed by local authorities. These duties are defined in the Housing Act 1996 (as amended), and the Homelessness Reduction Act 2017. In July 2018, 320,000 people were considered to be homeless in England, a rise of 300 per cent since 2010.[4]

Rough sleepers are a very small subset of homeless people who live out in public places to the extent that they have no place to sleep. Rough-sleeping numbers are literally counted once a year, and include those who are 'bedded down' for the

[3] These include Bury St. Edmunds*, Newcastle upon Tyne, Leeds*, Manchester, Ipswich*, Colchester*, Suffolk, Oxford*, Bath*, Stoke-on-Trent, Winchester, Woking*, Cambridge, Bristol, Liverpool*, Yeovil, City of London*, Tower Hamlets*, Westminster*, Croydon, Maidstone*, Kensington and Chelsea*, Nottingham, Cheshire West and Chester, Southampton, Taunton, Cheltenham, Brighton,* Preston* (* indicates Your Kindness Can Kill–inspired schemes). In a re-branding exercise in 2007, Thames Reach Bondway changed its name to Thames Reach.

[4] MCLG, Statutory homelessness and prevention and relief, January to March (Q1) 2018 England (Revised), 13 December 2018.

night: counts do not include day sleeping or, in fact, any daytime street presence or activities whatsoever, including begging. Rough-sleeper counts have been severely criticised for underreporting, masking a population of the 'hidden homeless'. These counts, for example, do not include a person who is in a hostel or night shelter, or managed to sleep for a night on a friend's couch. In 2018, 4,677 rough sleepers were counted, an increase of 165 per cent since 2010.[5]

There are no official counts of those begging, and the definition of begging used by officials and scholars is literally a 'dictionary' one. So, for example, the recent 2018 Public Health England literature review on begging and rough sleeping offered the following: 'Begging is defined in the dictionary as the solicitation of money or food, especially in the street'.[6] More typically, this definition is given further detail by scholars and officials who attach the proviso that the soliciting is carried out 'without expecting anything in return'.[7] The current criminal offence of begging, which remarkably remains in force in the Vagrancy Act 1824, was enacted to police certain types of people who were 'idle and disorderly'. No definition of 'to beg, or gather alms' was needed: people were presumed to know a slothful and undesirable person when they saw one cadging on the street.

Today, those who sleep rough are a small part of the total number of homeless, and those who beg, many of whom sleep rough, are a small subset of the rough-sleeper population.

The key aspect of this overlap is that rough sleepers tend to be the most victimised and desperate of the homeless population, and those who beg are generally the most despairing of those who sleep rough, who spend the majority of their time trying to survive in public spaces. The scholarly literature is nearly unanimous that there is a strong overlap between begging and rough sleeping, including the 'hidden homeless' in shelters and hostels. A comprehensive literature review of the research on begging and rough sleeping carried out by Public Health England and released in early 2018 noted:

> The relationship between street begging and street sleeping is a complex one, but what is clear from the literature is that those who street beg and/or are street sleepers are some of our most vulnerable individuals. They have a range of complex needs and experience severe and multiple deprivation over long periods of time.[8]

Perhaps the most extensive single research work on begging, commissioned by the Rough Sleepers Unit (RSU) and released in 2001, stated that of the 260 informants across five cities, 49 per cent slept rough in the past week, 33 per cent were in a hostel or night shelter, and 15 per cent stayed with friends. Only 2 per cent

---

[5] House of Commons Library, *Briefing Paper – Rough Sleeping England Number 020077*, 6 February 2019, 3.
[6] Public Health England, *Evidence Review: Adults with complex needs (with a particular focus on street begging and street sleeping)* (London, PHE Publications, 2018) 14.
[7] ibid.
[8] ibid, 29.

reported having their own home.[9] Other studies confirm the general trend that, while not all rough sleepers beg, the majority of those who beg sleep rough or have insecure or inadequate shelter.[10]

Two of the leading homelessness scholars in the UK, Catherine Kennedy and Suzanne Fitzpatrick, have pointed out the hesitancy of even some homelessness agencies to make explicit these connections between begging and rough sleeping:

> Such arguments are often encountered within our study amongst professionals working at a strategic or campaigning level within homelessness agencies, who felt that the link was damaging and stereotyped all homeless people as 'beggars' ... [i]n contrast agency interviewees working directly with rough sleepers commonly reflected that many of their users were engaged in begging.[11]

The result then is what the two scholars term a 'legitimacy crisis', in which those begging on the street are not being seen as a genuinely vulnerable population that is worthy of help and intervention. Those begging present a challenge to homeless advocates and charities that need to present a clear and morally uncomplicated figure that is deserving of assistance and financial support.

For the most victimised and despairing of the homeless, surviving on the streets involves abject human suffering that most people who live comfortable lives would have a difficult time understanding.[12] Rough sleepers and those begging often have to struggle to find food, to keep their bodies and clothes clean, to find private places to go to the bathroom or to use menstrual hygiene products. Those who are homeless and living on the pavement are often traumatised and deeply vulnerable, having suffered severe drug addiction, debilitating mental and physical health problems, sexual abuse and assault. Living on the street not only exacerbates the trauma of this violence and suffering but often provides conditions for further and more horrific victimisation.

Rough sleeping is a prolonged death sentence. A landmark study carried out by Bethan Thomas examined the mortality rate of homeless people, including the 'hidden homeless', of those who slept rough or who resided in night shelters (a population that is not included in rough sleeper counts). The study,

---

[9] S Jowett, G Banks, A Brown and G Goodall, *Looking for Change: The Role and Impact of Begging on the Lives of People Who Beg* (London, RSU, 2001) 26.

[10] In interviews conducted with 202 people who were street drinkers and who begged, Danzuk found that 51% of his informants slept rough, 28% stayed on a friend's floor, in a hostel, squat, or night shelter, and 20% had their own home. Moreover he found that 'Sleeping rough tended to be a long term rather than a temporary solution'; S Danczuk, *Walk on By ... Begging, Street Drinking and the Giving Age* (London, Crisis, 2000) 13–14. See also: S Johnsen and S Fitzpatrick, 'Revanchist Sanitisation or Coercive Care? The Use of Enforcement to Combat Begging, Street Drinking and Rough Sleeping in England', 47(8) *Urban Studies* 1703–24 at 1707.

[11] C Kennedy and S Fitzpatrick (2001) 'Begging, Rough Sleeping and Social Exclusion: Implications for Social Policy', 38(11) *Urban Studies* 2001–16 at 2002–03.

[12] S Fitzpatrick and C Kennedy (2001), 'The Links Between Begging and Rough Sleeping: A Question of Legitimacy?' 16(5) *Housing Studies* 549–68 at 566.

Homelessness Kills, commissioned by Crisis, showed that homeless people die 30 years younger than the national average, that they are seven times more likely to die from alcohol-related use, 20 times more likely to die from drugs misuse, and almost seven times more likely to die from HIV or hepatitis.[13] For those begging on the street (mostly men) for an extended period of time, and who have addiction issues, these numbers are probably understated. Not surprisingly, then, rough sleepers are in desperate need of multi-dimensional intervention, including addiction and trauma counselling. And even with this, the single overarching cause of homelessness and rough sleeping is structural: abject and often intergenerational forms of poverty, aggravated by a lack of affordable and accessible housing.

What has happened here? How is it that a primary response to some of the most poor and traumatised people, who make their suffering visible to us on a daily basis, are public campaigns that depict how *giving them money will kill them*? How is it that the primary legal response to them is to resurrect a centuries-old vagrancy law to police them as unwanted and illegitimate?

II. Counterfeit Coin

This book examines how the act of giving to those begging on the street has been formed into a powerful site of regulation and vagrancy law reform over the last two decades in England. Before I outline how this inquiry will proceed, I want to first reflect on the profoundly social and paradoxical character of street begging, qualities that can be located in the fact that, at the core, begging involves gift giving.

Marcel Mauss's classic book, *The Gift*, published in 1950, laid the foundation for how scholars have engaged the dynamics of gift giving across a range of disciplines and interests.[14] Mauss famously articulated the reciprocal character of gift giving in a range of 'archaic' societies, most notably in the potlatch of the Indigenous people of the American Northwest. His central insight is that a gift can never exist without the obligation to return it. As Mary Douglas reminds us in her reading of Mauss, despite the moral appearance of gifts being selfless and disinterested, the opposite is true, that 'there is no such thing as a free gift'.[15] Pierre Bourdieu captures this contradiction when he states that giving involves 'a lie told to oneself':[16] one knows full well that one cannot escape a personal economy of obligation when one offers a gift and how it will accrue some sort of debt for the recipient.

---

[13] B Thomas, *Homelessness Kills: An Analysis of the Mortality of Homeless People in Early Twenty-First Century England* (London, Crisis, 2018).

[14] M Mauss, *The Gift: The Form of Reason for Exchange in Archaic Societies* (London, Routledge, 1990).

[15] M Douglas, 'Foreword: No Free Gifts' in Mauss, *The Gift* (1990) ix.

[16] P Bourdieu, 'Marginalia: Some Additional Notes on the Gift' in D Schrift (ed), *The Logic of the Gift: Towards an Ethic of Generosity* (New York, Routledge, 1997) 232.

Almost all of us grapple with, and intuitively understand, this paradoxical character of the gift in a way that Mauss so brilliantly expressed. Gifts can wound, surprise, upset, heal and confuse. It is a very human thing to spend time thinking and fretting about gifts, or even conduct that appears gift-like, as giving and taking are intricately woven into questions of self-identity and social belonging. Indeed, for Mauss, 'a gift that does nothing to enhance social solidarity is a contradiction'.[17]

Does the gift, however, fraught with contradiction and paradox, really exist at all? The philosopher Jacques Derrida writes that Mauss 'speaks of everything but the gift'.[18] The gift for Derrida is 'the impossible': in order for there to be a pure gift, devoid of self-interest and expectation of return or exchange, it would require an immediate forgetting, an amnesia about why and how we give at all. The Maussian notion of a gift that will trigger exchange is, for Derrida, a 'madness of rationality'.[19]

Derrida's analysis is especially resonant with the themes of this book, as his central writing on the gift engages a one-page story by Charles Baudelaire, called 'Counterfeit Money'. Originally titled 'The Paradox of Alms', the tale revolves around two friends who, after leaving a tobacconist's shop, give to a beggar at their feet.[20] One of the men intentionally gives a 'counterfeit coin', leading his friend (the narrator of the story) into an examination of the ethics and meaning of such an act. In doing so, the narrator contends with the subversive nature of the beggar: if everyday gift giving within family and casual social relations is sometimes ambiguous and difficult, then the gift that those begging solicit is a triple moral threat: a gift of *money* that is *asked for* between *strangers*.

For Derrida, the only thing the gift can truly give is time: time for the coin to be scrutinised and accepted or rejected, time for some calculation of payback or return.[21] Indeed, the gift is about the time of the past as well: we cannot escape the expectations or attitudes we have about a beggar or the risk we may take in giving. In Derrida's analysis, the beggar becomes a sort of currency himself, to be inspected for signs of worth and authenticity. By its very nature, then, the debt of the gift can never be resolved; it is beyond rational calculation; it is a 'stranger to morality' and a 'stranger to the law'.[22] Begging is fundamentally an aleatory activity, and giving to someone begging is an act, above all, of moral uncertainty.[23] This book, then, is a study of how this open-ended act is both a target and a resource of regulation that has real consequences for poor people living on the street.

---

[17] M Douglas, 'Foreword' (1990), vii.
[18] J Derrida, *Given Time 1: Counterfeit Money*, trans P Kamuf (Chicago, University of Chicago Press, 1992) 24.
[19] ibid, 13.
[20] ibid, 127.
[21] ibid, 124.
[22] ibid, 156.
[23] ibid, 123.

William Carroll, writing of vagrancy in the Tudor era, comments that the beggar's body 'becomes a central site of semiotic conflict and interrogation'.[24] Carroll's observation remains an accurate description of the contested character of the beggar today. This book addresses two overarching questions. First, how did the encounter between the beggar and the passer-by become a sustained and durable site of gift regulation through appeals to public feeling? Second, how did this gift-crime movement, structured and energised by diverted-giving schemes, become an effective vehicle for otherwise unlikely reforms to archaic vagrancy law? Below the surface of these questions, this book becomes a study of something less tangible but perhaps more important: how one of the most admired qualities of being human – to be kind and relieve the suffering of strangers – has become perverted into a source of indifference and neglect.

III. Outline of Chapters

When did the feelings and conscience of the passer-by at the sight of someone begging – so provocatively targeted in Your Kindness Can Kill campaigns – emerge as a distinct site of regulation on public pavements in England? I explore this question in chapter one, and in doing so provide a historical backdrop that adds context and proportion to this study. While vagrancy law has for centuries encompassed a concern about fraud, mendacity and disguise, it was in the early nineteenth century that public feeling and the 'ill advised kindness of strangers' became a concrete object of intervention. This project became visible in the 1815 Select Committee on the State of Mendicity in the Metropolis and the 1821 Select Committee on Existing Laws Relating to Vagrants, which led to the 1824 Act that remains in force today. Even before these official inquiries, anti-mendicant societies had been formed to address the problem of careless public giving, one that would be taken up later on in the nineteenth century by the Charity Organization Society (COS). The effort to constitute a stable 'truth' about begging was particularly vexing in the new public spaces and crowds of the emerging metropolis. The result was a new mode of regulation that understood begging as a site that could be governed through the dynamics of giving.

In chapter two, I begin to examine the genesis of 'diverted-giving' programmes – and a wider gift-crime movement – that have been put in place over the last two decades: the provincial anti-begging 'experiment' designed in Winchester in 1995. Like early nineteenth-century anti-mendicant reformers, Winchester officials explicitly took public feeling as a major problem if they were to remove those begging from the street. I pay detailed attention to how officials grappled with the paradoxical character of the gift in forging a diverted-giving project, one that

---

[24] WC Carroll, *Fat King, Lean Beggar: Representations of Poverty in the Age of Shakespeare* (Ithaca, NY, Cornell University Press, 1999) 24.

attempted to directly intervene in the relationship between eyes, hands and pocket change at the sight of someone begging. This scheme involved customised charity boxes where the public could divert their donations to help 'genuinely' homeless people, by which they meant people who did not beg. Officials had to deal with the contradictions of marketing a scheme that involved an alternative 'real' gift to beggars that nonetheless discouraged actual face-to-face giving, a paradox that involved the awkward blending of both crime control and social welfare mentalities.

Before I return to how Winchester's Make It Count acted as the template for the gift-crime movement, I take the next two chapters to examine the much wider regulatory and policing landscape at that time.

In chapter three I take account of the activities of flag-day collections, busking and *Big Issue* vending during the early years of the Make It Count scheme. I examine how these three distinct forms of 'official begging' relied primarily on modes of self-regulation and *bona fide* accreditation to maintain a delicate legitimacy to the public eye and giving hands of the public. The regulation of these forms of soliciting expressed a central concern of vagrancy law – that of detecting disguise, mendacity and fraud in pavement requests for pocket change. These figures of acceptable importunity reinforce the criminal status of the beggar whose presence, appearance, and need are to be understood as a crime.

Chapter four brings criminal law into this analysis, in particular the begging and rough-sleeping offences of the Vagrancy Act 1824. In this chapter I examine the nature, use and limitations of the 1824 Act from about 1976 to the early years of the New Labour government, when diverted-giving schemes were just starting to be established.

I begin by examining the work of the formidable activist group End the Vagrancy Act (EVA), which carried out a sustained effort to have the Act repealed in the early 1990s. Drawing on the archives of EVA, I examine the contested moral and legal landscape around the begging and rough-sleeping offences, and detail the powers and limitations of how these sections were policed up to the early 2000s. I then shift to a more concrete analysis and examine three cases of specially tasked policing operations in the late 1990s: the 'Homeless Units' of the Greater Manchester Police and Metropolitan Police in Charing Cross, and British Transport Police operations against women begging with children on the underground. A particular focus across all three cases is the use of the preserved and archaic arrest powers, which were used in a punitive and capricious way. The fact that all three of these operations were presented as having an explicit 'social welfare' goal provides an even further point of comparison to the gift-crime-driven reforms initiated in 2003.

In chapter five I return to Winchester's Make It Count scheme and start bringing the discussion forward from 1996 to the period of legal reform that ended in 2005. This diverted-giving trajectory can be understood as occurring in two waves. The first (1996–2000) saw the migration of diverted giving to a handful of provincial cities, with a scheme that closely followed Winchester's message and approach. The growing town-centre management movement provided channels for this network to grow, as did local crime control infra-structures mandated by the 1998 Crime and Disorder Act. The second wave of diverted giving began in 2000 when the Rough Sleepers Unit (RSU) launched a nation-wide diverted-giving programme, 'Change A Life'. This 'death turn' in diverted-giving rationale, actively promoted by the RSU, was in fact an egregious misrepresentation of their own commissioned research, which found that the majority of money given to those begging by the public was in fact spent on food (not drugs), and that many of those begging were in fact rough sleepers. Nonetheless this 'new truth' that all those begging were drug-addled frauds who duped the public by pretending to be homeless would make gift-crime preven-tion a regulatory concern across England.

Given legitimacy by a national programme carried out in 2000 by the RSU that linked begging to drugs and death, a second wave of diverted-giving schemes expanded across most major centres in England. A wider gift-crime movement became visible that misrepresented beggars solely as drug addicts who were not homeless, and thus fraudulent in their street requests for money. The most formal consequences of this movement was the setting in place of conditions for reforms to vagrancy law powers that would have been politically fraught and techni-cally vexing only a few years earlier. Initiated by the 2003 white paper 'Respect and Responsibility', the goal of these reforms was to protect the public from aggression, while at the same time securing mandatory addiction treatment for 'persistent beggars'. I examine how these historic reforms created, in turn, a new offence of 'persistent begging' through the arcane structure of the 1824 Act; new abilities in making begging a recordable offence; a new classification as a 'trigger offence' in terms of drug crime; and new powers for police civilians.

Begging has not been a criminal offence in Scotland since 1991, a fact that has angered local officials in major cities, who have seen their efforts to re-criminalise begging thwarted by the Scottish government. In chapter six, I discuss how this Scottish case offers a stark contrast to the English one in ways that further illustrate the unique and punitive character of gift-crime order and vagrancy law reform in England. I discuss how since 1997 officials in cities such as Edinburgh and Aberdeen have tried to re-criminalise begging through the promotion of a model by-law. The Scottish government has refused, consistently arguing over the years that begging itself is not inherently conduct that may be alarming or distress-ing, and that in fact many people might consider those begging to be genuinely deserving of charity. I pay detailed attention to how officials in Edinburgh drafted an anti-begging law that they hoped would pass the scrutiny of the then Scottish Executive. The Scottish case throws further light on the remarkable extremes indulged in by the English Home Office in resurrecting a new begging offence, and the ways in which diverted giving and gift-crime regulation were central to driving the English reforms.

In chapter seven I attempt to weave together some themes and observations about the character and contradictions of gift-crime regulation, with particular attention paid to the consequences of the reforms that have taken place. I begin by reviewing how two Your Kindness Can Kill Campaigns in Bristol and Nottingham were challenged with complaints to the Advertising Standards Authority, which polices 'truth in advertising'. The details of these adjudications make visible the dubious and nonsensical aspects of gift-crime regulation.

Did the reforms started in 2003 provide mandatory drug treatment for 'persistent beggars'? Drawing on criminal justice statistics, I conclude that these reforms, including the new offence of persistent begging, had a practically non-existent effect in terms of getting those convicted of begging drug treatment through community sentences. Instead, the overall effect has been to vastly increase the surveillance and policing powers against those begging, with no discernible social welfare outcome. I argue that officials have simply extended and reaffirmed the real meaning of the 1824 Act to police 'idle and disorderly' people into the twenty-first century.

1

The Problem of the
Tender-Hearted Public

Begging: Watch Your Money Go To Fraud
Begging funds the misuse of drugs #givesmart
Nottingham City Council, #givesmart diverted-giving scheme poster, 2016

When did the feelings of the passer-by at the sight of a beggar first become an explicit target of regulation on public pavements? 'Begging is a species of extortion,' the famous police magistrate Patrick Colquhoun wrote in 1806, 'to which the tender hearted are chiefly exposed.'[1] This concern with the feelings of passers-by who carelessly indulged their kindness and compassion in gifts to beggars first emerged in the early nineteenth century. While not constituting a sharp break with long-standing concerns about the proper way to give, what was new was how the 'tender heart' of the passer-by was configured as an explicit, actionable regulatory object, one that could be targeted through the dynamics of gift giving. The consequence was what the historian MJD Roberts has called 'the volunteer professionalization of the gift relationship' in the early nineteenth century.[2]

I. Mendicity and Mendacity in the Metropolis

The beggar has been a central target of vagrancy policing since the enactment of the first specific prohibition in 1349,[3] and one of an astonishing range of offences that has covered an extraordinary swathe of English criminal law over the centuries. While vagrancy law has often been viewed as the 'penal side of the poor laws' and as 'an enforcer of economic and class relations',[4] one can read into it a second

---

[1] P Colquhoun, *A Treatise on Indigence, Exhibiting a General View of National Resources for Productive Labour* (London, J Hatchard, 1806) 75.

[2] MJD Roberts, 'Reshaping the Gift Relationship: The London Mendicity Society and the Suppression of Begging in England, 1818–1869' (1991) *International Review of Social History* 36, 231.

[3] 23 Edw 1.7; WJ Chambliss, 'A Sociological Analysis of the Law of Vagrancy' (1964) 12(1) *Social Problems* 68; United Kingdom, Parliamentary Papers [hereafter PP], vol 4, *Report from the Select Committee on the Existing Laws Relating to Vagrants* (1821) 129.

[4] Roberts, 'Reshaping the Gift Relationship' (1991) 228.

and equally prominent theme: that of a sustained concern about theatricality, counterfeit appearance, disguise and simulation. In her excellent book *Beggary and Theatre in Early Modern England*, Paola Pugliatti demonstrates that both begging and marginal street performances were subjected to an 'anti-theatrical' prejudice; the *mendicity* of the beggar and the *mendacity* of the itinerant actor were often conflated and subsumed into each other.[5] So while vagrancy laws of the fourteenth and fifteenth centuries are typically viewed as 'an attempt to make vagrancy a substitute for serfdom'[6] – by ensuring a supply of cheap labour for landowners after the Black Death in 1348[7] – Pugliatti points out that marginal street performers and their perceived power of simulation were the subject of repressive measures long before 1545.[8]

William Carroll notes that complaints about fraudulent and counterfeit beggars were 'already plentiful in the early 1500s'.[9] So, for example, while an Act of 1572 encompassed both repression of vagrancy and relief for the poor, it also targeted various forms of unregulated disguise. Suspicion of beggars as disguised performers of poverty and suffering constituted a 'philosophic threat'[10] as a protean character; begging vagrants appeared to be idle and slothful while at the same time they dramatised mobility and itinerancy.[11] This paradoxical character dramatised two of the greatest popular fears of early modern Europe: the spread of disease (particularly smallpox) and the danger of fire.[12]

Perhaps the most dramatic attempt to order this semiotic vagrancy – what Barry has called the 'crisis of the sign'[13] that vagrant beggars dramatised – was an attempt to permanently mark the flesh of their bodies to make their criminal status legible. The early labour-oriented statutes of Richard II[14] and Henry VII[15] which prescribed imprisonment and time in the stocks were to be replaced by laws authorising ferocious punishments – the burning, branding, cutting and whipping of vagrant flesh to mark a sign of infamy. These efforts at making immoral and deceitful figures readable to the public eye exemplify what Foucault has called 'penal semiotics', the marking of punishment as an external physical sign. Thus, in 1530 an Act of Henry VIII dictated that 'sturdy beggars' should be whipped and returned to 'their own places'. An Act five years later prescribed that on a second vagabondage offence, 'the offender should be again

[5] P Pugliatti, *Beggary and Theatre in Early Modern England* (Farnham, Ashgate, 2003) 10.
[6] Chambliss, 'Sociological Analysis' (1964) 69.
[7] ibid.
[8] Pugliatti, *Beggary and Theatre* (2003) 3.
[9] WC Carroll, *Fat King, Lean Beggar: Representations of Poverty in the Age of Shakespeare* (Ithaca, NY, Cornell University Press, 1996) 40.
[10] ibid, 3, 6.
[11] ibid, 4.
[12] D Marshall, *The English Poor in the Eighteenth Century* (London, George Routledge and Sons, 1926) 225–45.
[13] WC Carroll, 'The Crisis of the Sign: Vagrancy and Authority in the English Renaissance' *Semiotic*. 108, 381–388.
[14] eg, 12 R 2 c 3 (1388).
[15] eg, Henry VII H 7 c 2 (1495).

whipped, and to have the upper part of the gristle of his right ear cut off'; after a third offence the offender should 'suffer death as a felon'.[16] The Beggars Act 1531 prescribed punishment for 'vagabonds and idle persons': to be 'tied to the end of a cart naked and be beaten with whips and throughout the same market town or other place till his body be bloody by reason of such whipping'.[17] A 1547 Act of Edward VI deemed that those who refused to work and had lived idly for three days

> shall be branded with a red-hot iron on the breast (both men and women), with the letter V, and shall be adjudged slaves for two years of any person who shall inform against such idler; and it was left to the master to employ the slave in the vilest work ... and if the slave absented himself for fourteen days he became a slave for life, after being branded on the forehead or cheek with the letter S; and if he ran away a second time he was to suffer death as a felon.[18]

By an Act of Elizabeth I in 1571, beggars over the age of 14 were to be punished in the first instance by being 'grievously whipped, and burned the gristle of the right ear, with a hot iron of the compass of an inch about'.[19] This violent marking of the vagrant beggar was accompanied by the introduction of the category 'rogue' in an Act of 1571.[20] In 1604, under James I, the notion of the 'incorrigible' was introduced, a character status which would bring with it the punishment of being branded on the left shoulder 'with a hot iron of the breadth of a shilling having a Roman R upon it'.[21] If people with this brand were subsequently found begging, this punishment was to extend into the afterlife, as they would 'suffer death without clergy'.[22] This shift to a view of vagrants as dangerous threats who

---

[16] Colquhoun, *Treatise on Indigence* (1806) 66.

[17] As cited in FR Salter, *Some Early Tracts on Poor Relief* (London, Methuen, 1926) 123–24.

[18] 1 Ed 6 c 3, as cited in Colquhoun, *Treatise on Indigence*, 66. The first mention of the punishment of branding for vagrants occurred in 1361, when labourers and artificers 'who absent themselves out of their service' were to be imprisoned, outlawed or 'for the Falsity he shall be burnt in the forehead, with an iron made and formed to this letter F in token of Falsity' (34 Edw III c 10). Interestingly, the Act also contains a clause postponing the branding provision, which suggests that it was a desperate threat at a time of great labour mobility. I thank Alan Hunt for his comments on statutes of this period.

[19] 14 Elizabeth c 5; see AL Beier, *Masterless Men: The Vagrancy Problem in England, 1560–1640* (London, Methuen, 1985), 159, on this 'ferocious' punishment. A second tier of this aesthetic of vagrant and poor policing was the practice of badging. Wide-ranging legislation governed the badging and licensing of beggars as part of the systematisation of discriminate almsgiving. In Europe, legislation prescribing the device of a badge to signify a licence dates back to at least 1363 in Nuremburg. The conditions of these licences detailed the time of day, place and conduct of the legitimate beggar. Badges were stamped and engraved and had to be worn openly. For example, in France in 1544 this involved a yellow cross to be worn on the shoulder; in Middlesex, England, in 1694 the badge was to be worn 'at the end of the left sleeve' and was inscribed with the name of the parish from which the pauper came.

[20] 14 Edw c 5; Chambliss, 'Sociological Analysis', 74.

[21] The Act prescribes that the brand is to be 'so thoroughly burned and set on the skin and flesh, that the Letter "R" be seen and remain for a perpetual mark upon such rogue during his or her life'; as cited in Colquhoun, *Treatise on Indigence*, 67. See also WLM Lee, *A History of Police in England* (London, Methuen, 1901).

[22] Colquhoun, *Treatise on Indigence*, 67. See P Corrigan and D Sayer, *The Great Arch: English State Formation as Cultural Revolution* (Oxford, Basil Blackwell, 1985) on the relationship between moral regulation and English state formation.

deserved brutal, legible punishment is closely linked to the fact that, throughout the sixteenth century, the poor were losing the security of being smallholders as the feudal manorial economy dissolved.[23] The break-up of villeinage was aggravated by two factors: the population of England nearly doubled between 1541 and 1651, from 2.7 million to 5.2 million,[24] and the practice of enclosure further acted to erode customary tenancy and criminalised a wide range of subsistence activities, such as firewood collection and game hunting. 'By 1600 the English people,' comments AL Beier, 'had the country's major resources seized from their grasp; at a time, ironically, when their requirements for food and housing were increasing.'[25] The dissolution of the manorial estates, along with the decline of monastic charity – generated by replacement of the Franciscan ideal of noble poverty with Saint Paul's emphasis on how a good Christian 'worked to pay his way' – created a new object of vagrancy law, the 'sturdy beggar' who was 'able bodied'. The fact that the term *actor* was often used throughout this period to describe 'sturdy' beggars (those who could physically work) speaks to the continued anti-theatrical concern of vagrancy governance.[26]

The 12th Act of Queen Anne in the early eighteenth century modified the harsh penalties of the previous acts[27] and refined vagrant categories into three distinctions: 'Idle and Disorderly persons', 'Rogues' and 'Vagabonds'.[28] The Act of 1744[29] retained this distinction and consolidated the previous vagrancy statutes. While it is often commented that these categories were aligned to serve the labour discipline needs of 'eighteenth century masters',[30] they continued to encompass a broad range of street activity that speaks to disguise, simulation and fakery: gathering alms on the pretence of fire loss or on behalf of prisons or hospitals, fencers, bearwards, unauthorised 'players of interludes',[31] minstrels, jugglers, gypsies, fortune tellers 'using subtle craft', beggars pretending to be soldiers, or seamen illegally dealing in lottery tickets. In this refinement of vagrancy law, one continues to see a widespread concern with the theatricality embodied in pavement spectacles of chance, idleness and provocation of public feeling, of which the beggar was the most provoking actor.

---

[23] Beier, *Masterless Men* (1985) 20.

[24] ibid, 19.

[25] ibid, 22.

[26] Carroll, *Fat King*, 45.

[27] Colquhoun, *Treatise on Indigence*, 66.

[28] 12 Anne c 23.

[29] 17 Geo 2 c 5.

[30] eg, M Ignatieff, *A Just Measure of Pain: The Penitentiary in the Industrial Revolution, 1750–1850* (London, Macmillan, 1978) 25.

[31] Most notably the 19th Act of George II in 1737, which reads that 'all persons, whatsoever who shall for gain in any playhouse, booth or otherwise, exhibit any stageplay, interlude, show opera or theatrical or dramatical performance, or act any part, or assist therein, within the precincts of either of the said universities, or within five miles of the city of Oxford, or town of Cambridge, shall be deemed rogues and vagabonds; and that it shall and be lawful to and for the Chancellor of either of the said universities, or the Vice-Chancellor there of, or his deputy respectively, to commit any such person to any house of correction within either of the counties of Oxford or Cambridge respectively, there to be kept to hard labour for the space of one month, or to the common gaol of the city or county of Oxford.'

In the early nineteenth century, the ordering of beggars on the street was viewed to be in widespread disarray, according to inquiries into the state of 'mendicity in the metropolis', most notably in the evidence and reports of the parliamentary committees of 1815–1816 and 1821.[32] Despite the Act of 1744, which attempted to simplify vagrancy laws, many of its provisions were of 'very doubtful intendment',[33] and no fewer than 18 vagrancy-related statutes had been enacted since the mid-eighteenth century. 'The inadequacy of these acts,' noted the 1821 committee, 'to attain their object, numerous as they are, is clear from the increasing numbers of vagrants, and the enormous expense annually incurred by different counties in their apprehension, maintenance and conveyance by pass.'[34]

The 1821 committee frequently heard how magistrates were seen to be indifferent to the vagrancy law. In order to pass back convicted mendicants to their home parish, magistrates were required, by an Act of 1792, to have the convicted whipped or sent to the House of Correction for seven days before issuing a pass. Many magistrates chose instead simply to issue a pass without imposing punishment. Police magistrate Patrick Colquhoun testified to the 1815 select committee that the Act of 1792 was 'impractical' and that many magistrates ignored the punishment requirement and issued passes, as they were 'very glad to get them out of town'.[35] The few magistrates who did order strict street clearing – such as the City Magistrate – simply forced beggars into neighbouring parishes.[36]

Witnesses testified that the system of passes and conveyances underlying parochial relief was unworkable and subject to corruption and graft; a vestryman of the parish of St John's complained that passes were 'nothing but a licence to beg'.[37] Parishes which did not have workhouses 'farmed out' their poor to private entrepreneurs; contractors who ran poor farms came under detailed questioning from the 1815 select committee about the character of their operations, including the allowance paid, the type of work offered, diet, state of clothing, provisions for exercise, availability of a doctor and methods of punishment.[38] In dealing with beggars on the street, parish officers (such as constables and beadles) were afraid to 'overstock the workhouse' and were happy to either 'look the other way' or often collude

---

[32] The 1815 Select Committee on the State of Mendicity in the Metropolis and the 1821 Select Committee on the Existing Laws Relating to Vagrants both examined the current state of vagrancy governance. Specifically, the committees were charged with examining measures which might be adapted 'for a cure or an alleviation of the Evil which exists in the present state of Mendicity and Vagrancy'; PP, vol 5, *Report from the Select Committee on the State of Mendicity in the Metropolis* (1815), 3.

[33] PP, *Report from the Select Committee* (1821) 3.

[34] ibid.

[35] PP, *Report from the Select Committee* (1815) 54.

[36] ibid, 39.

[37] ibid, 68.

[38] The Committee was especially keen to have poor-farm contractors explain the source of any pocket money an inmate could expect to have. Certainly those who contracted poor relief from the parish were depicted in committee evidence as routinely letting offenders out to beg (particularly on Sunday, so they could apparently go to church), and in some cases, prisoners would be paid twopence half-penny if they agreed to forgo their daily meal, a practice that was known as 'slating'.

with those begging by way of payment to 'move them on out of their parish'.[39] The officers of the police (such as the Bow Street Runners) were issued with no specific directions for arresting beggars; it was, according to the chief clerk of the police office at Bow Street, 'a business appertaining to beadles and constables of the parish'.[40] Samuel Plank, an officer with the Marlborough Police Office, testified to the 1821 committee that he had never apprehended a vagrant and would apprehend a beggar only if he was disorderly, including a beggar being 'troublesome to a lady'.[41]

The continued concern with the faking of poverty and need was particularly evident in descriptions of the impostor, or 'lurk', who attempts to elicit sympathy by feigning an appearance of desperate hardship and suffering. A witness testified how one beggar was able to make a 'large sum' of money by begging for shoes, which were later sold. 'Their mode of exciting charity for shoes,' the committee heard, 'is invariably to go barefoot, and scarify their feet and heels with something or another to cause blood as it were to flow.'[42] Another beggar more simply walked around naked, gathering a great quantity of shoes 'and other habiliments' which were later sold. One well-known lurk described to the committee was John Collins, known among the beadles as 'the Soap-Eater' for chewing on bits of soap to make his mouth foam, then pretending to have a fit in the street.[43] The 1815 committee heard that beggars often attempted to evade the vagrancy law by adopting the pretence of selling toothpicks, cushions, matches, almanacs or cotton balls.[44]

Concern with the apparent mendacity of the beggar was jointly manifested in anti-vagrancy concern about the lotto, where idleness was rewarded through the exercise of chance in a pavement spectacle. 'Insurances in the lottery,' writes Colquhoun, 'constitute another form of indigence, which has produced at different times great misery and wretchedness.'[45] Warning against the harbouring of 'lottery insurers', Colquhoun suggests a series of rules and regulations for publicans that would stop the lottery from corrupting 'the morals of the labouring people'.[46] The lottery and other games of chance were seen to be a corollary of begging – and giving to those begging – as public expression of a careless and irrational

---

[39] PP, *Report from the Select Committee* (1815) 30, 40.
[40] ibid, 37.
[41] PP, *Report from the Select Committee* (1821) 87.
[42] PP, *Report from the Select Committee* (1815) 51.
[43] ibid, 84.
[44] ibid, 82.
[45] Colquhoun, *Treatise on Indigence*, 239.
[46] 'No publican shall hold out allurements to apprentices, journeymen, or labourers, by the introduction of unlawful games into his house ... such as cards, dice, domino, shuffleboard, what's o'clock, four corners, tables, missippi [*sic*], draughts, Sibley table, bumble puppy, ringing at the bell, or any other alluring game ... by which criminal, profligate, and disorderly persons shall be collected together, corrupting the morals of the labouring people, and seducing them from their useful occupations to waste time in idleness and dissipation'; ibid, 296.

expression of feeling and chance.[47] 'The spirit of gaming,' testified one witness to the 1815 select committee,

> is kept up by the object of the lottery being so obtrusively presented to the eye; and the common errand carts have lottery tickets placarded upon them. It is the objective of those interested in the lottery to make it as publicly known as possible as it can be; *it is obtrusive upon the public eye; it never ceases.*[48]

Given the confusion about how to discern mendicity from mendacity in the public eye of the new metropolitan crowd, it is not surprising that parish constables and beadles were often hesitant to arrest beggars for fear of provoking passers-by sympathetic to the sight of someone begging. Arresting street beggars 'is a very disagreeable office for an officer to take,' commented the clerk to the Lord Mayor in his testimony in 1815, 'for he is sure to get a crowd about him, and be ill treated; there is generally a serious struggle before any of these common beggars can be taken into custody, and conveyed to a place of security.'[49] Was the crowd of people obstructing the officer made up of those of the 'beggar's ilk'? the committee chairman asked. No, the clerk replied, adding that they were ordinary people acting on 'an ill advised kindness of individuals' which street beggars take advantage of. The witness observed that beggars learned to resist arrest 'by falling down and screaming', creating a scene, whereupon 'good natured people interest themselves' and come to the aid of the beggar.[50] Beadles willing to risk the abuse of passers-by and make an arrest were frustrated by the indifference of magistrates. 'I have taken many and many [beggars] down,' stated a beadle of St George's Bloomsbury to the 1815 select committee, 'and they have been discharged, and my brother beadles will give the same testimony.'[51]

Several witnesses testified to the presence of alehouses that acted as crucial meeting points for beggars, and gin shops were seen as especially dangerous. The chaplain at the London Bridewell complained to the committee that the gin shop was 'the first that is opened in the morning and the last that shuts at night: it is the most obtrusive evil, perhaps, that we have about the streets.'[52] The Rose and Crown, known in street cant as 'the Beggar's Opera', was mentioned as a notorious meeting place where beggars reportedly 'supped and drank all night, planning the next day's cadging.'[53] Beggars were thought to be organised to such an extent that they even established their own walks, which they treated 'as a sort of property'. Along with street beggars, there were 'two penny post' beggars, who wrote begging

---

[47] The clerk to the Lord Mayor, on examining an applicant for Soup Society relief, found out that the applicant had usually made his living as a translator but had recently lost his trade to the lottery.

[48] PP, *Report from the Select Committee* (1815) 44; emphasis added.

[49] ibid, 16.

[50] ibid.

[51] ibid, 82.

[52] ibid, 44. See also 21, 30.

[53] ibid, 43, 77.

letters, and 'knocker beggars', who made elaborate appeals for money at people's doors.[54]

The result of these inquiries, particularly that of the 1821 committee, was the Vagrancy Act of 1822, which was given permanence by Home Secretary Robert Peel in 1824. The statute repealed all other vagrancy legislation and consolidated the three types of vagrant categorised in previous statutes: 'Idle and Disorderly persons', 'Rogues and Vagabonds' and 'Incorrigible Rogues'. Section 3 laid out the offence of street begging, by which an offender could be marked with the status of 'idle and disorderly person'; it read in part:

> every Person wandering abroad, or placing himself or herself in any public Place, Street, Highway, Court or Passage, to beg or gather alms, or causing or encouraging any Child or Children to do so, shall be deemed an idle and disorderly person.

Every person capable of supporting himself and refusing to do so was guilty of being an idle and disorderly person, as well as anyone 'Sleeping in the open air, or in a wagon, cart, barn, tent, outhouse, or in a deserted or unoccupied building'. Not 'having any visible means of subsistence and not giving a good account of oneself' (s 4) was an offence as well. Unlicensed and unauthorised peddlers and petty chapmen and common prostitutes who behaved in a 'riotous or indecent manner' were also categorised as idle and disorderly (s 3). The category of 'rogue and vagabond' was reserved for those who had previously been convicted of being an idle and disorderly person, as well as those who offended by engaging in a wide range of activities that spoke to deceitful and fraudulent character.[55]

Gathering alms or procuring charitable contributions under 'false or fraudulent pretence' was illegal, as was leaving a wife and children chargeable to a parish, an offence which anticipated the reforms of the 1832 Poor Law.[56] In particular, any person found in an enclosed yard or dwelling house who had unlawful intent, and 'every suspected person or reputed thief' who frequented public places, including any 'quay, wharf or warehouse', was subject to conviction as a

[54] ibid, 24. For a detailed description of beggar types, see L Rose, *Rogues and Vagabonds: Vagrancy Underworld in Britain, 1815–1985* (London, Routledge, 1988) 23–48. For notable contemporary accounts, see JT Smith, *Vagabondiana; or, Anecdotes of Mendicant Wanderers Through the Streets of London* (London, Hatchard and Clarke, 1817) and CJ Ribton-Turner, *The Cries of London: Exhibiting Several of the Itinerant Traders of Antient and Modern Times* (London, John Bowyer Nichols and Son, 1839).

[55] 5 Geo. IV c 83. This included fortune tellers who used 'any subtle Craft, Means or Device', including palmistry, to 'deceive and impose on any of His Majesty's Subjects', as well as 'playing and betting' in the street, including the use of any 'Table or instrument of gaming at any Game or pretended game of chance' (s 3). These games of chance included forms of lottery such as street draws and little-goes, as well as card games such as lotto and tiddlywinks. The status of 'incorrigible rogue' was conferred on those convicted under the Act who escaped or attempted to get out of 'a place of legal confinement', those who committed an offence under the Act and had already been convicted as a rogue and vagabond, and those who violently resisted a constable apprehending a person for an offence which carried the status of rogue and vagabond.

[56] See M Dean, *The Constitution of Poverty: Towards a Genealogy of Liberal Governance* (London, Routledge, 1994).

rogue and vagabond.[57] This 'sus' (suspected person) power dramatised the core nature of the vagrancy police – to enforce offences based on social and economic status, sweeping up anyone who looked suspicious and out of place. The arrest powers in the Vagrancy Act 1824 were as capricious as the categories of vagrants the law policed; s 6 allowed for 'any person whatsoever to apprehend any person whatsoever who shall be found offending against this Act', provided that they be delivered to a justice of the peace. This arrest power (which, as I discuss in chapter five, was repealed only recently, in 2003) enabled both private and public anti-mendicant agents to arrest a wide range of disorderly types of people throughout the nineteenth century.

This refinement of vagrancy law in the early nineteenth century was influenced by English police intellectuals and their designs for governing the new metropolis. In the late eighteenth and early nineteenth centuries, the notion of policing – of 'the good order of public matters' – increasingly relied on the construction and ordering of specific populations.[58] Foucault has famously noted how these 'govern-mentalities' concerned themselves with 'the government of children, of souls, of families, of the sick' through institutions such as workhouses, asylums, prisons and schools.[59] The wearing of leg irons and the lashing of prisoners were viewed as less effective than specific time tasks such as the treadwheel, a labour calculated to reform the moral character of the offender, instilling industry, frugal living and self-control.[60] Indeed, the new Vagrancy Act was so closely associated with these new ideas of punishment that a main supporter of the 1822 Act, George Chetwynd, MP, was accused in parliamentary debates of inflicting 'treadmill cruelty'.[61] Described by Colquhoun as the 'art of conducting men to the maximum of happiness and the minimum of misery', the notion of policing involved widespread regulation of customs, habits, trades, commerce, buildings, streets, highways, poverty, peace and public order.[62] For Colquhoun, 'police' was understood to mean 'all those regulations in a country which apply to the comfort, convenience, and safety of the inhabitants, whether it regards their security against the calamity of indigence, or the effects produced by moral and criminal offences.'[63]

---

[57] The act of 'obscenely exposing his person … with intent to insult any female' or exposing any 'obscene Print, Picture, or other Indecent exhibition' was also an offence, as well as wandering abroad and 'endeavouring by the Exposure of Wounds or Deformities to obtain or gather alms' (s 4). Several commentators (eg, Rose, *Rogues and Vagabonds*) have noted that this latter section was a response to the sight of Napoleonic War veterans who exposed their wounds in order to solicit donations. While the sight of gangrene and field-amputated limbs must have been grisly indeed, the section was no doubt also a response to the widespread feeling that the most deceptive and skilled impostors and lurks were those who engaged in this form of exposing wounds.

[58] FL Knemeyer, 'Polizei' (1980) *Economy and Society* 9, 172–96.

[59] M Foucault, 'The Subject and Power' in H Dreyfus and P Rabinow (eds), *Foucault: Beyond Structuralism and Hermeneutics* (Chicago, University of Chicago Press, 1982) 221.

[60] Barry, *Alexander Maconochie*, 69–79.

[61] MJD Roberts, 'Reshaping the Gift Relationship', 202.

[62] P Colquhoun, *A Treatise on the Police of the Metropolis, etc.*, 6th edn (London, J Mawman, 1800), 72; Knemeyer, 'Polizei', 2; JL McMullan, 'The Arresting Eye: Discourse, Surveillance and Disciplinary Administration in Early English Police Thinking' (1998) *Social and Legal Studies* 7, 110.

[63] Colquhoun, *Treatise on Indigence*, 82.

Vagrants in 'the public eye' constituted a primary category that was targeted by police intellectuals such as Fielding and Colquhoun, who envisioned new forms of order which revolved around inspection, detection, prevention and deterrence. In the 1760s and 1770s John Fielding advocated close inspection and supervision of vagrants and itinerant characters, including ballad singers, whom he saw as a dangerous threat to public morality.[64] Fielding was concerned about the very sight of temptation and idleness which the beggar dramatised.[65] 'How disagreeable it is,' he wrote,

> to be attack'd at every corner of the street by beggars, most of whom make a trade of it; and how disadvantageous it is to shop-keepers to have every customer that stops in a coach at their door, to be importuned by these artful petitioners.[66]

Fielding proposed what he described as an 'arresting eye', a systematic police programme of surveillance and prevention carried out through a specialised knowledge of criminal populations.[67] In his *Treatise on the Police of the Metropolis*, Colquhoun advocated dividing the whole English population into seven classes, the lowest of which included 'paupers and their families, vagrants, gypsies, rogues, vagabonds, and idle and disorderly persons supported by criminal delinquency'.[68]

A prominent emphasis of the governmentalities that identified and classified populations was that of health and hygiene, as exemplified by the work of Johann Peter Frank and his eight-volume treatise *A System of Complete Medical Police*, completed in 1819. Frank was concerned about how specific populations could be governed through the linkage between private morality and public spaces. Thus Frank included under the rubric of 'medical police' the following:

> Human Procreation and Marriage Institutions; Preservation and Care of Pregnant women, their Fetuses, and of Lying-in Women; Food, Drink and Vessels; Laws of Moderation, Unhealthy Clothing, [and] Popular Amusements; Layout, Construction, and Necessary Cleanliness of Human Dwellings; Public Safety Measures as far as they concern Public Health; Interment of the Dead; Medical science and medical Educational Institutions; and the Examination and Confirmation of Medical Practitioners.[69]

The medical police linked the governance of private lives with aspirations of national wealth and prosperity. As Erna Lesky comments, 'Frank taught the monarchs that the greatest wealth of a state lies in its subjects, who should be as numerous, healthy and productive as possible.'[70] Public bypassing spaces were re-inscribed with the rational technologies of the medical police in walks, covered

---

[64] J Fielding, *An Account of the Origin and Effects of a Police Set on Foot* (London, A Millar, 1753); McMullan, 'Arresting Eye', 101.

[65] Fielding, *Account of the Origin*, ix.

[66] ibid, 35.

[67] McMullan, 'Arresting Eye', 104.

[68] ibid, 13.

[69] As cited in Carroll, *Fat King*, 145.

[70] ibid.

markets, theatres and swimming baths.[71] Paving projects and the widespread introduction by 1822 of gas lighting in public streets and malls literally opened up new ways for people to see each other.[72] By the 1830s the 'rational recreationist' movement was promoting the leisure pursuit of path-walking in new public parks, an activity which was thought to have an 'improving' and 'educational' effect on the population.[73]

II. The Humanity of the Population

The emerging public spaces of the nineteenth century presented new opportunities for strangers to encounter and engage with one another in streets and in parks.[74] Here the anti-mendicant forces would forge a new form of order to deal with the mendacity of begging, one that would attempt to stay the hands of both beggar and passer-by in an explicit project of 'tender heart' control. The problem of the public's relieving its conscience when faced with the beggar's hand was the focus of regulatory programmes developed first by the new anti-mendicant societies in the early 1800s and then more generally by the activities of the Charity Organisation Society later in the century.[75] This shift in the organisation of gifts to the poor, most visibly those giving to beggars on public pavements, was exemplified in the testimony of Matthew Martin to the 1815 select committee. A 'career philanthropist', Martin addressed what was widely viewed to be the central problem of mendicity, which lay not primarily in the character of the beggar but rather

> in that which is extremely creditable, the humanity of the population: people cannot bear to pass by distress without relieving it, but in fact they are only adding fuel to the fire. I really think that if it were possible to direct money which now goes in these various ways to support beggars, into one legitimate channel, coming into hands that would distribute it properly, it would more than supply all that are now in distress.[76]

Martin, who would later become a central figure in the London Anti-Mendicity Society, founded three years later, detailed his efforts to establish a ticket programme in London to stop the giving of money to beggars. The programme involved printing

---

[71] Roberts, 'Reshaping the Gift Relationship', 293; MJD Roberts, 'Public and Private in Early Nineteenth-Century London: The Vagrant Act of 1822 and Its Enforcement' (1988) *Social History* 13, 280; Carroll, *Fat King*, 161.

[72] See Roberts, 'Public and Private', for a detailed discussion of how the changing character of bypassing spaces is illustrated in a controversy that involves enforcement of the 'indecent exposure' section of the 1822 Vagrancy Act.

[73] H Cunningham, *Leisure in the Industrial Revolution* (London, Croom Helm, 1980), 93–96.

[74] ME Falkus, 'The Early Development of the British Gas Industry, 1790–1815' (1982) *Economic History Review* 35, 229–31; M Ignatieff, *The Needs of Strangers* (London, Vintage, 1994); Cunningham, *Leisure*; M Girouard, *Cities and People: A Social and Architectural History* (New Haven, Yale University Press, 1985), 339.

[75] This analysis is particularly indebted to the work of Roberts in 'Public and Private' and 'Reshaping the Gift Relationship'.

[76] PP, *Report from the Select Committee* (1815), 29.

and selling tickets that could be sold to subscribers, who could then gift them to those begging on the street. The circulating of these tickets would be a 'system practised in order to prevent the imposition of beggars on individuals, that individuals who are charitably disposed might give them to beggars instead of money'.[77]

Tickets in hand, the beggars would report to Martin's office, where he would 'ascertain whether the bearers were fit objects of charity'.[78] The beggars were subject to a 26-question survey and a surgeon was on hand to detect 'counterfeit lameness'.[79] In his testimony to the 1815 inquiry, Martin claimed to have sold 6,000 tickets at a cost of 3d each, 2,000 of which were returned to his office.[80] Keeping careful track of the applicants, he estimated that about 50 per cent of those who attended his office were fit for charity, and he complained that many of those who had a legitimate claim on parish support had no idea how to apply for relief. 'It is astonishing,' Martin told the committee, 'how ignorant poor people are.'[81]

Influenced by this work, the London Mendicity Society was established in 1818 under the direction of HK Bodkin. In his testimony to the 1821 select committee, Bodkin explained that the goal of the Society was to 'suppress mendicity by putting the laws in force against impostors, and by granting assistance to such persons as shall, upon investigation, be found to be deserving.'[82] Mendicity Society officers utilised the 'any person' arrest powers of the Vagrancy Act in carrying out their own arrests, and they appear to have had close working relationships with magistrates; at the Marlborough Police Office, mendicant officers were given the power to lock up prisoners on their own authority.[83] In addition to their Vagrancy Act arrest powers, mendicant officers were sworn in by magistrates as special constables, which gave them extra authority over those who resisted.[84] Mendicity Society officers were paid 20 to 30 shillings a week and were not supposed to take any other outside employment. Most notably, the officers were not allowed to collect the 10-shilling reward; instead it was paid to the Society by the county treasurer.[85] Between March 1818 and 1821, society officers reported apprehending 1,295 vagrants, of whom 967 were committed to gaol.

---

[77] ibid, 3.

[78] ibid.

[79] ibid.

[80] ibid.

[81] ibid.

[82] ibid, 5.

[83] PP, *Report from the Select Committee* (1821) 20. The fact that private mendicity officers, who would already have adequate 'any person' arrest powers, needed the further protection of being special constables suggests that arresting those begging was a 'very disagreeable task' in terms of resistance from both the person begging and the general public.

[84] ibid, 5.

[85] ibid, 20. This practice appears to be illegal, as the reward was payable only to the person who apprehended the vagrant, and the county treasurer was apparently not authorised to make those payments.

The society continued to provide evidence to police magistrates' courts from their own registry of beggars up until at least 1889.[86] In relation to the s 6 arrest power – that anyone could arrest anyone who violated the Vagrancy Act – the Mendicity Society noted in 1888 that 'it is not necessary that the person would be seen actually to "solicit alms" in order to carry out an arrest', an interpretation that no doubt suggests how the section had been used to round up a wide range of suspicious characters throughout the century.[87]

The London Mendicity Society was predated by developments in the provinces. In 1805 the Bath Society for the Suppression of Vagrants was established. The Society hired its own private 'beadle' to patrol the streets, kept a register of travellers, ran a system of home visits and circulated tickets among subscribers, who were encouraged to give them to beggars instead of money.[88] Within a few years, the Society was able to report 'the distress which demands charitable aids rarely to be found among street beggars: that almsgiving in the street, without investigation, are bounties on idleness and fraud; and that every shilling so received is a robbery from real distress.'[89]

In Edinburgh the Society for the Suppression of Public Begging was formed in 1812. In Oxford an Anti-Mendicity Society was founded in 1814, with strong support from the university, which had for a period in the late seventeenth century participated in running the city bridewell. Other societies were founded in Colchester and the counties of Ayr, Clackmannan, Dorset and Hereford.[90] As Bob Bushaway points out, this new emphasis on deservingness caused the practices of folk charity and calendar doles (for example, at Christmas and Easter) in rural communities to be discontinued.[91] Customary giving to an open community gave way to the application of documentary evidence and legal proof. Practices such as the distribution of Christmas boxes and the opening of rectories on Boxing Day for unlimited suppers of ale, bread and cheese were seen as indiscriminate and were brought to an end.

With the decline of anti-mendicant societies in the second half of the nineteenth century, a more dynamic and substantive movement emerged in the form of the Charity Organisation Society (COS). Originally established under the name Society for Organising Charitable Relief and Repressing Mendicity, the Charity Organisation Society would act as the 'consciousness of sin'[92] and promote

---

[86] Mendicity Society, 'Seven Reasons for Supporting the Above Society', 3 June 1889, John Johnson Collection, Bodleian Library. The Society claimed to have apprehended 64,500 'beggars and street impostors' since it was founded in 1818 and to have a registry of 210,000 begging-letter cases.

[87] Mendicity Society, 'Specimens of Constables' Cases' in *Annual Report for the Year 1888*, John Johnson Collection, Bodleian Library, 4.

[88] Roberts, 'Reshaping the Gift Relationship', 207.

[89] As cited ibid.

[90] CL Mowat, *The Charity Organisation Society, 1869–1913* (London, Methuen, 1961) 5–7.

[91] B Bushaway, *Custom by Rite: Custom, Ceremony and Community in England, 1700–1800* (London, Junction Books, 1982) 253–59.

[92] Mowat, *Charity Organisation Society*, 1.

a science of charity whose guiding principle would be 'no relief without inquiry'.[93] The COS retained its concern with anti-mendicity work throughout the century.[94] COS officers argued that indiscriminate almsgiving in the streets was a primary cause of demoralisation and pauperism,[95] an argument that was often unpopular with the public.[96] A further target of the COS was the number of charities in operation which were viewed as indiscriminate; beggars were thought to be overfed in the soup kitchens of London,[97] and even those that charged a token penny or two were considered to be encouraging begging.[98] 'The greater the poverty,' comments Jones, 'the more the public were warned by the society to watch for fraud.'[99] As the Mendicity Society instructed its subscribers, 'the more plausible the story exhibited by those in pursuit of charity, the more necessary it is that those of whom it is sought should be on their guard.'[100]

While it never achieved a system of charity offices located in each Poor Law division, as it had first aspired to, the COS nevertheless established a network of programmes that encompassed the policing of a wide range of charity efforts. Control of the street beggar was the subject of periodic committees and publications and the object of a permanent committee on mendicity established in 1877.[101] In 1875 the Society named 'the repression of mendicity and imposture, and the correction of the maladministration of charity' as one of its five mandates.[102] Funded by subscriptions and donations, the COS pioneered the 'case work' method of inquiry,[103] prosecuted fraudulent and bogus charities and became especially well known for the investigation of begging letters, work which it continued until 1956.[104] By the end of the nineteenth century, the feelings and conscience of the public at the sight of beggars were firmly installed as a rational object of intervention. An address by the Archbishop of Canterbury to the Society in 1891, titled 'The Science of Charity', provides a vivid example:

> There is a story of a great man – a great philosopher – a great Churchman. In his dying moments he was seen upon his sofa smiling placidly, moving his hand quietly up and down, and murmuring something to himself over and over again. His friends stooped

[93] Roberts, 'Reshaping the Gift Relationship', 215.

[94] Some of the most noteworthy include Dr Barnardo's Homes (1870), the YMCA (1849), the National Institute for the Blind and the Salvation Army (1878). See Beveridge (1948) for a listing of nineteenth-century charities and friendly societies.

[95] D Garland, *Punishment and Welfare: A History of Penal Strategies* (London, Gower, 1985), 115.

[96] W Beveridge, *Voluntary Action: A Report on Methods of Social Advance* (London, George Allen & Unwin, 1948), 147.

[97] D Jones, *Crime, Protest, Community and Police in Nineteenth Century Britain* (London: Routledge & Kegan Paul, 1982) 189, 53, 189.

[98] ibid, 53.

[99] ibid, 189.

[100] Mendicity Society, 'Specimens of Constables' Cases', 3.

[101] Mowat, *Charity Organisation Society*, 53.

[102] ibid, 25–26.

[103] The 43rd edition of 'How to Help Cases of Distress' was published in 1950; ibid, 176.

[104] ibid, 37; see also JS Heywood, *Children in Care: The Development of the Service for the Deprived Child* (London, Routledge & Kegan Paul, 1959), 105.

close to his lips to catch what he was saying. With closed eyes he was saying: 'Thank God, I never gave a penny to a beggar in the street! Thank God!' When he was gone, it was disclosed that he had given very vast sums in charity. Now that is not a very attractive saying, but the force and meaning is this: It is an evil thing to be charitable for the sake of giving careless and idle relief to one's feelings. It is [as] detrimental to give careless and idle relief to those feelings as to give careful and idle relief to any other of the emotions that possess us, without putting them under the *judgement of conscience and the guidance of reason*.[105]

By the end of the century, the COS rationale of 'no relief without inquiry' had produced extraordinary ticket systems by which passers-by could exercise 'Scientific and Sympathetic Charity' to those they saw begging. As the Mendicity Society reported in 1889,

> If food tickets distributed to Subscribers were universally used, *and money never given to street beggars*, the nuisance of street begging would gradually cease, as money is the only object of the professional beggar, who often makes five shillings a day by begging.[106]

It is notable, Roberts suggests, that the Society never dared take the advice of the Metropolitan Police commissioners who suggested in 1853 that an offence of giving to beggars should be enacted.[107] To do so would have been to remove a central social field within which the exercise of benevolence, and the accompanying dramatisation of social status, could take place.

An objection that one might enter at this point in my argument – that there emerged a mode of regulation in the early nineteenth century that manifested itself in the explicit targeting of public feeling and gift giving to the poor on public pavements – is what about the use of poor boxes? As Robert Bernasconi points out, the poor box was used as an instrument from at least the sixteenth century to persuade people not to give to people who were begging.[108] As far back as the second century, chests were kept in churches to receive voluntary contributions to the poor as well as 'orphans, aged servants, ship wrecked sailors and Christians imprisoned for their religion'.[109]

In his attempt to construct its genealogy, Bernasconi argues that, starting around the sixteenth century in Europe, the poor box became more ubiquitous and was explicitly linked with attempts to discourage people to give to those

---

[105] Charity Organisation Society, 'The Science of Charity: An Address Delivered by the Archbishop of Canterbury at the Annual Meeting of the London Charity Organisation Society, April 23, 1891', Occasional Paper 19, 1891 (Bodleian Library, John Johnson Collection), emphasis added.

[106] Mendicity Society, 'The Mendicity Society', *Charity* (June 1889) (John Johnson Collection, Bodleian Library), emphasis original.

[107] Roberts, 'Reshaping the Gift Relationship', 225. To my knowledge, the only known legal prohibition against giving to beggars occurs in 1349 with 23 Edw 3 c 7, which prohibits almsgiving to able-bodied beggars. It is notable that this prohibition was not re-enacted even when governance of vagrancy shifted to the more dangerous notion of criminality.

[108] R Bernasconi, 'The Poor Box and the Changing Face of Charity in Early Modern Europe' (1992) *Acta Institutionis Philosphiae et Aestheticae* 10, 33.

[109] ibid, 38.

who begged.[110] Chained inside the entrances of churches, hospitals and public buildings, poor boxes became a central instrument in the dramatisation of piety and religious devotion. A Venetian statute of 1529 required every church to have a poor box and to submit accounts; it included detailed prescriptions for emptying of the box.[111] In addition, legislation in 1506 and 1543 prohibited begging with one's face covered,[112] for the beggar's face was a cipher to be read for signs of wickedness and evil.[113] At the same time, legal provisions were made for alms to be personally delivered to noble families who were suffering hardship, known as the *poveri vergognosi*, or shamefaced poor.[114] Luther's ordinance for a common chest[115] prohibited begging and almsgiving while prescribing one or two council chests in which food could be left, along with the provision for a 'box or two wherein money may be put'.[116] Similar 'chest ordinances' followed in 1536 and 1542[117] and were often tied to sumptuary regulations prohibiting the wearing of costly clothes.[118]

In the public imagination, poor boxes played an important role in the dramatisation of penitence and atonement. As Herbert writes in his poem 'Praise', part of the 'literature of tears' of the seventeenth century,

> I have not lost one single tear
> But when mine eyes
> Did weep to heav'n, they found a bottle there
> (As we have boxes for the poore)
> Readie to take them in; yet of a size
> That would contain much more.[119]

In France, poor boxes were a legitimate enough form of charity to be the object of wills, as was the case of the Paris printer Charlotte Guillard, who in her will left £10 to the church and £10 to the 'poor box', with instructions that if any person challenged the will, then that person's portion was to go to the poor box as well.[120] In eighteenth-century France, communal poor boxes, along with the state

---

[110] ibid, 39.

[111] B Pullan, *Rich and Poor in Renaissance Venice* (Oxford, Blackwell, 1971); Salter, *Some Early Tracts*, 111–17.

[112] Pullan, *Rich and Poor*, 254.

[113] Bernasconi, 'The Poor Box', 35–36.

[114] ibid, 35.

[115] M Luther, 'Ordinance of a Common Chest' in HJ Jaroslav Pelikan, HJ Grimm, HT Lehman and HC Oswold (eds), *Luther's Works*, vol 45 (Philadelphia, Muhlenberg, 1962), 182.

[116] Salter, *Some Early Tracts*, 87.

[117] In England, an Act of 1536 stated that 'every parish of this realm shall in good and charitable ways take such discreet and convenient order, by gathering and procuring of such charitable and voluntary alms, of the good Christian people within the same with boxes every Sunday, Holy Day and Festival day'; cited in ibid, 125.

[118] ibid, 81.

[119] Cited in R Strier, 'Herbert and Tears' (1979) *ELH: A Journal of English Literary History* 46, 242.

[120] P Beech, 'Charlotte Guillard: A Sixteenth-Century Business Woman' (1983) *Renaissance Quarterly* 36, 355.

regulation of 'gleaning',[121] played a central role in efforts of church officials to make farmers responsible for the needs of the poor.[122]

So while the shift in the early nineteenth century that I have outlined did not then constitute a sharp break with a centuries-old trajectory of discriminate almsgiving, what was new, in England specifically, was how anti-mendicant officials configured the tender heart of the passer-by: as a site that could be governable as an object of rational calculation and acted on through specific projects such as ticket programmes and relief inquiries. The eye, hand and coin could be formed into a locus of order, an actionable site of regulation where giving 'idle relief to one's feelings' could be combatted by placing both the passer-by and the beggar within a wider economy of inspection, surveillance and deservedness. And while there is no doubt that the anti-mendicity movement was shaped by the evangelical spirit of the nineteenth century – a period which Boyd Hilton characterises as being imbued with the notion of Christian atonement[123] – this evangelical emphasis coloured the policing of early nineteenth-century begging rather than subsumed it. The fact is that early anti-mendicity efforts, and later the COS, were surprisingly secular as compared with other moral reform movements.[124] While poor boxes continued to play an important role in practices against discriminate almsgiving and the struggle over the responsibility for poor relief, they remained chained within the private religious space of the hospital and church until very late into the nineteenth century. Like the booth of the confessional, poor boxes facilitated a charitable act whose piety and atonement were generated by its private and anonymous character, qualities that would be destroyed when it was unchained from the church vestibule. The fact that, as Roberts points out, for its first operational structure the COS used the eight Metropolitan Police districts as a guide, rather than parish boundaries, illustrates how this movement was imbricated in the wider field of 'police' rather than in any particular strand of religious belief.[125]

III. A Man of the Crowd

The emergence of 'the humanity of the population' as a vexing problem for anti-mendicant reformers in the early nineteenth century – one to be addressed with a refined vagrancy law and charity programmes that might relieve public distress at the sight of a beggar – took place at a time when questions of disguise and

---

[121] Gleaning is the customary right of the poor to pick the fields for leftovers after reaping has been carried out. It is most famously depicted by Jean-Francois Millet in *Les glaneuses*, completed in 1857.

[122] L Vardi, 'Constructing the Harvest: Gleaners, Farmers, and Officials in Early Modern France' (1993) *American Historical Review* 98, 1435.

[123] B Hilton, *The Age of Atonement* (Oxford, Clarendon Press, 1992).

[124] Roberts, 'Reshaping the Gift Relationship', 211.

[125] ibid.

identity were being acutely felt and puzzled over in the new social spaces of the metropolis. This explicit emphasis on the problem of public feeling can be viewed as part of what Raymond Williams has called the crisis of a 'knowable community' in the first half of the nineteenth century. For Williams, the growth of cities and the metropolis, the changing character of labour, and shifting relations between and within social classes all brought into relief questions of community and identity. 'There is a direct though very difficult relationship between the knowable community and the knowable person.'[126] The new crowd of the metropolis[127] – in which the narrator of Wordsworth's poem wanders only to find that 'the face of everyone that passes by me is a mystery' – opened up opportunities for people to see and encounter one another while passing by on the pavements and during park strolls. The result was the manifestation of a particularly theatrical realm of self-presentation tied to an acute self-consciousness, what Elaine Hadley has characterised as a distinctly 'melodramatic mode'.[128] And given how begging was targeted as a problem of legibility – of discerning the authentic poor – the result was, as Murdoch notes, that the 'theatrical elements' of begging were exaggerated 'and applied to nearly all mendicants'.[129]

The place of the beggar in dramatising a much wider social 'crisis of the sign' is vividly illustrated in how the beggar was conflated with another archetypal figure of the early nineteenth century: the gentleman. The suspected fraud of gentlemanly appearance is vividly captured by Edgar Allan Poe in his short story 'The Man of the Crowd', published in 1840.[130] Watching the jostling passing crowd from a coffee house in London, the narrator observes a wide variety of characters teeming in a way 'which jarred discordantly upon the ear, and gave an aching sensation to the eye'.[131] In this cacophony of the senses that is the new crowd of the metropolis, Poe's narrator observes 'many individuals of dashing appearance' who, while appearing to be gentlemen, in fact belong to 'the race of swell fat pick-pockets'.[132] Respectability and probity in the public eye could so easily be counterfeited that, as Poe's narrator observes, even gentlemen themselves could not discern those who were counterfeiting their appearance. 'How difficult to imagine how they should ever be mistaken for gentlemen by gentlemen themselves.'[133]

---

[126] R Williams, *The Country and the City* (London, Hogarth Press, 1975), 124.

[127] ibid.

[128] E Hadley, *Melodramatic Tactics: Theatricalized Dissent in the English Marketplace, 1800–1885* (Palo Alto, Stanford University Press, 1995).

[129] L Murdoch (2003), *Begging 'imposters', street theatre and the shadow economy of the Victorian city*, unpublished paper presented at the North American Victorian Studies Association (NAVSA) Conference, Bloomingdale, IN, 5.

[130] EA Poe, 'The Man of the Crowd' in *The Unabridged Edgar Allan Poe* (Philadelphia, Running Press, 1983) 647–54.

[131] ibid, 650.

[132] ibid.

[133] ibid, 649.

The beggar and the gentleman were two figures who 'did not work' in the typology of Mayhew's poor,[134] for the public was deeply suspicious both of the well-to-do 'man about town' who looked after his invisible shares and of the beggar's hands, which accumulated coin without any visible labour.[135] As Murdoch argues, beggars were feared 'because they were so seemingly adept at manipulating modern economic practices … thereby highlighting the potential corruptibility of England's modern market economy.'[136] At a time when capital was reorienting the relation between hands, labour and coin, beggars, like the gentleman, were particularly upsetting in how they 'seemed to play the game of capitalism too well.'[137] As Audrey Jaffe observes in her brilliant study of 'scenes of sympathy' in nineteenth-century literature, 'the anxiety about false beggary, like that about gentlemanliness, is also an anxiety about the theatricality of the social world, the susceptibility to manipulation of social identity.'[138] The beggar, like the gentleman – both of whom rely on an appearance that can easily be manufactured and feigned – endangers the social identities of those who encounter him.[139]

Giving to people begging in the new crowd of the metropolis would, as Jaffe notes, embody an act of exchanging 'identity for coin'. This disconnect among knowable character, labour and coin was perhaps most clearly marked by the prevalence of begging letters, which penetrated the status-seeking consciousness of the middle class. Handwriting itself was viewed as being representative of character, and written letters could be read for the marks of a respectable educated man. But the gentleman's hand, like his appearance and idiom, could easily be forged. As the Charity Organisation Society warned its subscribers later in the century, the fraudulent beggar writer could very well appear to be a 'man of education and good address'.

[134] A Jaffe, 'Detecting the Beggar: Arthur Conan Doyle, Henry Mayhew, and "The Man with the Twisted Lip"' (1990) *Representations* (Summer 1990), 96–117.
[135] ibid, 101.
[136] Murdoch, 'Begging "Imposters"', 2.
[137] ibid, 4.
[138] Jaffe, 'Detecting the Beggar', 101.
[139] ibid, 102.

2

The Genesis of Gift-Crime Regulation: Winchester's 'Make It Count'

The beggar's hand is Christ's poor box, for whatever a poor person accepts, Christ accepts.

Peter Chrysologus, Bishop of Ravenna (fifth century)[1]

This chapter explores how the genesis of diverted-giving schemes in England, and the wider gift-crime-movement that now warns 'Your Kindness Can Kill', can be traced to the city of Winchester in 1995. Like anti-mendicant officials in the early nineteenth century who took the 'ill advised kindness of individuals' as a central problem to be overcome, Winchester city officials explicitly set out to order both public feeling and pocket change at the sight of someone begging. Named 'Operation Diverted Giving', this 'experiment' involved officials who took particular care in designing a scheme that involved a central paradox: a form of charity that would give to those begging by not handing anything to those begging on the streets. This first diverted-giving project was immediately viewed as a success, resonating with emerging ideas of urban renewal and crime reduction. The Winchester experiment would migrate to other cities and become the central driver of a much wider regulatory movement, one that held a new truth about beggars, and giving to people begging.

I. An Experiment

The city of Winchester is a well-heeled provincial community known for an educated and conservative population, which one national newspaper referred to as the 'smart set'.[2] The affluent character of Winchester is complemented by a dazzling historical heritage, making it one of the most desirable tourist destinations in southern England. It was used as a capital of ancient England under King Alfred the Great, and the medieval Gothic cathedral (the longest in Europe) is

---

[1] B Ramsey, 'Almsgiving in the Latin Church: The Late Fourth and Early Fifth Centuries' (1982) *Theological Studies* 43, 226–59.
[2] A Millington, 'Beggared in the Name of Charity', *The Observer*, 17 March 1996.

the burial place of Jane Austen. A medieval ethos of charity remains, including a former almshouse on the High Street; the Hospital of St Cross on the outskirts of the city, founded in 1136, remains the oldest charitable institution still occupied in England. History-hungry tourists today can walk from the city centre to St Cross, across a wet meadow where Keats once strolled, and receive a customary 'wayfarer's dole' at the gate, consisting of some bread and a horn of ale.

In explaining the impetus for the diverted-giving programme, local officials cited a growing concern, crystallising in the summer of 1995, that Winchester's High Street was in a state of decline. City officials, traders and the police spoke of a 'growing consensus' that something had to be done about the number of 'drunks', 'winos' and 'beggars' hanging around the city centre.[3] There was a feeling in Winchester – a 'law-abiding and well-heeled community' – that there were 'too many [beggars and street drinkers] sitting around, littering the streets up thoroughly'.[4] As the deputy mayor commented, 'even three or four young people lying around the streets begging and drinking was an offence to some people, so they said, "What is the city council going to do about it?"'[5]

This concern for the declining character of the pedestrianised city centre – viewed as being in direct competition with the new Tesco superstore on the outskirts of the city – prompted the formation of a City Centre Forum in 1995. This forum operated by means of bimonthly meetings which ostensibly presented an opportunity for community members to discuss city-centre issues. A steering group composed of representatives from the police, city council and trading communities was established to direct the forum agenda. The presence of begging, street drinking and other forms of behaviour considered to be 'antisocial' was immediately identified by the steering group as a major threat to the economic health and civilised experience of the pedestrianised city centre. Guided by these concerns, the steering group established what the police would later call a 'basket of measures' to address the presence of people who were drinking and begging.[6]

A scheme in which off-licences were asked to remove from their shelves especially strong lager – a favourite purchase of street drinkers – was set in motion, and the council, backed by the Traders' Association, pledged to spearhead a bid to the Home Office for funding of a CCTV system for the city centre. The Hampshire Constabulary came under pressure to assume a more visible presence on the street and was urged to support the council in passing a by-law that would ban drinking from the city centre. A tactic that immediately appealed to the City Centre Forum was the implementation of a buskers code, which was adapted from one being used in the city of Bath.[7]

---

[3] Interview with deputy mayor, City of Winchester, June 1997; interview with tourism director, City of Winchester, June 1997.

[4] Interview with deputy mayor.

[5] ibid.

[6] Interview with police inspector, Hampshire Constabulary, Winchester, November 1996.

[7] Winchester City Council and Hampshire Constabulary, 'Winchester Buskers Code', C\U\Az\ Cbusk.cdr.08.96, 1996.

Begging in the pedestrianised city core was seen to be a particularly troublesome problem. While the buskers code targeted those who were seen to be begging under the pretence of entertainment, the forum viewed the 'very generous and affluent population' of Winchester as the main problem which had to be addressed if the city was to get rid of beggars.[8] The pedestrian public was, according to the city estates officer, constantly being faced with the dilemma 'Do I or don't I give?' to someone begging in the street.[9] City officials believed that the crisis of conscience the passer-by felt when presented with a beggar's outstretched hand could be addressed by diverting donations away from those begging into specially designed and strategically located charity boxes. As Winchester's tourism director pointed out, such a programme would be a way to

> deal with the issue of people in the city who felt that they wanted to be charitable, consequently they could be assured that their money was going where it needed to go, and therefore that took out the thing of 'Should I give someone money or shouldn't I give someone money?' What is incredibly important and differentiates this [diverted-giving scheme] from other ventures is that it *actually deals with a person's guilt or compassion.*[10]

In problematising the feelings of the public as the key issue that had to be addressed, Winchester officials went about designing what Foucault identifies as a 'technology of the self', which he describes as the efforts of

> individuals to effect by their own means or with the help of others a number of practices on their bodies and their souls, thoughts, conduct, and way of being, so as to transform themselves in order to attain a certain state of happiness, purity, wisdom, perfection, or immortality.[11]

The impulse to give to someone begging was to be targeted with a specific technology by which people could, with the help of the officials, 'respond to their conscience in a positive way', as the deputy mayor commented.[12] By self-regulating their wisdom and emotions, officials hoped the public could align their conduct with that of being a 'good' and 'responsible' citizen who would not give to the 'drunks' and 'beggars' littering the street.

In justifying the development of this technology, Winchester officials cited a range of concerns that resonate in the popular and widespread stereotypes about homeless populations across England. Officials frequently mentioned that because of their affluent and generous population, the city centre had become a Mecca for antisocial and often dangerous beggars who would take advantage of the public to feed their drug or alcohol addiction. They worried that Winchester

[8] Interview with police inspector, Hampshire Constabulary, July 1997.
[9] Interview with estates officer, City of Winchester, June 1997.
[10] Interview with tourism director, City of Winchester, June 1997, emphasis added.
[11] M Foucault, 'Technologies of the Self' in LH Martin (ed), *Technologies of the Self: A Seminar with Michel Foucault* (Amherst, University of Massachusetts Press, 1988) 18.
[12] Interview with deputy mayor.

was considered to be a 'soft touch', an easy hit for undesirables who wanted to take advantage of people, especially those who were seen to be vulnerable, such as the elderly. This sentiment was often evoked in relation to the 'tougher' approach that the city of Salisbury – Winchester's closest competitor for tourist commerce – had taken by enacting an alcohol ban by-law for the city centre.[13] The 'soft touch' theme would be emphasised later in media interviews given by city officials on the diverted-giving and off-licence schemes.[14]

Closely joined to the 'soft touch' theme was evocation of the 'professional beggar', depicted as a stranger from out of town who earns a steady income by preying on the tender hearts of an unsuspecting public. A common sentiment expressed by city officials was that the begging-box programme would act as a deterrent to professional beggars who were 'ripping people off',[15] a view supported by a Hampshire police inspector, who believed that a beggar in Winchester could collect as much as £100 a day.[16] According to the city's tourism director, the begging-box programme would be 'putting in place barriers to make it difficult for people to abuse the system'.[17] What is notable about this widespread sentiment is that it posits a 'real', recognisable beggar in the public imagination who is worthy of support. In this view, begging itself is considered a legitimate form of charitable appeal, an organised 'system' that can be abused. Evocation of the professional beggar who accepts benefit at the expense of the real beggar mimics the construction of the 'welfare scrounger' who takes advantage of the system at the expense of those in real need. As the vice-president of Winchester's Chamber of Commerce noted,

> The problem with begging is that it is very difficult to differentiate between those who really need the money and those who do it because it is lucrative and a professional business: professional beggars. But what you couldn't determine is if they were actually really in need, [or] if they were professionals operating. The police were very clear that there are a number of people doing it as a way of living because it was very lucrative.[18]

Synonymous with evocation of the professional beggar was the concept of 'aggressive begging' as a form of antisocial behaviour. In justifying the diverted-giving project, aggressive begging was evoked by officials to describe behaviour that ranged from simply looking destitute and unsightly to criminal acts such as robbery, assault and menacing.[19] In a nostalgic turn, an official noted that a recent shift had taken place: beggars who had previously sat with a cap, calling out,

[13] Interview with receiver general, Winchester Cathedral, June 1997; interview with owner, McDonald's restaurant, Winchester, June 1997.
[14] eg, A Napier, 'Stopping Beggars, Helping Homeless', *Hampshire Chronicle*, 28 January 1997, 1.
[15] Interview with tourism director.
[16] Interview with police inspector, July 1997.
[17] Interview with tourism director.
[18] Interview with vice-president and chair, Winchester Chamber of Commerce, June 1997.
[19] Interview with police inspector, June 1997.

'Can you spare a few pennies, governor?' had now turned to forms of begging which were more threatening.[20] When probed about the ambiguity of the term *aggressive begging*, one official admitted that it was 'hard to put into words' but nonetheless said:

> The term is ambiguous but it is not: reality-wise you have to remember that Winchester is quite charitable in its nature. We actually have a situation where half the people say, 'We don't want these people here,' and the other half of the residents giving them money, encouraging it by the nature of what they were doing.[21]

And another official stated: 'When you encounter aggressive begging you may give money, but often it is because of a feeling of guilt. The public give because they feel embarrassed not to. They are cornered in a narrow passageway going through the square.'[22]

Closely linked to evocation of the 'aggressive' and 'professional' beggar was the perception that most people begging were drug abusers and 'drunks' who would simply 'drink their money'. As the deputy mayor explained, the 'worst thing you can do is give money directly' to those begging, because they would just spend it on alcohol so they could indulge in one of their 'favourite pastimes'.[23] This romantic outlook, which evokes heavy street drinking as a form of time-passing leisure rather than as a condition that might receive the attention of social services, was particularly widespread. Indeed, the attitude of many officials towards the figure of the 'drunk' as unworthy beggar was especially common, as typified by comments such as this:

> If they haven't got money and they're down on their luck, what are they doing spending it on alcohol, because that's going to do them no good at all. If you're down on your luck and short of money, [why] spend it on alcohol?[24]

Absent from such comments is an awareness of conditions which might dispose people to addiction – that, for example, drinking heavily might be a perfectly understandable response to the violence and degradation of living on the street.[25]

An overarching theme of these justifications was how the antisocial nature of begging was actively linked with the economic health and competitiveness of the city of Winchester. This linkage was most effectively expressed by city tourism officials, who played a crucial role by evoking the city-centre area as a 'product' that could be blighted by antisocial behaviour. The tourism director claimed that behaviour such as begging would intimidate 'the marketplace' and would damage the economy: 'For us to be competitive in the marketplace we need to take out

---

[20] Interview with tourism director.

[21] ibid.

[22] Interview with Chamber of Commerce vice-president.

[23] Interview with deputy mayor.

[24] Interview with manager, Sainsbury's store, Winchester, July 1997.

[25] See J Healy, *The Grass Arena* (London, Faber and Faber, 1988) for a biographical account of social conditions which led to the brutal violence and alcoholism of the 'grass arena' of street life.

the negative aspect of what's there'; 'Aggressive appeals to people [by beggars] are destroying our product.' In explaining the notion of diverted giving, the director explained: 'We are taking measures to move these people out of the range of the tourists.'[26] This motivation to remove the negative aspects from the city centre stemmed from the city's hope of cultivating what tourism officials claimed from their own research to be 'sustained visitors' to Winchester: the 15 per cent of visitors who stayed three or four nights and generated 61 per cent of visitor revenue.[27] Certainly this concern about the tourist 'product' of Winchester resonated within a business community which was deeply worried about the presence of the new Tesco superstore on the outskirts.[28]

Officials suggested that a programme which could divert the pocket change of passers-by from the beggar's hand into a network of charity boxes would move beggars 'out of the range of the tourists'. According to city officials, beggars who truly needed money for food and accommodation – those whom officials considered to be 'real' beggars, deserving of assistance – would no longer need to beg on the street, as they could avail themselves of services supported by money that had been diverted to the begging boxes. And those who did not need to beg for money for food or shelter – who begged to support a drug or drink habit or begged 'professionally' – would simply move on to another location, as the diverted-giving scheme would dry up donations. A central tenet of diverted giving's logic was that beggars on the streets after the diverted-giving programme was initiated could be considered undeserving and justifiably moved on by the police, a strategy characterised by the city's estates officer as an 'economic tool to reduce begging', one that would 'target the undesirables'.[29]

The steering committee of the City Centre Forum developed a mission statement which set out three main goals for what the committee called 'Operation Diverted Giving':

(1) To have a number of donation boxes in readily accessible locations within the city centre to receive donations from people who would otherwise give to those begging on the street.

(2) To direct the donated money to those agencies best placed to help those in greatest need.

(3) To encourage the public not to give to beggars and pseudo-buskers by way of ongoing publicity and raising awareness of the donation boxes and the work of voluntary groups.[30]

There was little initial difficulty in securing participants, with prominent retailers such as Marks & Spencer, Boots and WH Smith agreeing to take a box. 'I saw

---

[26] Interview with tourism director.
[27] ibid.
[28] Interview with Chamber of Commerce vice-president.
[29] Winchester Estates Office, 'Operation Diverted Giving: Aim', 1997. This approach is an interesting reflection of regulatory ideas popular in the 1980s, when economic incentives and disincentives were seen as a more efficient way to regulate conduct than more overt efforts of command and control.
[30] Winchester, 'Operation Diverted Giving: Aim'.

it as an initiative,' commented the WH Smith store manager, 'that could aid the fact that if we are doing this and people are giving to us and not giving to people in the street, there should be less people that are actually involved in that [begging].'[31] He viewed the scheme as particularly targeting hard drinkers and 'travelling beggars who actually make a living at it.'[32] The Marks & Spencer manager described the scheme as a community effort that would 'give givers an alternative route' to provide 'resources for those most in need'.[33] Other locations agreed to accept posters and flyers that would publicise the scheme and direct pedestrians to the nearest box. The participation of Winchester's famous cathedral would have added an air of legitimacy to the charitable ethos of the project. However, despite the efforts of the estates officer to place a box in the close, cathedral officials refused, explaining that it would be unfair to be seen to favour one charitable cause over another.[34] The cathedral was nevertheless supportive of the 'charity of diverted giving', as its receiver general reported, and agreed to place a poster on its notice board in the close entrance nearest to the pedestrianised city centre.[35]

Securing of the co-operation of 'agencies best placed to help those begging on the street' was a more contentious issue. The benevolent face of the project depended on securing the assistance of voluntary agencies which could offer services that, according to the diverted-giving logic, the real and thus worthy beggar could use. The scheme was considered to be controversial in the volunteer community, where some agencies were suspicious of the motivations of the police and city merchants. When asked to participate, the Winchester Council of Community Services (which acts as an umbrella group for about a dozen small agencies) decided that it was simply not practical to divide the money among its members, some of which had 'ethical' objections to the programme.[36]

Nevertheless, the city estates officer was able to secure participation of the two homeless shelters in the city, the Trinity Day Centre and Winchester Churches Nightshelter. The participation of both a day and a night shelter was essential to the marketing of the scheme as a legitimate 'compassionate' alternative that would apparently offer comprehensive support to people begging on the streets. A brief summary of the characters of both the night and day shelters during the first two years of the Winchester scheme is useful for understanding the nature of diverted-giving coin. A registered charity, Winchester Churches Nightshelter provides 17 beds a night and offers modest common room facilities and a primary health-care unit. Approximately 100 centre volunteers are supplemented by paid staff, comprising a project manager, a part-time administrator and four part-time

---

[31] Interview with manager, WH Smith store, Winchester, June 1997.
[32] ibid.
[33] Interview with manager, Marks & Spencer store, Winchester, June 1997.
[34] Interview with cathedral receiver general.
[35] ibid.
[36] Interview with housing manager (1998).

project supervisors. The shelter employs no professional social workers. Located within the city-centre area, the night shelter has been described as embodying 'tough Christian love' and has a reputation for a strictly enforced regime of rules.[37] Its stated mission, 'to provide overnight shelter and food to anyone who is homeless', is a qualified one.[38] First, the accommodation is not free, as guests are 'requested to pay something towards their accommodation'; the 'guest contribution' fee is £2.00 per night, with a concessionary fee of £1.00 for those under 25.[39] Second, the shelter will deny accommodation to those who refuse to pay the fee.[40] As the shelter manager comments in the 1996/97 annual report,

> Though not the easiest part of our daily duties, we managed to persuade our guests to contribute almost £10,000 towards the shelter's running costs. We have never subscribed to offering 'free' accommodation, and I personally consider that a 'give-away' society in no way helps guests become responsible citizens.[41]

This policy of 'persuading' the guests to pay a fee is enforced by the shelter through surveillance of how much money those guests have received from social security. Those who are registered as guests are required to provide their Department of Social Security (DSS) number and date of birth to the shelter manager, who enters the information on a computer spreadsheet used to keep track of guests.[42] The shelter uses the information to check with the local DSS office to see which guests are in receipt of benefits and to ban anyone on benefit who owes more than one week's contributions.[43] The manager explained that this surveillance often leads to the DSS's telling him how much 'pocket money' individuals have. In the spring of 1997, 72 people were excluded from the shelter, the majority of those for non-payment, although others were banned for offences such as possessing alcohol, smoking in their room or not making their bed.[44] Certainly it is easy to see how a shelter that does not believe in a 'give-away' society would be attracted to a diverted-giving scheme.

Unlike the night shelter, the Trinity Day Centre has struggled to maintain a secure existence. Located outside the city centre in a residential area behind the railway station, the day centre offers a 'place to go where our project workers seek

[37] Interview with Trinity Day Shelter team leader, July 1997.

[38] Winchester Churches Nightshelter [hereafter Nightshelter], *Annual Report, 1996/1997.*

[39] ibid.

[40] ibid.

[41] ibid.

[42] In January 1997, 107 registered individuals had used the shelter in the past six months.

[43] The manager provided the example of recently discovering that one individual who owed the shelter £35 had just been paid £140 by the DSS; interview with Nightshelter manager, January 1998.

[44] Interview with Nightshelter manager, July 1997. In 1996/97, £9,900 was raised through contributions 'requested from guests'; Nightshelter, *Annual Report, 1996–1997.* In 1997 this informal surveillance of social recipients' money was formalised in a form titled 'Winchester Night Shelter Guest Contributions', which guests were required to sign on their arrival. It reads in part: 'I, the undersigned, give my permission for the Nightshelter administration to approach the DSS/JSA to obtain information deemed necessary to check the details that I have given you relating to my benefit level or date of payment.'

to create a welcoming, non-judgmental atmosphere'.[45] Hot lunches are served for a charge of 50p a person. Washing, bathing and laundry facilities are available, as well as clothes, blankets and sundry items such as razors and soap. The most visible contrast with the night shelter in the late 1990s was the centre's permissive open-door policy, in keeping with its 'non-judgmental atmosphere'. Users were excluded only under the most exceptional circumstances, and the centre tolerated individuals who had been drinking or who were accompanied by dogs. The relationship between the day centre and its residential neighbours was strained; the neighbours were openly hostile to plans to expand services at weekends.[46] This tension, exacerbated by lack of funding, led the manager to reorganise the centre's operations early in 1997. Along with staff redeployment from full-time to part-time, the centre moved to more prohibitive rules: the main entrance door was kept locked, dogs were banned, and those who had been drinking were excluded.

Prior to their participation in the diverted-giving programme, and perhaps as a reaction to concerns about their clients' visibility, both the night shelter and the day centre had previously attempted to implement token and voucher schemes to provide an alternative to cash for those who wished to give to people begging. The Trinity Day Centre created luncheon vouchers for 50p with the intention of selling them to church groups, which would distribute them to members of the public, who could hand them out to those begging as an alternative to money. The luncheon tokens were first made of paper but were later laminated after worries about their being easily forged.[47] The scheme was an immediate failure; as the centre's manager commented, it was a 'puff of smoke; it disappeared as quickly as it came up'.[48] There was 'no take-up' of the vouchers; they did not circulate from the pedestrian giver to the beggar and back to the day centre. Indeed, the few vouchers that arrived at the centre caused suspicion. As the manager explained,

> One or two people turned up with a token [voucher], and we weren't sure where they got them from, whether there was a black market, or whether they got one from the drawer [of a desk in which they were stored]; then there was a notion that maybe we should number them. From our point of view it was a nightmare to administer.[49]

The day centre's manager was left with a desk drawer full of 'a hundred of them'.[50]

The night shelter organised a similar scheme at about the same time, to be able to 'offer a form of help other than cash to those persons begging for money'.[51] One hundred and fifty tokens, each worth 50p off the shelter fee, were produced and bought by St Peter's Church to be distributed by the church to those who

---

[45] Interview with Trinity Day Centre team leader, 1997.
[46] Interview with Nightshelter manager, 1998.
[47] Interview with Trinity Day Centre team leader, January 1998.
[48] ibid.
[49] ibid.
[50] ibid.
[51] Nightshelter, *Annual Report, 1995/1996*.

appeared in need of shelter services. The notice on the tokens that they could not be exchanged for money is a reminder that this, like nineteenth-century anti-mendicant tickets, was an effort to create a surrogate for the morally dangerous character of money placed in the beggar's hand. The project was thought to work well at first, but soon the shelter management became worried about street people stealing tokens from one another.[52] The scheme was discontinued after shelter users seeking tokens started lining up for them in the mornings at the church – which sits across from the night shelter – camping out on the lawn and causing damage to trees and shrubs.[53]

With the participation of the two homeless shelters secure, the most practical task facing the project committee was the design of posters and publicity material which would provide visual instructions for pedestrians walking through the city centre. The officials considered diverted-giving posters not only important for educating tourists that there is an alternative to giving to beggars, but more specifically as a visual aid that could literally guide members of the public to a box, should they suffer pangs of conscience upon seeing someone begging. The original posters, titled 'City Centre Begging', read in part:

> You are asked not to give money to beggars. If you have sympathy with these people please make your donation where you can be SURE that it will help. Collection boxes are located around the city for the Night Shelter and Trinity Centre ... The nearest collection box is in [space for retailer name].[54]

A flyer displayed and given out to pedestrians at various city-centre locations reads:

> Begging has become a real concern for the public, local traders, the City Council and visitors to our beautiful city. There is also an understandable concern for the plight of people at risk. However, giving to beggars and poor quality buskers provides no guarantee that the money will be spent on food, shelter and other basic essentials. The City Council ... has decided to give people a convenient alternative way to give by organising collecting boxes in the city ... By giving this way you can be SURE your money goes where it will help most.[55]

The poster is a prominent example of a type of 'technology of the self', of an inscription or 'official graffiti' that makes the reader responsible for self-regulation, often in the context of risk.[56] It effectively presents a mode of wisdom to the passer-by that provides an alternative to the 'risk' of giving to beggars, a jeopardy that can be solved through the insurance of safe official charity boxes where people can be *sure* about the use their money is put to.

---

[52] Interview with Nightshelter manager, 1998.
[53] ibid.
[54] Winchester Estates Office, 'City Centre Begging', poster, 1996, capitalisation original.
[55] ibid.
[56] J Hermer and A Hunt, 'Official Graffiti of the Everyday' (1996) *Law and Society Review* 30, 455–80.

While local traders and council officials were enthusiastic about the programme, they were reluctant to spend very much in the way of start-up costs for something the city estates officer considered to be an experiment.[57] Five wooden boxes were 'cobbled together' by a local carpenter at a cost of £20 each, paid for by the city as a 'Town Centre management' initiative.[58] The boxes had to be affixed to the wall in each store – a feature that would later be considered undesirable – and were secured by a small, toy-like lock; the names of the two recipient shelters were displayed on the front of the box. With two local charities and a number of High Street retailers on board, there was still the matter of how donations deposited in the boxes would be administered. The council did not want to be responsible for the costs of emptying each box and preparing a deposit; the city 'did not need the hassle'.[59] Each retailer who participated in the scheme agreed to be responsible for retaining a box and keeping it secure, emptying the box, recording the amount in a 'pay-in' book and depositing it into an account held by the treasurers of each charity. There were no accounting procedures to monitor the collections and deposits; shops with boxes were trusted to be accurate about recording and depositing the exact amounts donated.

Figure 2 Launch of the Winchester diverted-giving programme at Marks & Spencer, Winchester, 2 December 1995 (photo courtesy of the *Winchester Chronicle*)

The programme was launched on 2 December 1995 at the Marks & Spencer store, which had played a key role in promoting diverted giving as a solution to the problem of begging. A photo opportunity was arranged with the store manager and an Environmental Health Committee member demonstrating the proper response to the sight of people begging on the High Street (see Figure 2).

---

[57] Interview with estates officer.
[58] ibid.
[59] ibid.

The begging-box programme was immediately considered a success; stories abounded of people leaving 'notes rather than coins' and that the boxes were over-flowing with money.[60] A police inspector noted that someone had deposited a £35 cheque, and commented that diverted giving was thus shown to be successful, as a passer-by 'wouldn't have given that to a beggar'.[61] The *Hampshire Chronicle* ran a story one week after the programme began, titled 'Shoppers' Seasonal Generosity' and reported that WH Smith had raised £100 in the first two days.

The campaign gained modest attention in the national media[62] and the estates officer wrote a 'good practice' note for the newsletter of the Town Centre Management Association, of which he was a member.[63] The only visible expression of resistance was a petition organised and signed by several users of the Trinity Day Centre, who complained that the programme unfairly targeted those who cadged pocket change, and suggested that they should have access to free services. That shelter users expected improved and accessible services did not seem unreasonable, given that this was the official goal of the programme as promoted to the public by the council. In responding to the organiser of the petition, Winchester Council's chief executive replied that it was

> The Council's belief that more money is being given via the boxes than would otherwise be given to people begging on the street, and that by distributing it through support agencies it can be better targeted to assist those in real need. The Council is confident that all money given is used to best effect by the charities.[64]

For the city estates officer, the petition suggested something else: 'I think the petition is an acknowledgement,' he wrote to the manager of the day centre, 'that the scheme is having an effect.'[65] The city's response to the petition is curious. Why would a project presented as helping those who used the day centre be considered a success when the users were upset at being stigmatised? The answer becomes clear in the next phase of diverted-giving development that officials carried out. Encouraged that their experiment was a success, the steering committee felt that, with some changes, the charity of diverted giving could be significantly improved. The estates officer formed a Diverted Giving Committee to redesign the programme and plan a relaunch for the summer of 1996. The committee was composed of the Trinity Day Centre manager, a city tourism officer, a city-centre police inspector, an official from the city planning department and, perhaps most notably, a regional Marks & Spencer security manager.[66] Meeting minutes reveal

---

[60] ibid.

[61] Interview with police inspector, November 1996.

[62] Millington, 'Beggared'.

[63] Winchester Estates Office, 'Operation Diverted Giving', 1997.

[64] Letter to Trinity Day Centre team leader from Winchester estates officer, 'Diverted Giving Campaign: Winchester City Centre', 20 March 1996.

[65] Letter to petition organiser from Winchester chief executive, 'Collecting Boxes: City Centre Begging', 19 March 1996.

[66] Winchester, Minutes of Diverted Giving Scheme Project, May [nd], 22 May and 23 June 1996, with attachments: three technical drawings of begging boxes and brackets with Tuskguard

that the Committee believed the scheme could generate as much as £10,000 a year and that as many as 15 boxes could be fixed inside stores, with an additional 24 external boxes located on the street.[67]

The participation of the Day Centre's manager is notable, as it was the first time that someone from the volunteer sector had actively participated in the diverted-giving scheme. While his co-workers at the shelter (where users had organised the petition) were not enthusiastic about his involvement in the programme, the manager took a conciliatory approach: 'I didn't come in there [to the committee] to say, "You mustn't do that, this is an outrage, taking away people's right of choice." I thought there was nothing I am going to do with this powerful group'.[68] The manager viewed his participation within the larger context of public relations, in which he had to solicit financial help for the shelter:

> I wanted to keep them [the press] on board. There are times when I need them, and that's helped, because since then they do phone up and say, 'Got any news for us?' or I phone them and give them a story, and then when that happens we occasionally get a cheque through the post.[69]

The Diverted Giving Committee focused on improving two aspects of the programme: the poster's message and the charity boxes. The Committee felt that the posters were unattractive and awkwardly written and did not effectively emphasise the notion of social responsibility. Committee members believed that public opinion about the programme was fragile and that they had to be 'very careful about how things were written'.[70] In considering options for refining the poster's message, the idea of using some type of illustration to depict the notion of giving was agreed on. The task of redesigning the poster was given to the police inspector, who employed a police artist from general headquarters to work up the Committee's ideas of a diverted-giving image. A basic template was established using a border with the familiar Winchester King Alfred icon and a circular window where an image could be inserted to accompany the poster text.

Over several meetings, the Committee struggled to devise a suitable image to represent the diverted-giving message to the public. The police inspector asked the artist to provide an illustration of giving and came to the next meeting with an image of a homeless 'down and out' character crouching on the street. The Day Centre manager described it as a Ralph McTell character,[71] a 'scruffy-looking drunk with a dog and a couple of bottles,[72] while the tourism manager thought the

---

watermark; Diverted Giving Project Group membership list, May 1996; 'Making It Count', press release for relaunch, 25 July 1996.

[67] ibid.

[68] Interview with Trinity Day Centre team leader, July 1997.

[69] ibid.

[70] Interview with manager, Tourism Services, City of Winchester, July 1997.

[71] Ralph McTell is a well-known folk singer whose best-known work, 'Streets of London', evokes the down-and-out side of street life. The approximate North American equivalent appears to be country singer Willie Nelson, popularly known as 'Boxcar Willie'.

[72] Interview with Trinity Day Centre team leader, 1997.

image looked 'really hideous'.[73] It was considered so offensive by the Day Centre manager that he took a copy back to the shelter to show his skeptical staff that there was some value in his being there to counter offensive stereotypes of the homeless.[74]

The police artist responded to this criticism by producing a second, similar graphic with the addition of someone in a suit 'throwing money' at a homeless figure sitting on the pavement wrapped up in a blanket.[75] Again the tourism manager and Trinity Day Centre's manager balked at this stereotype of homelessness, although they did agree with the other Committee members that it was important to depict the actual act of giving. The problem the Committee faced, according to the tourism officer, was to illustrate giving in such a way that it did not look like someone 'distributing largesse' to a beggar.[76]

After some discussion about how giving could be more specifically represented, the police artist responded with an image of two hands, one moving towards the other in a 'reaching, helping' act. The Committee liked this 'Good Samaritan' depiction, but after reflecting on the image further they worried that the helping hand also looked like a hand reaching out to apprehend someone. This realisation caused much 'jocularity' among Committee members, who joked about the image's evoking the 'long arm of the law'.[77] In order to address the ambiguity of the two reaching hands, the Diverted Giving Committee decided to introduce objects that would clarify the relationship between them: coins dropping from one hand into the other, a depiction that was chosen for the final poster (Figure 3).

The design of the diverted-giving icon is notable for the semiotic awareness the Committee members exercised in negotiating the moral character of the diverted gift, and in doing so, the moral characters of both the passer-by and the beggar. The first image considered – a stereotypical image of the homeless person as drunkard – suggested a charitable object who was undeserving, one who might 'drink his money', a connotation that went against the idea that the diverted-giving programme would help 'real' beggars who would not just spend their money on alcohol or drugs. The second version, of a passer-by throwing money at a sympathetic image of homelessness – a prostrate figure wrapped in a blanket – was nevertheless considered inappropriate because of the overly generous, perhaps even reckless gift that was not morally discriminate ('distributing largesse'). This image also presented the public-relations risk of assuming a rather cynical view of public charity in which giving to those who begged was not a generous, heartfelt act. The solution to these unclear images was one of synecdoche, of representing the

---

[73] Interview with Tourism Services manager.
[74] Interview with Trinity Day Centre team leader, 1997.
[75] ibid.
[76] Interview with Tourism Services manager.
[77] Interviews with Tourism Services manager and Trinity Day Centre team leader, 1997.

Figure 3 Relaunch poster, 'Make It Count' programme, Winchester 1997 (photo by author)

passer-by and the beggar with only their hands, each reaching towards the other. But while this reduction made it easier to refine the message of discriminate almsgiving by literally erasing the bodies of the beggar and passer-by – and by doing so the social position of each – it opened up a new ambiguity: was this an image of helping or of arrest, of assistance or coercion? The solution was to add the coins dropping from one reaching hand to another.

The image represents a perverse paradox: an icon designed to discourage handing pocket change to someone begging consists of an image of the direct exchange of coins between two hands. This stark contradiction speaks to how the Committee struggled to evoke the personal and spontaneous generosity that is often associated with giving to someone begging, while at the same time promoting a form of charity that is impersonal and bureaucratic. Officials understood that they had to carefully evoke the moral leverage of generosity that is implied in giving to a beggar, but in a way that nevertheless involves not giving at all to someone begging. To accompany this image, the poster text was edited to present a softer, less pedantic message, summed up in the new catchphrase 'Make It Count'. This slogan further emphasised the morally discriminate character of diverted giving while at the same time suggesting that giving to someone begging wouldn't count for anything.[78]

Officials envisioned the posters as a network of visual stimuli to compete with the sight of people begging, acting to break the immediate link between eye, hand and coin. The original drab green poster colour was initially replaced with a scheme of red on blue. However, the Committee worried that, like the reaching hands, the blue was 'too police-orientated', and that might make people 'think of the Hampshire Constabulary'.[79] Red was instead chosen as the primary colour – the same shade of red that Winchester used for its city letterhead and civic publications.[80]

A striking feature of the creation of the Make It Count icon is that the officials reproduced a centuries-old discourse: of the hand as an organ of expression and feeling and, more specifically, as an instrument of discriminate almsgiving. Perhaps the most notable treatise on the hand as a tool of expression is John Bulwer's *Chirologia: or the Natural Language of the Hand*, the first English writing on the role of the body in rhetoric, published in 1644.[81] Taking up Bacon's observation that 'As the Tongue speaketh to the ear, so the gesture speaketh to the eye,' Bulwer provides an extensive survey of all possible movements of the hands and fingers, which are 'external expressions of man's intellectual and emotional nature'.[82] The gestures of the hand are 'the only speech and general language of human

<hr/>

[78] Interview with Trinity Day Centre team leader, 1997.
[79] ibid.
[80] ibid.
[81] J Bulwer, *Chirologia: or the Natural Language of the Hand and Chironomia: or the Art of Manual Rhetoric* (1644), ed JW Cleary (Carbondale, Southern Illinois University, 1974).
[82] JW Cleary, 'Editor's Introduction' in J Bulwer, *Chirologia*, xiii and xv.

nature', one that escapes the confusion of Babel, one through which God speaks to us in a holy language.[83] Nature provides a universal language of the hand; in public speaking, Bulwer observes, 'nature's gestures must be made subject to the requirements of art'.[84] Drawing on ancient and contemporary sources, he sets out to chart the 'active elocution of the hand':[85]

> In all the declarative conceits of gesture whereby the body, instructed by nature, can emphatically vent and communicate a thought, and in the propriety of its utterance express the silent agitations of the mind, the hand, that busy instrument, is most talkative, whose language is as easily perceived and understood as if man had another fountain of discourse in his hand.[86]

Figure 4 *The Natural Language of the Hand: Auxilium fero* (Bulwer 1644)

Figure 5 *The Natural Language of the Hand: Mendico* (Bulwer 1644)

Figure 6 *The Natural Language of the Hand: Munero* (Bulwer 1644)

In Bulwer's catalogue of 48 gestures, three have a particular resonance with the work of the diverted-giving committee. First, the effort to evoke the 'helping, reaching' act of diverted giving has a remarkable correlation with *auxilium fero*, or 'I bring aid' – of a 'helping hand', of 'an expression of intention to afford comfort and relief ... an expression much desired by those who are in distress and are

---

[83] ibid, xv.
[84] ibid, xxiv.
[85] ibid, xxx.
[86] Bulwer, *Chirologia*, 15.

not able to shift for themselves' (Figure 4).[87] Indeed, this depiction of assistance, of taking by the wrist, is resonant of the connotation that Winchester officials feared in the first of the three sample poster designs – that of the 'long arm of the law' coercing the helpless supplicant. The ambiguity of this image led officials to portray two of Bulwer's related gestures, those of *mendico* (Figure 5) and *munero* (Figure 6). The first, *mendico* ('I beg'), demonstrates for Bulwer an 'unusual capacity' of the hand: 'to hold out the hand hollow in [the] manner of a dish is their habit who cravenly beg, covet and show a greedy readiness to receive.'[88] Contrasted to the beggar's hand is that of *munero* ('I reward'): 'to put forth the right hand spread is the habit of bounty, liberality, and a free heart; thus we reward and friendly bestow our gifts.'[89]

Munero and *mendico* have played a central role in prescriptions around almsgiving as an activity which is central to the exercise of Christian atonement; almsgiving was considered by the Church Fathers to be one of two 'fonts of mercy', a 'kind of washing of the souls'.[90] And unlike the other font of mercy, exercised in baptism, almsgiving could be repeated an unlimited number of times in order to maintain spiritual hygiene.[91]

With the centuries-old iconography of *munero* and *mendico* thus reproduced in the diverted-giving poster, the second, closely related task of the Committee was to develop and obtain new charity boxes. These, like representations of the hand as 'signifying faculties of the soul', have a central place in the history of discriminate almsgiving, as I briefly touched upon in the previous chapter. The original wooden boxes (Figure 2) were seen by the officials as quaint and amateurish-looking and were now considered neither big nor secure enough. As one member of the Diverted Giving Committee stated,

> They needed to be big enough so that you didn't have to empty them every week – if we are encouraging retailers to take them, then they have other things to do than run to the bank with the money – but not so big that you couldn't move them.[92]

Concerns over the charity box's being so large that retail staff might not be able to move it when full speaks to how the officials believed they could tap into such a vein of guilt and compassion in the public conscience that the coin produced might well be physically unmanageable. In addition, retailers had concerns about how the original wooden boxes were anchored; simply using screws to attach the box to the wall was insecure and inconvenient for store managers, who had a limited amount of available wall surface to work with.[93]

---

[87] ibid, 58.

[88] ibid, 53–55.

[89] ibid, 55–58.

[90] Peter Chrysologus, Bishop of Ravenna, cited in B Ramsey, 'Almsgiving in the Latin Church: The Late Fourth and Early Fifth Centuries' (1982) *Theological Studies* 43, 226–59.

[91] Ramsey, 'Almsgiving', 228.

[92] Interview with Tourism Services manager.

[93] ibid.

The Committee felt that the boxes should be unique and co-ordinated to produce a visually consistent brand within the space of the city centre and the network of stores. As one committee member stated,

> We could have gone and bought a dozen plastic boxes and stuck a little notice on it and shoved it [onto a retail counter]. We wanted it to be more of a scheme that was co-ordinated, so if you maybe saw one in Marks & Spencer and didn't think very much of it, and then saw one in [another shop], then it encouraged the idea.[94]

The job of researching and co-ordinating the effort of finding new boxes was taken up by the Marks & Spencer security manager. He turned to a security installation company called Tuskguard, which produced a series of technical drawings of a steel box and attachment brackets which the security manager brought to the meetings for discussion.[95] The boxes, which could be attached to floors, walls or counters with customised stands and brackets, were designed to be adaptable to different store interiors in a way that would provide consistent diverted-giving options for pedestrians wandering around Winchester's city centre. As one member of the Committee commented,

> The colour scheme of the posters was integrated with the boxes. The boxes were bigger and more colourful and could be mounted on a variety of surfaces and positions; they were highly mobile and adaptable to specific environments. The committee wanted boxes that were 'big and bright'; there were lots of collecting boxes on people's counters from various charities, [and] we didn't want it to be anything like that.[96]

Both the posters and the boxes made the absent present, both in terms of officials who wanted to discourage giving and by creating a relationship through space and time where handed-out pocket change could be diverted into an alternative shelter gift. Retailers were urged by the City Traders Group to act in unison with the diverted-giving posters by physically 'pointing would-be-givers to the collection boxes'.[97]

Fifteen cylindrical charity boxes were ordered from Tuskguard at an invoiced cost of £1,970.95.[98] Despite the Committee's ambitions to expand the number of box locations, they could find only one additional site that would participate. Nine of the new boxes (valued at about £1,000) were stored in the City Council's basement.[99] No 'external' boxes were mounted in public spaces. The relaunch costs – for the boxes and new publicity posters – were covered by a £2,000 donation from the Hampshire Constabulary and a £500 donation from Marks & Spencer.[100]

---

[94] ibid.
[95] Winchester, Minutes of Diverted Giving Scheme Project.
[96] Interview with Tourism Services manager.
[97] City Traders Group [Winchester], 'Winchester News', December 1996.
[98] Invoice from Tuskguard Ltd to Winchester estates officer and Marks & Spencer security manager, 'To design, supply and fit: 15 No. Cylindrical Charity Boxes', invoice no. 3413, 1 October 1996.
[99] Interview with estates officer.
[100] ibid.

The Marks & Spencer location was used for the relaunch on 25 July 1996. A press release quoted the mayor of Winchester:

> Winchester City Council and the City Centre management steering group are delighted to be pioneers of this new initiative, believed to be one of the first in the country. We are pleased it has gained the support of many local businesses and been welcomed by visitors and residents.[101]

The most notable aspect of Operation Diverted Giving was how the boxes guarded the pedestrianised space and attempted to create a network of surveillance and regulation that would order the interactions and feelings of High Street pedestrians. The Marks & Spencer box was located at the end of the food tills, mounted with a wall bracket in the same place as the original wooden box. The location was just beyond the cashier, where, according to the store's manager, customers would 'come off the food tills with change in [their] hands or return the trolley, which has a pound coin system. These are two triggers which encourage our customers to put money in the boxes.'[102]

At WH Smith the box was mounted with a floor bracket at the checkout leading out to the High Street, where there was, according to the manager, the 'highest customer flow'.[103] The diverted-giving box competed with two other charity boxes: a Hat Fair box, which raised money for a local summer street fair, and a British Heart Week box. At waist height, the diverted-giving box appeared perfectly positioned to compete with those other charities and intercept change received after a purchase. The Committee was certainly aware that the diverted-giving boxes would have to compete with other static charity boxes inside the retailers' premises, most usually on the counter at the cash tills. Similarly, in McDonald's the box was mounted on a side wall parallel to where people lined up to order their food. Competing with the box was a coin-activated game box which contributed to the McDonald's charity fund. The game was popular with children who were growing impatient with queueing for their food.

In the Sainsbury's location, the box was mounted on a floor bracket chained to trolley rails at the far front corner of the shop (Figure 7). While the box was highly visible, it was not near one of the 'giving triggers' found at Marks & Spencer, directly across the pedestrianised street. As the Sainsbury's manager commented on the box's location, 'The problem we've got down here is that the store just isn't big enough, so we've had to put it in a little corner where it would be out of the way.'[104]

The Boots store posed a special challenge: while the cash tills near the front of the store exited onto the High Street, the rear entrance, which had no change-making

---

[101] Winchester, Minutes of Diverted Giving Scheme Project.
[102] Interview with Marks & Spencer manager.
[103] Interview with WH Smith manager.
[104] Interview with Sainsbury's manager.

Figure 7 'Make it Count' box mounted in Sainsbury's, looking out across the pedestrianised high street to Marks & Spencer, Winchester, 1997 (photo by author)

tills, led into the cathedral close, a prime pedestrian area for visiting tourists. And it was at this rear exit, away from the cashiers, that the box was mounted. The store manager located it there on the suggestion of the city's estates officer, as it would 'service the square and the cathedral area'.[105] The manager wanted to re-site the box to what he felt was a more lucrative position near the tills at the front store entrance. 'I'm embarrassed about it,' the manager admitted.

> The box is in the wrong place. That's where I was asked to put it – [the estates officer] had a look around and said that's where he would like it. And I said, 'Okay, but you're not going to get much in it there, mate. No one's got money on them there.'[106]

[105] Interview with manager, Boots Drug Store, Winchester, June 1997.
[106] ibid.

Figure 8 'Make it Count' box and poster, Guildhall Tourist Information Centre, Winchester, 1996 (photo by author)

Certainly the positioning of this box at the back of the store, near the cathedral close, suggests that the estates officer was more concerned about educating soft-hearted tourists as they passed through from the cathedral close into the pedestrianised area than maximising the potential of change in hand at the tills.

The sixth box was located in the tourist information centre at the Guild-hall, mounted on a stand which could be moved freely across the public counter (Figure 8).[107] Like the box at Boots, which was placed to cover pedestrian traffic from the cathedral area, this box was meant to greet the estimated 250,000 tourists who visited Winchester each year.[108] As the city's tourism director commented, the diverted-giving box educated information-seeking tourists walking into the city centre 'that they should be prepared to see' people begging and not to feel intimidated into giving when there was an alternative.[109] Like the trinkets and postcards displayed around it, the box was there primarily to manage and promote Winchester as a tourism product.

II. A Lot Better than Nothing?

Did the Winchester charity of diverted giving, Make It Count, provide 'resources for those most in need', as officials such as the Marks & Spencer manager claimed? Did the city ensure that every penny from the hands of the public would 'count' towards providing 'direct support, accommodation, and food' for those 'really in need'? In examining the financial character of the scheme, one is immediately drawn to the manner in which the programme was administered. Despite the fact that the diverted-giving programme was presented as an accountable public scheme, the city council made no real attempt to administer or oversee the programme in any meaningful way. With the new Make It Count campaign launched, the Diverted Giving Committee, which had designed the scheme in such detail, was simply disbanded. Even 18 months into the programme, the council had not collected any information on the amount that each location was depositing at the bank. Only after repeated requests to the city for information did the estates officer circulate a form, asking retail participants to volunteer the deposit information they had recorded in their pay-in books.

This absence of oversight is especially significant considering the extent to which the council made authoritative statements about the success of the programme to other cities and to users of the day shelter who had complained in their earlier petition. It is unclear how, in responding to the day shelter users, the Winchester chief executive could claim 'the council is confident that all money given is used to best effect by the charities'[110] when the city had no firm idea at that point how much money had been raised or how it was benefiting anyone in the shelters. Because of this lack of participation by the city in administering the boxes, Make It Count was operated as a private charity: each participating retailer emptied its box, counted the money, recorded the amount in a pay-in book and deposited the money into an account shared by the treasurers of each charity.[111]

[107] Interview with Tourism Services manager.
[108] ibid.
[109] Interview with tourism director.
[110] Letter to Trinity Day Centre team leader from Winchester estates officer, 20 March 1996.
[111] The account was held at a Winchester High Street bank.

While the programme was ostensibly a public scheme, it operated as a loosely co-ordinated network of private charity boxes under the control of the retailers. And because the boxes were inside the private spaces of the retail shops, they were exempt from accountability to public charity law.[112]

An analysis of the bank statements detailing deposits made by the scheme participants, along with the year-end financial reports of the day and night shelters, provides a picture of the diverted-giving money generated over the first two-year period of the programme.[113] The highly irregular deposit patterns of the five locations makes it impossible to construct detailed patterns of giving; however, by averaging out these deposits per month, we can tell that officials consistently overestimated the actual amounts being raised by diverted giving. For example, officials reported that the scheme raised £500 per month[114] when in fact it averaged £258 per month in the first six months of the programme, an amount which would drop to £110 per month in the last six months of 1997.[115] A review of the operational budgets of the charities[116] demonstrates that the amount contributed was negligible. For the operating year 1996/97, diverted-giving cash accounted for 1.8 per cent of expenditures of the Trinity Day Centre and 1.4 per cent of the expenditures of the night shelter[117] – a 'drop in the ocean', according to the Winchester Churches Nightshelter manager.[118] And while officials admitted that the diverted-giving money accounted for only a fraction of the operating costs of the shelters, the overall opinion was that (as a cathedral official noted) the diverted-giving change was 'a lot better than nothing' for those who used the shelter services.[119]

But was it really 'a lot better than nothing'? Not only did the programme generate a negligible amount of revenue for the shelters, there is considerable evidence that the diverted-giving project created a backlash within the shelter communities. Both shelter managers reported that, shortly after the programme started, individuals began showing up at their centres – not unreasonably, given the stated goals of the scheme – asking for free or reduced charges for services. The night shelter manager reported that users routinely asked if the nightly fee could be waived

[112] This may explain in part why the plans of the Diverted Giving Committee to permanently mount 24 boxes in public spaces were never carried out. Mounted boxes would have been illegal under street-collection legislation, most notably because Make It Count was not a registered charity.

[113] Trinity Day Centre, bank statements, Winchester City Centre Collection account, 10 February 1997 to 9 January 1998; Winchester Estates Office, completed 'Make It Count' forms from several merchants, 1997.

[114] Interview with deputy mayor; Winchester, Minutes of Diverted Giving Scheme Project.

[115] Trinity Day Centre, bank statements; Winchester, completed Make It Count forms.

[116] Trinity Day Centre, *Trinity Day Centre Annual Report, 1996/1997*; Nightshelter, *Annual Report, 1996/1997*.

[117] For the financial year 1996/97, diverted-giving funds contributed £1,798 towards an expenditure of £98,179 for the day shelter and £1,200 towards an expenditure of £89,300 for the night shelter. Trinity Day Centre, *Annual Report, 1996/1997*; Nightshelter, *Annual Report, 1996/1997*.

[118] Interview with Nightshelter manager, January 1998.

[119] Interview with cathedral receiver general.

because the shelter had received money from the scheme; the manager character-ised these requests as 'crap' and refused to change an already rigid fee scheme.[120] This position is not surprising, given the ethos of the night shelter, which does not believe in a 'give-away' society.

In the case of the day centre, the programme exacerbated an already under-funded and stressful work environment. After the diverted-giving programme started, several of its users who had been subjected to a harsher policing regime came into the day centre and made their displeasure known to the staff.[121] The most concrete expression of this tension is illustrated in the use of the shelter manager's small welfare fund (about £20 a week), usually used for emergency requests. Typically the centre manager frequently had to say 'Not this time' to users who came to him for money. With the introduction of the diverted-giving boxes, the manager had a much more difficult time saying no to people: 'Now when they come and ask for something and I'm saying, "No, we haven't got enough," [they say,] "Just read in the *Chronicle* that you got £2,000 from the begging boxes. What you have done with the money?"'[122]

These sorts of confrontations happened several times a week at the peak of media awareness of the programme. The demands heightened an already tense environment at the day centre, to the point where staff felt they had to justify charging 50p a meal for lunch; the centre's management decided to lower the price to 25p so that staff could 'have something to tell them'.[123] The fact that Make It Count had become a liability to the day centre's operations in particular, with no tangible benefits to shelter users, compelled its manager to insist that the shelter's association with the scheme not be publicised on the new boxes or in publicity material. Subsequently the relaunch poster (Figure 3) did not identify the agencies which would offer 'direct support, accommodation and food', as the original box had for the two shelters (Figure 2).

A more serious event widely seen to be related to the diverted-giving programme occurred when the day centre shut down for two weeks after two of its users became violent with staff. While there is no evidence to suggest that this inci-dent was directly linked to frustration over the diverted-giving scheme, the closure of the centre was nevertheless seized upon by proponents of the programme as a sign that the scheme was having the desired effect. As one trader commented, the shutdown was inevitable because the centre users '[understandably] saw their income disappearing – they [the Centre staff] got quite a lot of grief – people that were giving them money were not now [after diverted giving]'.[124]

Was the programme successful in removing the 'professional' and 'aggressive' beggars from Winchester's High Street? Retail and city officials believed that it

[120] Interview with Nightshelter manager, January 1998.
[121] Interview with Trinity Day Centre team leader, 1997.
[122] ibid.
[123] ibid.
[124] Interview with Chamber of Commerce vice-president.

was and attributed the apparent absence of beggars on the street to an increased police presence and public hesitation to give to people begging.[125] There is, however, no evidence that the scheme had any impact on the giving habits of the public, that it 'dried up' pocket change in the beggar's hand. As would become common in promotion of other schemes in the years to come, its success was measured through anecdotes and soft public relations impressions; in Winchester this comprised a tourism department survey of tourists' perceptions in terms of, for example, how many people knew about the scheme.

More substantively, there is a consensus among city officials that the police did, in various phases, initiate a crackdown in the pedestrianised area as part of the package of city-centre improvement measures which included the diverted-giving scheme. The response of the police was complex, but there is little doubt that, in conjunction with a number of 'management' initiatives (such as the off-licence and CCTV schemes), they followed through with what a local police inspector described as 'robust enforcement of legislation' as an expression of the 'increased level of support' which the police had agreed to provide with implementation of Make It Count.[126] 'What we are trying to do,' the inspector explained, 'is educate the public and say, "You don't like aggressive begging, you don't like vagrants and antisocial behaviour? We don't like it either."'[127]

In the words of the city's deputy mayor, the police would have 'something positive' to say in dealing with those begging: 'They didn't need to beg around here. If you're short of food or a bed, we've got a place for you to go.'[128] The consequence was displacement of visibly indigent individuals from the pedestrianised central area to a park outside the city centre, an area near Andover Road.[129] And despite officials' insistence that the programme would simply 'dry up' street donations and drive the 'professionals' out of town, this police-generated displacement was in fact anticipated by members of the Diverted Giving Committee from the outset. As a committee member commented,

> We determined early on as part of that group that what was going to happen [was] that it [diverted giving] was going to shift our problem to somewhere else, that we couldn't solve social problems and that this might have to be a measurable success.[130]

The police seemed as unwilling or unable as anyone else (including the two shelters) to deal with the hard core of street drinkers which the programme appeared to be targeting. As the police inspector stated, those individuals were 'low-quality prisoners'; they smelled and were dirty and their arrest provided

---

[125] This was not a unanimous perception. One box-site participant suggested that people who usually gave to beggars would continue to do so, while the provision of more social services would in fact increase the perception that Winchester was a 'soft touch'; interview with McDonald's owner.

[126] Interviews with police inspector, 1997 and 1996.

[127] Interview with police inspector, 1997.

[128] Interview with deputy mayor.

[129] Interviews with Sainsbury's manager and Tourism Services manager.

[130] Interview with Tourism Services manager.

little status for young officers keen to deal with 'real' crime.[131] Along with this 'measurable' goal of displacement was the admission by both shelters that street drinkers who beg – often identified as the most problematic group – are the least likely to avail themselves of shelter services; this is especially true of the night shelter, which has much stricter rules.[132] Perhaps the reason why the Committee was so sensitive about not evoking an image of coercion when designing the diverted-giving image is that it accurately reflected the intentions of the scheme – one that, far from 'helping those most in need', did nothing to address the needs of those on the street; in fact it seemed to be viewed as a success particularly in terms of the perceived punishment that the day centre users experienced. And while officials understood the fake character of 'helping those most in need', those who begged and used shelter services did indeed expect that passer-by pocket change would be diverted to them in terms of increased and improved shelter services.

While officials publicised how every penny would count, the reality is that authorities exhibited little interest in where the money was going and how it might be making a difference in tangible shelter services or serving the needs of those on the street. The 'success' of the diverted-giving programme in Winchester, which would be emulated in major cities and tourist destinations across England, had little to do with extending the charitable coin of public generosity to those who beg. What it was successful at was making the explicit policing of those who were begging on the street an acceptable and legitimate activity in a consciously affluent and historically charitable community.

---

[131] Interview with police inspector, 1996.
[132] Interviews with Trinity Day Centre team leader and Nightshelter manager.

3

One Remove from Beggary: Flag-Day Collectors, Buskers and *Big Issue* Vendors

Why is it generally better to give money to an organised charity than to a street vendor?

Question on Weschler Children's IQ Test, 1949

In his 1806 work *A Treatise on Indigence*, Patrick Colquhoun complained of the 'idle employments' of 'the lower orders of peoples, such as ballad-singers and minstrels' who could not be suppressed.[1] His contemporary Thomas Smith complained of 'that lower order of street-musicians, who so frequently distract the harmonious ear with their droning bag-pipes, screaming clarionets, and crazy harps. These people, with the match, toothpick, and cotton-ball vendors, may be considered, but as one remove from beggary.'[2]

In the centuries-old history of vagrancy policing, street characters who are 'one remove from beggary' have proved to be a consistent source of frustration and annoyance for officials. Today one can see the descendants of this wide collection of importuners in the figures of flag-day collectors, buskers and *Big Issue* vendors, particularly in how each of them relies on a particular theatricality to colour their performances with a message of worthiness, skill, or industry.

This chapter briefly explores how these activities are constructed as desirable gift opportunities that are differentiated from vagrant begging. My discussion of these forms is brief and limited to the time period of the first few years of Winchester's Make It Count scheme. Such a comparison is useful to this study when one considers how each of these activities is intricately regulated to be outside the gift crime of giving to the vagrant beggar. This regulation that makes them 'one remove' from begging is carried out in two forms, through 'body idiom', the appearance and conduct of the importuner, and second, through the visibility of *bona fides* that evoke some sort of official authority.

---

[1] P Colquhoun, *A Treatise on Indigence, Exhibiting a General View of National Resources for Productive Labour* (London, J Hatchard, 1806) 74.

[2] JT Smith, *The Cries of London: Exhibiting Several of the Itinerant Traders of Antient and Modern Times* (London, John Bowyer Nichols and Son, 1839) 45–46.

I. Flag-Day Collectors

Street collections, as carried out on annual 'flag days', are one of the most visible aspects of the multi-million-pound charity industry, which also uses direct mail, radio and television appeals, telephone soliciting and inserts in paper media. Charities compete with one another to get noticed in a visually noisy world and rely on established formulas specifically designed to startle the conscience. Fundraisers intentionally target the emotions of the potential donor, as illustrated by three of the most effective advertising styles recommended by a leading charity consultant:[3]

1. The 'shock/horror' advertisement: Classically it features big-eyed, starving children in famine-relief appeals. It hits people hard and therefore gets results.
2. The 'guilt-inducing' advertisement: Perhaps people need to feel guilty before they respond, but this style can easily put people off.
3. The 'professional amateur' advertisement: For years Help the Aged, Britain's biggest charity advertiser, admirably typified this style with simple text advertisements without illustrations. They appeared to be written by honest, unsophisticated charity supporters working with low overheads but high commitment, and they worked.

Such tactics enable charities to be depicted as helping the helpless – the old, the sick, the abused, the handicapped – in representations that intentionally pander to a public belief that these individuals are all hapless victims.[4] The key to forging this linkage is vividly suggested in the training material for collectors produced by the Royal National Institute for the Blind (RNIB; now Royal National Institute of Blind People), which asks: 'Why do people give to charities?'

> Donations are often influenced by a number of factors, including demographic trends, the state of the economy and the general willingness to give. The latter is often heightened by the incidence of natural disasters, media coverage, etc. People often feel closest to causes which are most likely to affect an individual's sense of well being and security, or most likely to affect immediate family and friends (eg cancer, heart-related causes).[5]

During the 1990s the notion of 'relationship fundraising' was promoted in the British charity scene, most notably by Ken Burnett in his two popular and influential books.[6] Burnett advocates promotion of a 'professional relationship fundraiser'

---

[3] K Burnett, 'Creating Successful Advertising' in K Burnett (ed), *Advertising by Charities* (London, Directory of Social Change, 1986) 32.

[4] M Morris, 'Why Advertise?' in K Burnett (ed), *Advertising by Charities* (London, Directory of Social Change, 1986) 10–11.

[5] Letter to author from fundraising development officer, Royal National Institute for the Blind, 16 January 1998, enclosing RNIB information sheet (October 1997), 3.

[6] K Burnett, *Relationship Fundraising: A Donor Approach to the Business of Raising Money* (London, White Lion Press, 1992) and *Friends for Life: Relationship Funding in Practice* (London, White Lion Press, 1996).

who can adapt commercial fundraising techniques to the charitable sector and transform the donor into a 'customer'.[7] 'We have to see donors,' he comments, 'as co-owners of the organisation, partners in a common aim'.[8] Professional relationship fundraisers 'make caring possible by enabling donors to realise their capacity and potential to support good works'.[9] Charities rely on demographic profiling of donors and attempt to establish long-term donations with devices such as deeds of covenant.

Within this industry, street collections are perhaps the most visible of an almost endless number of charity activities carried out in public and semi-public spaces. In its guidelines for fundraisers, the City of London lists 62 types of fundraising activities in 1997, including 'miles of pennies', wastepaper drives, bar jars in pubs, and coffee mornings.[10] In support material for its fundraisers, the World Wildlife Fund (WWF) recommends the following A-to-Z list of possible fundraising activities:

> Appeals, auctions, art exhibitions
> Bike rides, barbecues, 'bring and buy'
> Concerts, coffee mornings, cricket matches
> Dances, discos, diving competitions
> Exhibitions, empties collecting
> Fêtes, fun runs, football matches
> Garden parties, guessing the weight of the cake
> Home-made goodies, Halloween parties
> 'I did it for Wildlife'
> Jumble sales, jumpathons, jars of pennies
> Knit-along (sponsored)
> Market stalls, morning coffee, money boxes
> Nature trails, 'nearly new' sales, naming the doll
> Outings, outgrown clothes sale, 'odd job' days
> Pantomimes, pram races, plant sales
> Quizzes
> Raffles, readathons, record funds, 'run for the fund'
> Sports days, sponsored silence, sponsored spells
> Tombolas, treasure hunts, toy sales
> Used stamp collections, used can collections
> Volunteers, Valentine dances
> Walk for wildlife, waste paper collecting
> Xmas draw, Xmas card sale
> Yo-Yo competitions, your own ideas
> Zany ideas.[11]

---

[7] Burnett, *Relationship Fundraising*, 4.

[8] ibid, 7.

[9] ibid, 9, original emphasis removed.

[10] Letter to author from chief trading standards officer, City of London, 6 November 1997, enclosing fundraising guidelines.

[11] World Wildlife Fund [WWF], 'Fact Card: A–Z of Fundraising' (1997).

There appears to be no form of risk, endurance activity or skill too mundane or trivial (eg, guessing the weight of a cake) not to be considered worthy for fundraising. Often fundraising has been seen as an opportunity for particular groups to get away with behaviour that otherwise might be questionable, the paradigm example being university 'rag days' with their slightly penitential character, whereby students are seen to be making up for out-of-place behaviour by raising money.

A recurring theme in fundraising is efforts that attempt to take advantage of loose change, which is viewed as being a nuisance. Events which target small change (such as 'penny miles' and penny jars) are the most obvious examples, including the collection boxes placed on retail counters which attempt, like the Winchester Make It Count boxes, to prompt giving after change has been made from a purchase. Charities occasionally target money whose currency has expired, such as the *Sunday Sun's* campaign to collect out-of-circulation 50p pieces for the Diana, Princess of Wales Memorial Fund shortly after her death in 1997.[12] Charities routinely make arrangements with banks to cash in currency which has become out-of-date for public use.[13]

A variation on this technique is campaigns carried out by airlines which involve soliciting money from passengers, with envelopes passed out by the cabin crew during the flight's descent. Such schemes cleverly take advantage of the inconvenience of small amounts of foreign currency which passengers have not exchanged (or are unlikely to exchange). One such scheme, called 'Change for Good', carried out by Cathay Pacific, reportedly raised £1.5 million for UNICEF in 1998.[14] A more static scheme has been used at Heathrow Airport in London, where a series of charity boxes greet travellers and invite donations in any currency. The donations are counted, changed into pounds sterling and distributed to allocated charities by the BAA Heathrow Corporation.[15]

In chapter two I noted in a discussion of poor boxes that organised street collections did not emerge until late in the nineteenth century. The Royal National Lifeboat Institution (RNLI) has a defensible claim to establishing the first modern street collection to be sustained at a national level; it can be considered a forerunner of the modern flag day. Responding to the need to set up a relief fund for the orphans and widows of the *Mexico* shipwreck, which caused the death of 13 lifeboat men from St Annes, Lancashire, in December 1886, the

---

[12] The *Sun* promoted the campaign with the phrase 'For Diana's sake give a big'un to save a little'un' and sent out stickers to be placed on containers for workplace or home collection.

[13] Letter to author from regional manager, Royal National Lifeboat Institution (RNLI), 2 February 1998, enclosing minutes of City of London Branch annual general meeting, 28 May 1997.

[14] Cathay Pacific, 'Cathay Pacific and UNICEF announce $3.6 Million Change for Good Result', press release, 9 March 1998.

[15] Letter to author from public relations officer, British Airports Authority Heathrow, 20 February 1998, enclosing 'Charity Boxes at Heathrow' fact sheet.

RNLI engaged in a programme of fundraising that made direct appeals to the public for assistance.[16] Led by the cotton-industry magnate Sir Charles Macara, the RNLI initiated its first 'Lifeboat Saturday' on 17 October 1891 on the streets of Manchester.[17] A 'grand procession was formed', according to a contemporary account,

> consisting of the two boats, three bands, the fire brigade, the ambulance corps, representing the mode of saving life on land as well as water. The procession proceeded from the centre of the city to Belle Vue Gardens, and was witnessed by enormous crowds on route. A number of collectors accompanied the boats ... and large collecting boxes were placed in the main thoroughfares, at the railway stations, and places of amusement. These were tended by boys from the Strangeways Refuge in their uniforms, the boxes being so made that money could not be extracted. Sheets were also erected at various prominent places; these being guarded by policemen. A sum of £600 was got in the streets, largely in coppers.[18]

Of particular note is how this event has the markings of modern street collections: systematic collection of pocket change on the public pavement and the use of secure boxes. Lifeboat Saturdays were abandoned during the First World War, during which charities in both the United States and Britain produced cloth flags to be sold to the public to support war widows and orphans. The RNLI quickly followed, reproducing its insignia in 1915 as a flag to be given out during pedestrian collections when Lifeboat Saturdays were resumed after the war.

The flag-day collector is governed by two intersecting forms of order: formal regulations that charities must follow after being granted a permit by local authorities, and informal training and guidance. The result is that specific *bona fides* are created that can be presented and communicated to strangers through non-verbal ways. The central way in which *bona fides* are performed is what Goffman calls 'body idiom'. 'These comprise bodily appearance and personal acts', Goffman writes, and include 'dress, bearing, movement and position, sound level, physical gestures such as waving or saluting, facial decorations and broad emotional expression'.[19] In 1997 flag days were ordered by regulations made under s 5 of the Police, Factories etc (Miscellaneous Provisions) Act 1916. The regulations are administered through local councils, which adopt model regulations approved by the Home Office.[20] Applications for collections are received by local authorities, and only those registered as charities with the Charity Commissioner are considered for street collections.

---

[16] AJ Dawson, *Britain's Lifeboats: The Story of a Century of Heroics* (London, Hodder and Stoughton, 1923), 156.

[17] CW Macara, *Getting the World to Work* (Manchester, Sherratt and Hughes, 1922).

[18] As quoted in Dawson, *Britain's Lifeboats*, 158.

[19] E Goffman, *Behaviour in Public Places: Notes on the Social Organization of Gatherings* (New York, Macmillan, 1963), 33.

[20] City of London collections are administered by the Commissioner of Police for the City of London; collections within London councils are administered by the Commissioner of the Metropolitan Police. The regulations under this Act are almost identical across all jurisdictions.

The street collection regulations focus on two main aspects of flag-day conduct: the character and conduct of the collector and the design, use and emptying of the collection box. In addition, prominent charities carry out their own detailed regulation of flag-day activities through the training, supervision and appearance of collectors and their collection boxes. Not surprisingly, the probity of the collectors is a primary concern of the regulations. Each collector, states the City of London, 'is to be a fit and proper person of good character'.[21] This notion of good character is further enforced in the prescription that collectors must be volunteers and cannot be paid in any way from the proceeds of the collection.[22] However, this reliance on unpaid volunteers provides a security risk to charities; volunteer guidelines often address the possibility of volunteers' using charity material to collect illegally for themselves. The Multiple Sclerosis Society (MSS) warns flag-day promoters to check the name, address and telephone number of new recruits, never to let them collect on their own, and to make sure collection materials such as boxes and badges are given out and handed in just before and after the collection.[23] This concern is especially relevant for charities that must recruit collectors by using newspaper advertisements or through a local volunteer centre or university rag club.

Good character is manifested visually through a trustworthy appearance and the behaviour of the collector. Each collector must carry written authority of the promoter for inspection by the police, and charities usually provide collectors with customised badges that are worn as part of the co-ordinated brand of the charity. This appearance of good character is further enforced by the regulated conduct of the collector, who must carry a collection box, remain stationary while collecting, and not stand within 25 metres of other collectors.[24] In addition, 'no collector shall importune any person to the annoyance of such person', which effectively means tin rattling and shouting should be avoided, and no collection shall be made in a manner likely to cause danger, obstruction or inconvenience to any person.'[25]

Charity fundraising manuals provide detailed guidelines to order the body idiom of flag-day collectors, including ordering the appearance and conduct of collectors in a way which constructs them as polite, trustworthy and dependable. These specific instructions are the most detailed efforts at ordering 'body idiom', where the collector is expected to embody and present a good character through position, posture and conduct.[26] 'Consider your appearance,' comments one

---

[21] In the City of London this vetting of good character is carried out through an application form that requests information about any court convictions; letter from chief trading standards officer, London.
[22] ibid.
[23] Letter to author from marketing assistant, Multiple Sclerosis Society (MSS), 4 February 1998, enclosing fundraising guidelines.
[24] Police, Factories etc (Miscellaneous Provisions) Act 1916, ss 14, 11.
[25] Letter from trading standards officer, London.
[26] Goffman, *Behaviour in Public Places*, 34.

flag-day manual, 'as you will be a representative of the British Red Cross.'[27] Following police regulations, the National Society for the Prevention of Cruelty to Children (NSPCC) advises its collectors to remain 'in one place' and to 'be aware that your posture when collecting is very important. We suggest that you stand as upright as possible, so making yourself easier to notice.'[28] They should also refrain from smoking, drinking or eating while collecting, lest they look slovenly.[29] The collector must be morally upright and able to control his own impulses, giving full attention to acting on behalf of the distant victims. He should also be friendly and should 'try to catch people's eye with a smile and offer a cheerful greeting,'[30] as this often 'prompts them to give.'[31]

Fundraising guides often suggest that collectors attract attention to themselves with a 'fancy dress costume' that 'can make collecting more fun and draw in members of the public'.[32] Street collectors are urged to position themselves at 'the busiest point possible' on the pavement in order to maximise giving opportunities.[33] As the NSPCC fundraiser manual suggests, collectors should strategically locate themselves on the pavement to expose themselves to as much pedestrian foot traffic as possible:

> Stand away from the wall of the building – ie: within the flow of pedestrians. A collector standing near the edge of the kerb, with his back to the traffic, has the advantage of being able to judge the flow of people from either direction. This position also guarantees that people should be forced to walk in front of him/her or risk being run over on the road. It is hard to resist giving in these circumstances.[34]

Faced with being run over by traffic, pedestrians would have little choice but to give to this charity, which is concerned with preventing forms of human cruelty. While annoying tin-rattling is illegal, collectors are often encouraged to shake their boxes 'gently' in order to get attention.[35] 'It is a good idea,' suggests the NSPCC fundraising manual, 'to insert two or three coins in each box. These are known as "rattlers"; and, as the name implies, help when shaken, to make the collector noticed when he/she begins the shift.'[36] Indeed, collection boxes act as a sort of acoustic instrument, reminding the passing pedestrian of the change so far donated by other strangers.

[27] Letter to author from Regional Fundraising department, British Red Cross, 5 March 1998, enclosing 'Collection Pack' containing 'Helpful Hints for Collectors'.
[28] Letter from administrator, Regional Appeals, National Society for the Prevention of Cruelty to Children (NSPCC), 20 February 1998, enclosing volunteer handbook; letter from British Red Cross.
[29] Letter from British Red Cross.
[30] ibid.
[31] Letter from NSPCC.
[32] Letter from MSS.
[33] Letter from British Red Cross.
[34] NSPCC volunteer handbook, 5.
[35] ibid; letter from RNLI.
[36] NSPCC volunteer handbook, 5.

The body idiom of flag-day *bona fides* relies on a commercially branded appearance to communicate a carefully crafted charity image. Collectors are to be properly outfitted with appropriate collection paraphernalia and material, which often uses distinctive corporate colours and logos.[37] Indeed, a whole array of customised collection media is available for the official collector to wear, including sashes, pins, tabards, armbands, banners and badges.[38]

Collection boxes act as an officially sanctioned and secure conduit by which pocket change can be channelled as a good gift into the bureaucratic hands of the charity. Flag-day boxes create an accountable, authorised space for the relationship between *munero* and *mendico*. According to the regulations, every 'collection box, receptacle or tray' must be sealed in a way that opening it would break the seal, and all monies received by the collector 'shall be immediately placed in a collecting box'.[39] The box must be numbered and 'securely closed and sealed' during the collection.[40] Sealing the collection boxes not only provides a visual assurance to passers-by of the trustworthiness of the charity but, more importantly, acts as a way of ensuring that the volunteer collectors do not pocket any donated money for themselves. Flag-day manuals warn that collectors should never 'ask for money'[41] nor 'open your collection box to give change'.[42] Each box must be numbered and display the name of the charity, and a list must be maintained that notes the name of the collector.[43]

The emptying of money from the sealed box is prescribed in some detail. The seal of each box can be opened only in the presence of a promoter and 'another responsible person' or a bank official.[44] Each numbered collection box must be accounted for and the contents recorded and certified.[45] Collection expenses must be noted and are expected to be kept below 10 per cent for first-time collections (to pay for the boxes) and 5 per cent after that. 'Any expense ratio above 10 per cent,' states the City of London, 'is sharply questioned and promoters are reminded that extraneous expenses should be financed by donations or central funds.'[46] In addition, the promoter of each charity may be required to report financial details of the flag day in a designated newspaper. These requirements are a sharp contrast to diverted-giving schemes, which literally have no safeguards in place to either secure the handling of the money or scrutinise the economic transparency and efficiency of the charitable effort.

---

[37] Letter from MSS.

[38] Letter from director, Angal Service to Fundraisers, 11 August 1998, enclosing 'Angal: Make Ideas Work for Fundraisers' package with marketing materials.

[39] Police, Factories etc (Miscellaneous Provisions) Act 1916, s 14(3).

[40] ibid, s 14(2).

[41] Letter from NSPCC.

[42] Letter from British Red Cross.

[43] Police, Factories etc (Miscellaneous Provisions) Act 1916, s 15.

[44] ibid, s 16(1, 2).

[45] ibid, s 16(3).

[46] Letter from trading standards officer, London.

In the sector of street-collection media, the company Angal Collecting Boxes and Devices dominates the flag-day market in the United Kingdom. Angal provides a wide range of collection services, from various types of boxes and stands to the production of specific flag-day media. The firm does a wide range of custom work involving retail-counter boxes which greet people 'when they are at their most receptive and generous', with change from making a purchase in their hand.[47] Often these counter boxes use 'eye catching coin actions', which are especially attractive to children.[48] One of the most evocative devices is the 'begging dog' box of the RSPCA: a wooden dog sitting upright in front of a doghouse with a tray balanced on its front paw. According to the RSPCA, this box 'appeals to children particularly as they love putting money on the red tray held by the dog, tipping it into a slot at the front of the kennel.'[49]

The most specialised and popular product that Angal has produced is the Polybox Handbox, which can be used in street collections to enable pedestrians to carry out what the company refers to in its marketing literature as 'direct giving' between the collector and the passer-by.[50] Hand-moulded in 'tough polythene', the Handbox long ago replaced the collection tin. It is specially designed to cater to the requirements of collection regulations concerning how a container should be sealed and emptied.[51]

The most significant aspect of the Handbox, which is used almost exclusively by major charities that collect on the street, is how it is specifically designed to funnel loose change efficiently from the hand of the passer-by in a way that does not involve actually placing it in the hand of the collector.[52] The Handbox acts to discipline both the licensed hand of the collector and the giving hand of the passer-by. For the collector, the waisted shape of the Handbox makes it 'comfortable and convenient to hold and shake' and 'makes coins seem lighter'.[53] 'This is an interesting point with the design of the "flag day collecting units"', comments the World Wildlife Foundation, as they are 'designed to be comfortable to hold for a long period of time.'[54] Angal claims that the box is capable of holding three kilograms of 'mixed coins', which the company estimates would constitute about £200 in donations. In addition to this carrying capacity, the Handbox also has a 'generous area for appeal message'.[55]

[47] Letter from Angal Service to Fundraisers.
[48] ibid.
[49] Letter from NSPCC.
[50] Letter from Angal Service to Fundraisers.
[51] Angal Limited, 'The Legal Requirements and Commonsense Practice Relating to the Use of Collecting Boxes Generally', Angal Service to Fundraisers, December 1993.
[52] Letter from Angal Service to Fundraisers.
[53] ibid.
[54] WWF, 'Fact Card'.
[55] Letter from Angal Service to Fundraisers.

'Key features'

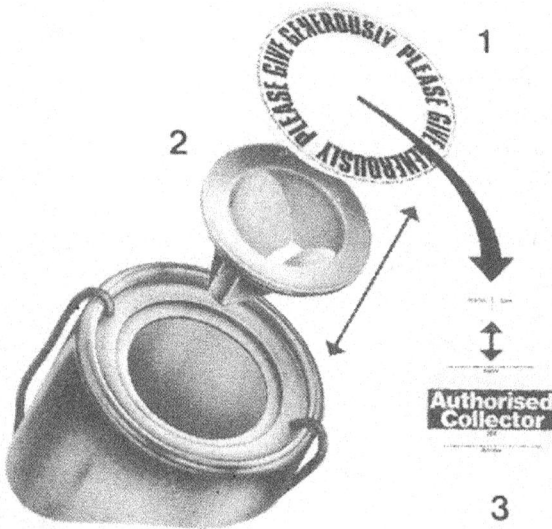

The Angal patented sealing system

To open the Polybox Handbox®, slit the Ringseal® (1) all round the edge of the Funnel Slot Closure® (2). Lever the closure out with a screwdriver or similar tool, pushing it well under the closure. After removing the contents of the box, press the closure back into place and apply a new Ringseal®. The Box Identity Sticker (3) should be filled in with number, date, etc., and stuck to the side of the box where visible. New Ringseals® can be stuck on top of old and removed en bloc only as necessary. Stubborn fragments can be left.

Figure 9 'Key features' of the Angal Polybox Handbox (reproduced with permission)

Not only is the Handbox comfortable to hold and shake for a collector stand-ing in one place, it also ensures secure funnelling of handed-over change. The box is equipped with a customised 'opening and sealing system and a patented slot design that literally funnels coins into the box by the handful' (Figure 9).[56] A patented feature of the box's opening is the 'Funnel Slot Closure', which has a wide opening to accept 'multiple coins and notes' so there is no need 'for donors to hesitate to "select" coins'.[57] An excerpt from the patent description for this closure and sealing system (as illustrated in Figure 9) vividly illustrates the role of the Handbox in constructing a legitimate and trustworthy giving opportunity to the public.

> Many persons donating money, tokens or saving stamps prefer to be able to see that their donations are secure. Similarly, many collectors prefer to use a container which is such that their integrity is not questioned. In order to go some way towards meeting the above problem, the known container is provided with an aperatured [*SIC*] security ear on the body, and an aperatured security tab on the lid. The security ear and the security tab are such that they are connectible together by a sealing arrangement.[58]

The patent notes that the baffle created by the sealing system makes it difficult to shake money out of the container, while at the same time making it difficult to 'insert a probe such as a knife blade through the slot' in order to obtain 'coins, bank notes or cheques'.[59] An important aspect of the Funnel Slot Closure is a special-ised 'tamperproof Ringseal', which uses a 'special adhesive' that can reseal the slot closure after the box has been emptied. The Ringseals come with the message 'Please Give Generously' in five languages. A 'Polybox emblem dispenser', which can be used to 'load' flag-day emblems, can be attached to ensure easy dispens-ing. For collections in large crowds (such as those outside football stadiums), 'where even a Polybox Handbox cannot collect fast enough', Angal also produces a collection bucket with a patented 'Bucket Security Lid'.[60]

The Polybox Handbox acts as an extension of the hand – change from the pedestrian's pocket can easily be deposited into a handheld security system and delivered to a 'responsible person' to be accounted for. The polythene box acts as a prosthesis, transforming the *mendico* hand of the collector into a standardised conduit that funnels loose change from pedestrians into a sealed, tamperproof space. Designed for the comfort of the collector's hand, the Handbox enforces what Goffman refers to as 'limb discipline'.[61] As an extension of the hand, the Handbox can be used to gesture to the passer-by with an appeal message, evoking the giving

---

[56] ibid.
[57] ibid.
[58] UK patent GB2304333A.
[59] ibid.
[60] Letter from Angal Service to Fundraisers; UK patent GB2317165A.
[61] E Goffman, *Behaviour in Public Places*, 27.

Figure 10 The Angal Polybox Flag Day Collector (reproduced with permission)

of change as a controlled gift. Equipped with the prosthesis of the Handbox, the official collector becomes a sort of cyborg[62] to be deployed amidst pedestrian flows, branded as friendly and trustworthy, able to capture and secure loose change while efficiently dispensing recognition with a thank-you emblem which then marks the anonymous donor.

What is most immediately striking about major street collections is the fact that they are generally limited to a particular type of charity, one that is able to evoke a worthy victim who suffers at a distance. Major street-collection efforts by organisations such as the Red Cross, Save the Children and the Cancer Society evoke not just good causes but also victims who are blameless for their situation. Indeed, street-collection charities often portray the victims as heroic, most often those who are seen to face especially terrifying illnesses, such as cancer, that can be 'fought' with technology.[63] It is notable that street collections are not carried

[62] DJ Haraway, *Simians, Cyborgs and Women* (London, Free Association Books, 1991) 149–81; I Hacking, 'Canguilhem amid the Cyborgs' (1998) *Economy and Society* 27, 202–16.

[63] Of course, the construction of 'victim' can have profound consequences for those who are expected to perform this role in dealing with their condition. See R Scott, *The Making of Blind Men* (New York, Russell Sage Foundation, 1969) for a fascinating analysis of how those who have difficulty seeing or who cannot see at all are socialised by various agencies into the role of 'the blind'.

out in any organised way on behalf of those who might be viewed as contributing to their own affliction. There are no major flag-day collections for the homeless, alcoholic, drug-addicted or suicidal. Neither are there collections for general causes that cannot easily portray personal victimhood. Thus the National Trust does not carry out street collections, although it does rely extensively on static collection boxes.[64]

Indeed, street-collection charities rely on a semiotics in which the needs of the absent victim can be expressed for the glance of a passer-by, constructing a mode of recognisability, of *bona fides*, which does not require sustained evaluation or inspection. Street-collection gift encounters are designed to be instantly identifiable and as fleeting as possible. The homogeneity of presentation – all the charity's collectors are outfitted with similar boxes, sashes, badges and so forth – makes the representation of legitimacy easy to reproduce. Ironically, the more that charities brand themselves to look legitimate by using homogeneous collection media, the more easily they expose themselves to being impersonated by bogus collectors, a fact often reflected in warnings from local councils and the Charity Commission on the dangers of fraudulent collections.

The licensed gift encounter of street collections capitalises on the anxiety most of us have that, through no fault of our own, we will be struck by some illness, accident or violence. This evocation is dramatised by the fact that street collections are carried out by 'normal', healthy bodies. Indeed, people would be outraged if, for example, cancer patients actively collected for the Cancer Society, or if accident victims (or people dressed as bloodied accident victims) solicited donations for the Red Cross. By acting on their behalf, official collectors act as 'normals' to mediate the social stigma of the imagined victim.[65] Of course, exceptions to this are notable, such as the British Legion's Poppy Day, when both veterans and active soldiers collect for fallen and disabled comrades.[66] A variation on this is the Royal National Lifeboat Institution's flag day, when collectors dress in yellow slickers to resemble lifeboat crew members and shake miniature lifeboats into which money can be inserted. The RNLI has perhaps the perfect charitable appeal, evoking community, sacrifice and heroism in a way that taps deeply into the nostalgia of a seafaring nation.

However, this mediation must be carefully managed. A charity must evoke guilt, sympathy and pity in the potential donor without offending the individuals for whom the appeal is being made. This tension is often present in efforts to re-brand charities with a co-ordinated, easily recognised message. For example, the Spastics Society changed its name to SCOPE, the rationale being that even though the word *spastic* is a medically accurate term in relation to cerebral palsy, being 'a spastic' is also a term of derision and stigma. The name had rightly

---

[64] Letter to author from supporter fundraising co-ordinator, National Trust, 5 February 1998.

[65] E Goffman, *Stigma: Notes on the Management of Spoiled Identity* (1963).

[66] Letter to author from head of Poppy Appeals, Royal British Legion, 22 January 1998.

become untenable in an era of increased sensitivity and activism around the rights of those who are physically challenged. However, when the new name SCOPE was introduced, it was completely uninformative; it was not immediately clear what it meant or who the charity served.[67] The fact that the most visible condition of cerebral palsy, the spastic seizure, is not a symptom that can easily be signified in the semiotics of a branded corporate entity speaks to the extremely narrow representational band within which charities can communicate a worthy recipient with a 'good cause' message.

The 'flag' (the charity's emblem) given to those who donate is a token of a gift that will be channelled to the imagined victim in the future. The flags are no longer pieces of cloth to be pinned on the lapel but are rather adhesive stickers that can easily be dispensed from the base of the Polybox Handbox.[68] The fact that the collector is often expected to place the sticker on the donor's lapel is further evidence of the trusted character of the collector, in that one stranger is thus allowed to touch another. The wearing of the emblem on a particular flag day does not just mark the donor as generous but also relieves the wearer of the emotional burden of ignoring the overtures of subsequent collectors who are trying to catch their eye.[69]

II. Buskers

When I lived in Oxford, I frequently saw a man who, in an apparent bid to entertain passers-by, stood upside down in the middle of the pavement with his head in a bucket, his hat lying close by primed with a few coins. As I discuss in chapter two, this very modest piece of theatre illustrates a major category that has historically often been synonymous with street begging. As Paola Pugliatti notes, the Underground sign that states 'Busking and begging is not allowed' conjugates two activities which are intricately connected in the governance of vagrancy.[70] Certainly the origin of the word *busker* speaks to this theatrical ambiguity, having its root in the nineteenth-century word *buskin*, a type of shoe worn by peripatetic stage actors,[71] particularly in Shakespearean productions. Today, buskers and other

[67] It is notable, then, that on the SCOPE collector's badge there is an explanation that reads: 'To provide care, education, training, employment, accommodation and social services for people with cerebral palsy'; letter to author from marketing researcher, SCOPE, 5 February 1998, enclosing 'Introducing Fund-Raiser Services' handout.

[68] As a volunteer collector for the RNLI, I must confess to having suffered considerable anxiety at the expectation of many strangers – especially women – that I will place the sticker on their lapel. While this anxiety was addressed somewhat by giving the emblem to the donors to place on their own lapels, many simply paused and waited for the sticker to be pressed onto their outerwear. Fur and leather-like coats were of particular concern.

[69] Goffman, *Behaviour in Public Places*, 116.

[70] P Pugliatti, *Beggary and Theatre in Early Modern England* (Farnham, Ashgate, 2003).

[71] *Oxford English Dictionary*, 2nd edn.

street entertainers are a common feature of public pavements, often promoted by town and city officials as a desirable aspect of city-centre experience.

Musical buskers on British pavements range from accomplished amateur musicians who play classical instruments to those who might play a penny whistle in an attempt to exhibit themselves as worthy through their display of talent and skill. Buskers do not establish a set price for hearing their performance; they sometimes receive donations that are a sort of hybrid between a tip or gratuity and payment for a service that exists in the realms of both charity and itinerant labour. This ambiguous status is often evoked in tales of successful recording artists who got their start playing on the street. In a song by Long John Baldry, he remembers being a busker hauled into court for playing 'boojie-woojie' (boogie-woogie) music on a London street.[72] On the other hand there are individuals, like the man in the Oxford High Street, who appear anxious to colour their begging for change with almost desperate attempts to 'give something back' to the passers-by. To what extent his performance required any particular talent or was actually entertaining the public is hard to ascertain, given the range of public opinion about what is 'art' and entertainment. Nevertheless, busking and street entertainment are a form of conduct that is troublesome to order, precisely because of its ambiguity about being 'one remove from beggary'.

The legal status of busking is precarious. There is no right in English common law to busk, or in fact to do anything other than pass along the 'Queen's Highway', as established in the famous case of *Harrison v Duke of Rutland*.[73] And as we have seen, the Vagrancy Act 1824 makes no distinction between begging by the visibly indigent and conduct involving street entertainment. This point has often been noted in discussions about the vagueness of the vagrancy law; local officials who feel that buskers are too close to beggars cite the fact that it is illegal.

However, the case of *Grey v Chief Constable of Greater Manchester*[74] suggests that buskers considered to be professionals may not fall within the meaning of s 3 of the Vagrancy Act. In this 1983 case, the busker had previously been convicted of setting himself up in a public place to 'beg or gather alms'. The initial conviction was based on the evidence of two police officers, who watched him play his guitar while several passers-by threw money into the open instrument case in front of him. On appeal, counsel for the busker argued that no solicitation of payment was taking place, that he was not begging or gathering alms, because he was giving 'value for money' to the passers-by, and that the appellant was not the type of disorderly and idle itinerant who was being considered by the Act.

The respondent argued that singing and guitar playing should be regarded as 'begging and gathering alms' because persons passing by were throwing money into the guitar case out of pity, on a charitable impulse, after realising that the

---

[72] Long John Baldry, 'Don't Try to Lay No Boogie-Woogie on the King of Rock and Roll' (1971).
[73] 1 QB 142 (1893).
[74] CLR 45 (1983).

busker had no proper employment. The court held that the busker was soliciting payment by his actions, and that because he was offering something in return for the money given by passers-by, he was not begging or gathering alms. The appeal was allowed. This case is significant in how it distinguishes the busker as a person 'one remove from beggary' who offers 'value for money' in a service. It does little, however, to establish how any particular busker might be considered a professional based on the character of his performance. How, for example, does one formally delineate between a man soliciting coins by standing on his head in a bucket and a student practising Beethoven behind an open violin case on the High Street?

The central strategy for regulation of buskers is the widespread use of informal codes administered by city-centre management partnerships to enable busking while at the same time emphasising the illegal and unwanted character of begging. In Winchester, city officials used an informal code during development of the diverted-giving campaign, constructing a distinction between buskers or 'street entertainers' and those who were viewed as 'pseudo-buskers'. The code was used to 'educate' buskers and construct them as self-regulating objects who would control the content, quality, duration and location of their performance.[75] In practice, police and city officials admitted that they left buskers alone if their performance was of 'reasonably good quality' and if shopkeepers agreed that it represented 'good entertainment'.[76] Underlying the code was a widespread belief that many beggars attempt to mask their begging with some sort of demonstration of musical skill. Thus the handbook of 'useful police powers' issued to constables who policed Winchester's city centre reads: 'Vagrants making feeble attempts to play musical instruments or singing are not busking and consideration should be given to dealing with them for begging'.[77]

In Winchester, environmental health officers, who can enforce obstruction and noise pollution legislation against buskers, did not move on those who were 'passively' soliciting loose change.[78] Council officers rationalised this approach by appealing to the notion of choice: 'Everybody's got the right to choose, and if you choose to put money in the hat, then that's fair enough'.[79] The Winchester environmental health officer I interviewed argued that buskers are not soliciting contributions by leaving a cap on the pavement; instead they are simply allowing passers-by to exercise their choice to 'contribute' to a performance. As he explained,

> Soliciting is really going up to someone and sort of saying 'Come on,' putting them under pressure to give. Most of the buskers I have seen have their violin box or have a hat down and it's up to you – it's like a passive thing if you want to put money in.

[75] Interview with environmental health officer, City of Winchester, July 1997.
[76] Interview with police inspector, Hampshire Constabulary, November 1996.
[77] Hampshire Constabulary, 'Useful Police Powers and By-Laws for Dealing with Offences in Winchester City Centre' (1995).
[78] Interview with environmental health officer.
[79] ibid.

You're not drawn out to put money in; if you've enjoyed the music you put money in. They are 'part of history'.[80]

This widespread view – that the busker should be free to benefit from passers-by who choose to give money – is not one in which the beggar is given latitude. The talent, skill and entrepreneurialism displayed by the busker construct an acceptable, sanitised form of street life which evokes the minstrel lifestyle of the itinerant stranger in a way that is not viewed as a nuisance. Local authorities and police, while suggesting that busking is strictly illegal, nonetheless usually tolerate buskers because they are 'one remove from beggary' through some demonstration of talent or skill. This approach is exemplified, for example, by the chief executive of the City of Carlisle, who stated: 'Busking for private gain is still regarded as begging but this council takes a more relaxed view of it provided that the busker can actually play the instrument and they are not causing a public nuisance or obstruction.'[81] Similarly, the chief executive of South Ribble Borough Council stated: 'Buskers or street entertainers also operate outside the law ... traditionally they have been allowed to ply their trade, on condition that the entertainment provided does not go beyond that which is morally acceptable, and that passers-by are not harassed.'[82]

A. Buskers Codes

The use of buskers codes has become a standard technique of town-centre management strategies, particularly with the pedestrianisation of city-centre areas. Such codes are in place in major cities across England.[83] They are concerned primarily with ordering aspects of the 'body idiom' which intersect to create a performance: (1) the conduct of the busker and the content, quality and duration of the entertainment, and (2) the location of the busking. For local councils, codes of practice enable buskers to provide 'music to shop by' with carefully regulated performances at varied locations, or 'pitches', including tuneful playing and singing. For many local councils, buskers are seen as creating a cosmopolitan street scene that is attractive to city-centre visitors. They produce an 'enhanced atmosphere' in Blackpool, 'liven up the streets' in Brighton and 'add to the enjoyment and atmosphere of town centres' in Halton.[84]

---

[80] ibid.

[81] Letter to author from chief executive, City of Carlisle, 11 February 1997.

[82] Letter to author from chief executive, South Ribble Borough Council, 17 February 1997.

[83] Buskers codes are in place in the cities of Bath, Winchester, Peterborough, Cambridge, Blackpool, Brighton, Taunton and Gloucester. They have also been established by the Halton, Erewash, Solihull and Brighton borough councils and the Charing Cross Police Division in London.

[84] Blackpool Town Centre Forum, 'Street Entertainment in Blackpool: A Code of Practice' (1995); Brighton Borough Council, 'Busking in Brighton' (1997); Halton Environmental Services, 'Code of Practice for Street Entertainers' (1997).

Buskers codes generally prescribe that street entertainers should perform either on designated sites or in such a way that pedestrians are not inconvenienced. For example, they 'must not perform directly outside shop doorways, shop windows or by public telephones'.[85] There should be no 'clustering' of buskers,[86] and 'a minimum of 100 metres should be maintained between performance/entertainment areas'. Some codes prescribe specific 'entertainment areas', while others simply allow buskers to choose their own pitch.[87] The duration of busking activity is also frequently prescribed by the codes, being anywhere from one to three hours, including setting-up time.

With the location and duration of busking activity thus prescribed, codes often also establish detailed guidelines for the actual character of the performance. Many restrict the use of amplifiers, while others suggest that the noise level be kept 'reasonable'. The codes emphasise that buskers' performances should involve a 'repertoire' that is 'varied and attractive'.[88] They often mention the fact that a repetitive beat can be annoying, especially the use of drums. The Brighton code, for example, suggests that buskers 'have plenty of variety in [their] set – the same song or beat all day can get tedious. Djembe drumming is not welcomed in Brighton because it causes too many complaints.'[89]

Buskers are also asked to 'sing or play tunefully'[90] and 'should demonstrate an appropriate level of skill and/or talent during their performance.'[91] A paradoxical aspect of buskers codes is that buskers are implicitly expected to 'solicit contributions' but not to do so in a way that resembles begging. Thus the codes vary in the degree to which buskers may actually solicit contributions. Some simply prohibit the use of signs, as in Blackpool: 'No sign shall be displayed inviting payment, except where a collection for charity has been authorised by the Borough Council.'[92] Similar proscriptions exist when it comes to the selling of recorded music; some codes remind musicians that they 'must not sell items without a trader's licence'. While some codes state that the performer should not ask for money, there is clearly an expectation that it is acceptable for the public to contribute by dropping money into a hat or instrument case. Some codes even go so far as to legitimise the collection of money: 'You can obviously collect money,' states the Brighton code, 'just don't put up a huge sign asking for it.'[93] In Erewash and Peterborough, 'Money collection containers should be so placed as to ensure they do not act as an obstruction to passers-by.'[94] And in Taunton, 'neither street

[85] Halton, 'Code of Practice'.
[86] Erewash Borough Council, 'Street Entertainers Code of Practice' (1997).
[87] Taunton Deane, 'Taunton Street Entertainers Code of Practice' (1997).
[88] Solihull, 'Buskers Code of Practice' (1998).
[89] Brighton, 'Busking'.
[90] Solihull, 'Buskers Code'.
[91] Halton, 'Code of Practice'.
[92] Blackpool, 'Street Entertainment'.
[93] Brighton, 'Busking'.
[94] Erewash, 'Street Entertainers'; Peterborough Environmental Services, 'Busking in Peterborough: A Code of Conduct' (1998).

entertainers, nor their money collection containers should be so placed as to act as an obstruction to the passers-by.'[95]

An overarching feature of these codes is a disclaimer that the code in itself does not imply a 'right to perform' and that it does not 'confer immunity' from any relevant legislation which may make busking illegal.[96] The Blackpool code provides a vivid example:

> IT SHOULD BE CLEARLY UNDERSTOOD THAT THIS DOES NOT IMPLY ON THE PART OF THE BOROUGH COUNCIL OR POLICE ANY SANCTIONING OF BUSKING OR OTHER STREET ENTERTAINMENT IN THE TOWN, SINCE THE COUNCIL IS UNABLE TO GRANT SPECIFIC PERMISSION FOR STREET ENTERTAINERS.

However, the Blackpool police and borough council will not normally institute legal action where the code is being observed.[97]

In other words, buskers codes manufacture a space of permission for particular types of 'talented' entertainers while at the same time retaining more formal modes of control for anyone who does not conform to the ideal type that the codes construct. And at the same time as this permission is being manufactured, the codes work to imply that within the context of city-centre management, a wide range of officials has the authority to exercise policing power against buskers. This informal surveillance and regulation are enforced by the way buskers are frequently required to wear an official badge to confirm their *bona fides* as approved collectors.[98] For example, in Bath, 'Entertainers must stop performing immediately when requested to do so by a Police Constable or Council Officer.'[99] In Peterborough, 'Buskers shall immediately stop their activities in that place [their pitch] when requested to do so by a police officer, the Pedestrian Area Manager, City Centre Inspector, or an appropriate City Council Officer.'[100]

B. Legal Controls

Some local authorities went further than simply issuing informal codes which include a form of permission and have attempted to set up licensing and permit schemes. A notable case involving a formal attempt to license a busker in a public place is the Court of Appeal decision in *R v Bow Street Magistrates' Court*

---

[95] Taunton Deane, 'Taunton Street Entertainers'.
[96] Erewash, 'Street Entertainers'.
[97] Blackpool, 'Street Entertainment', capitalisation original.
[98] Interview with assistant city-centre manager, Bath, October 1998; Gloucester City Environmental Services, 'Approved Street Entertainers' Scheme' (1998).
[99] Interview with Bath assistant city-centre manager.
[100] Peterborough Environmental Services, 'Busking in Peterborough: A Code of Conduct' (1998).

and Another ex parte McDonald.[101] A well-known busker, Bruno McDonald, had played in London's Leicester Square on a regular basis for some years, usually with amplification equipment. Westminster Council believed that under the London Government Act 1963, the square constituted a 'premises' and was subject to being licensed according to paragraph 1(2) of Schedule 12 of the Act, whereby no premises shall be used for 'public dancing or music and any other public entertainment of the like kind, except under and in accordance with the terms of a licence'. The Council secured a warrant empowering its agents to enter and search the 'premises' at Leicester Square and seize equipment belonging to Mr McDonald. He in turn applied to the Metropolitan Stipendiary Magistrate for a judicial review of the warrant; his application was in the first instance refused but he was granted leave to appeal. At issue was whether the public space of Leicester Square could be considered a premises for the purposes of the Act. The Council argued that because the 1963 Act stated premises to be 'any place', this should include Leicester Square and any other public street; it also noted that 'a place' could be confined to 'any area capable of demarcation'.

Lord Justice Schieman prefaced the Court of Appeal judgment by observing that buskers could add to or detract from the enjoyment of daily life, depending on the tastes of the listener and the skill of the busker. In finding against the Council, the Lord Justice found that it had attempted to use powers in a 'wholly artificial way' against the busker in a public space. The fact that the Council made a point of obtaining entry into a public place which it already owned vividly illustrated this. Further, Lord Justice Schieman noted that Schedule 12 had not been designed to cover a public place where entertainers could come and go, and that the Act could be used to create a criminal offence of which the public would have no reasonable expectation.

This case clearly established that any licensing scheme must take into account the precise legal character of the 'public place' that a council attempts to claim a regulatory authority. And while most authorities agreed that they have no actual authority to license busking, some jurisdictions did attempt to go further than simply instituting informal codes. Chichester District Council issues 'letters of no objection' to those who wish to busk; it emphasises that the letter does not in itself constitute a permit.[102] The councils of Lewisham and Bromley use the London Government Act 1963 to license buskers: 'Since the designated busking areas are located on the public highway', comments Lewisham Council's licensing officer, 'in effect, the Council is licensing itself'.[103]

Portsmouth City Council and Southampton City Council operate a licensing system (£11 per permit), claiming authority under section 145 of the Local

---

[101] Judgment, 20 March 1996, as reported in C Clayson, 'Street Wise' in *Justice of the Peace and Local Government Law* (3 August 1996) 573–75.

[102] West Sussex, 'Activities in Precinct' (1997).

[103] Letter to author from principal licensing officer, Lewisham Environmental Health, 1 September 1998; letter to author from section leader, Environmental Services, Bromley, 19 November 1997, enclosing attachments concerning 'street entertainment'.

Government Act 1972, in order to control busking in their entertainment areas.[104] However, the Act very clearly applies only to parks and theatres and not to public highways, a point that West Sussex County Council noted when it examined the issue.[105] Nevertheless, the Council issued a detailed letter of objection which, while stating 'THIS IS NOT A PERMIT', contains a long list of conditions. It reads: 'The County Council have no objection to the [busking] activity taking place ... provided you comply with the following conditions':

> The County Council have always taken the view that there is no law which allows them to give anyone permission to carry out an activity on the highway as, in effect, this would be authorising someone to cause an obstruction. In view of this a system has been evolved where up to 4 buskers at a time are allowed in the precinct and each of them is given a letter which clearly states that it is not a permit; it simply states that the County Council have no objection to them carrying out their activity provided they comply with the conditions attached.[106]

This strategy led to a situation which 'somewhat got out of hand' when the police were unwilling to enforce what the Council called a 'system of non-permits'. The police felt that the letter of no objection 'negate[d] any power which they might have'.[107] Certainly it put the police in an awkward situation in which the Council appeared to be condoning illegal activity in an effort to 'lend colour to the street scene'.[108]

Horsham District Council admitted that there was no 'specific statutory base for the granting of a licence or consent for events in the Town Centre', including busking.[109] The Council nevertheless set up an application and licensing system for buskers, claiming that

> the conditions imposed on applicants are enforceable as a contract (provided the Council has the power to impose them) because the applicant signs a document stating that he agrees to abide by them. Additionally, if the conditions are contained in the bylaws or statute, then they are enforceable as such.[110]

While these creative legal efforts to permit and license buskers are uncommon, they nevertheless speak to the extent to which officials attempt to both encourage and control busking as part of their efforts to create an attractive and lively city centre. Through the use of informal codes, permits and even licensing, officials attempt to further moralise 'untalented' forms of begging, providing city-centre managers with the ability to control exactly how colourful the street scene can be.

---

[104] Letter to author from corporate projects manager, Portsmouth, 28 August 1997, enclosing attachment on 'Street Entertainment Permit'; letter to author from head of Legal Services, Southampton, 11 November 1997.

[105] West Sussex, 'Activities'.

[106] ibid.

[107] ibid.

[108] ibid.

[109] Horsham, *Horsham Town Centre Activities* (1997) 67.

[110] ibid, 68.

III. The *Big Issue* Vendor

The sight of *Big Issue* vendors has become a familiar part of British street culture. Started in 1991 with funding from the Body Shop, the magazine is sold on the streets exclusively by homeless vendors, who keep part of the sale price for themselves. It is now sold in almost every major UK city and is part of an international 'street paper' movement (similar newspapers operate in Canada and the United States). Set up as an 'alternative to begging for homeless, ex-homeless and the vulnerably accommodated', the *Big Issue* promotes itself as a self-help initiative through which the homeless can 'help themselves' by earning an income as vendors.[111] *Big Issue* sellers, with their call of 'Help the homeless – buy a *Big Issue*', occupied a particular place in the public imagination during the years of Conservative government, nicely captured by John O'Farrell in his memoir as a Labour supporter:

> People who were embarrassingly left-wing in the eighties still bare [*sic*] the soul-tortured scars of those years. If we buy a *Big Issue* we carry it on the outside of our briefcase in case we meet another vendor who might not believe us when we say we have already bought one. We buy over-priced dusters at our front door and hope the vendor hasn't etched a special mark that denotes 'sucker' on our front gate.[112]

Unlike buskers, *Big Issue* vendors carry out their work on a sound legal basis as news vendors: under local legislation, news vendors are exempt from being licensed as street traders and are allowed to sell their products 'from hand' on the pavement, subject to certain spatial restrictions.[113] In order to bolster the status of its sellers as news vendors, the *Big Issue* has registered itself as a newspaper with the Royal Post, despite the fact that the magazine is sold exclusively on the street.[114] The exemption enjoyed by news vendors has provided the *Big Issue* with a powerful tool for exerting the right of its vendors to set up a pitch on public pavements.[115]

  Within this legal status as a vendor, the *Big Issue* administers and controls vendors through the practice of visual *bona fides* and a self-regulating form of

[111] *Big Issue*, 'Tony Blair', *The Big Issue* 214 (6–12 January 1997).
[112] J O'Farrell, *Things Can Only Get Better: Eighteen Miserable Years in the Life of a Labour Supporter, 1979–1997* (London, Black Swan, 1999) 68.
[113] Letter from chief trading standards officer, London. The various powers which exempt news vendors are complicated. In London, the exemption is located in the City of London (Various Powers) Act 1987, Part III, s 19(1), which reads: 'Nothing in this part applies to a person who sells or exposes for sale newspapers or periodicals in a street unless he uses for that purpose a receptacle which occupies a stationary position in a street and, in a case where he sells or exposes for sale one daily, weekly or Sunday newspapers, such receptacle (a) exceeds 3 feet in height; or (b) occupies a position extending over a portion of the carriageway of the street measuring more that 2 feet 6 inches in any direction exceeding 3 square feet in area; or (c) occupies a position extending over a portion of the carriageway of the street.' Similar exemptions are found in the London Local Authorities Act 1990 and the street-trading provisions of the Local Government (Miscellaneous Provisions) Act 1982. The newsstands which newspaper vendors typically sell from are designed to fit the space requirements of this exemption, and *Big Issue* sellers in London occasionally utilise these newsstands.
[114] *Big Issue*, 'The Big Issue: Helping the Homeless Help Themselves' (1997).
[115] ibid.

body idiom. Those who wish to sell the *Big Issue* apply to 'badging up' sessions at one of their offices. After presenting written proof of their homelessness, they have a brief meeting with a caseworker, followed by a session on how to sell the *Big Issue*, where they sign a code of conduct which they agree to abide by. They are then issued a *Big Issue* badge which entitles them to buy magazines from their local office and sell them to the public, enabling a profit. In 1999, the price of a *Big Issue* was £1.00, with 45p of that going to the vendor. (In 2018 it was sold to the vendor for £1.25 and sold to the public at £2.50). There are no apparent limits on the number of magazines any particular vendor can buy.

The allocation of selling pitches varies by city and according to the local practices of regional offices. In London, vendors establish their own pitches with the assistance of vendor-support teams. In Bath, pitches have been established in consultation with local retailers; a place for the vendor to stand and pitch is marked on the pavement with a *Big Issue* emblem (Figure 11).[116] In Manchester in 1999, vendors were assigned pre-established pitches throughout the city, with newer, more vulnerable vendors being given the more lucrative pitches within the city centre.[117] In 1999, The *Big Issue* estimated that as many as 800 to 1,000 vendors were working in London at any given time.[118]

Figure 11 Official *Big Issue* pitch pavement stamp, Bath 1997

---

[116] Interview with Bath assistant city-centre manager.
[117] Interview with manager, *Big Issue* in the North, Manchester, December 1997.
[118] *Big Issue*, 'Helping the Homeless'.

The *Big Issue*'s Code of Conduct acts as a second point of control in assuring that the vendors present a polite, disciplined face to the public.[119] The Code states:

> As a vendor of the *Big Issue*, disciplinary action will be taken if any of the following offences occur:
>
> 1. Using aggressive or bad language towards the general public.
> 2. Using aggressive or harassing behaviour towards *Big Issue* staff – in or out of the *Big Issue* building.
> 3. If you are found drunk or under the influence of drugs whilst selling or buying the magazine.
> 4. Fighting over pitches with other vendors, or those earning a living from the streets, eg buskers and beggars.
> 5. Violence towards general public, *Big Issue* staff or other vendors.
> 6. The *Big Issue* magazine cannot be sold on: (a) public transport, (b) public transport concourses without prior permission or (c) on the way to your pitch.

The badging of vendors allows the public to feel assured that they are making their purchase from a legitimate homeless person; 'Please buy from badged vendors only', readers are warned on the cover of the magazine. It also allows local authorities, including town-centre managers, to monitor the activities of particular vendors. In addition, the magazine itself encourages the public to report any complaints about vending behaviour to the regional office, as well as warning readers that they should never give money to someone who appears to be collecting for the *Big Issue*, as 'we do not collect money on the street'.[120] *Big Issue* vending, while centred in commercial exchange for a reputable product, depends on the vendor's selling himself as a 'positive and worthy' homeless person who, unlike the criminal beggar, does not believe in getting something for nothing.

---

[119] *Big Issue*, 'The *Big Issue* Code of Conduct' (1998).
[120] *Big Issue*, 'Britain's Best PM?' *The Big Issue* 218 (3–9 February 1997).

4

The Vagrancy Act 1824, 1976–2000

I begin this analysis by reviewing the extensive work done by the activist group End the Vagrancy Act (EVA) in the early 1990s to have the 1824 law repealed. While EVA was unsuccessful in having the begging and rough-sleeping sections abolished, the group did contribute to a continuing diminishment of Vagrancy Act powers that had been occurring over the previous two decades. I then examine three unique cases of vagrancy law enforcement in the late 1990s that flesh out the archaic character of the 1824 Act that EVA so vigorously challenged: the first two dedicated police 'homeless units' in England, based in London and Manchester, and a British Transport Police operation that targeted women begging with children in the Underground. Each of these cases demonstrates that before the reforms of 2003, the 1824 Act remained a capricious and punitive policing resource, even when used in operations that claimed to be sensitive to the social welfare of people begging in public.

I. The EVA Challenge

With the implementation of the National Assistance Act in 1948, beggary and homelessness were vastly diminished for the next three decades. Those who lived on the street were entitled to welfare payments, and with the availability of rehabilitative programmes and labour exchanges and the achievement of full employment, begging became unnecessary in postwar Britain.[1] By the early 1960s, however, there were signs that what were then known as 'reception centres' and 'Part 3 accommodation' provided by local authorities were seriously deficient in dealing with increasing numbers of the long-term homeless. The squalor and violence of the hostels (many were former workhouses) were given full public airing in 1966, in the television play *Cathy Come Home*, which galvanised public attention and led to the formation of the homelessness advocacy charity Shelter.

In the 1970s the Department of Health and Social Security (DHSS) often provided one-way train tickets to the nearest 'spike', or hostel, to people claiming benefits who had no fixed address. This practice was coercive in the sense that

---

[1] L Rose, *Rogues and Vagabonds: Vagrancy Underworld in Britain, 1815–1985* (London, Routledge, 1988) 175–81.

those who did not take up the offer could be barred from receiving their benefit from the social services office the next day. With the Conservative government of Margaret Thatcher espousing the virtues of voluntarism, the DHSS shut down the hostels in the early 1980s in favour of 'care in the community' – styled small hostels run by voluntary organisations, of which the night shelter in Winchester is a typical example. This situation, described as 'ill thought-out' and 'chaotic', signified the withdrawal of government from hostel services and was no doubt a contributing factor in the widespread increase of people living on the street throughout the 1980s.[2]

By the late 1980s the increasingly common sight of people begging and sleeping rough on London pavements had become for many a potent symbol of the anti-welfare measures of Thatcherism. Homeless shelters such as Centrepoint reported significant increases in the number of rough-sleepers, and Labour opposition benches evoked the presence of beggars as emblematic of the human cost of Tory economic policies.[3] Troubled by the increase in Vagrancy Act prosecutions that they had observed in inner London magistrates' courts, two barristers from Gray's Inn, Matthias Kelly and Mark Grindrod, decided to actively lobby for repeal of the Act, which they viewed as 'morally indefensible'.[4] On 4 December 1989 they launched the End the Vagrancy Act campaign, with the specific purpose of repealing section 3 (on begging) and section 4 (on sleeping rough), which read, respectively:

> Every person wandering abroad, or placing himself or herself in any public place, street, highway, court or passage, to beg or gather alms, or causing or procuring or encouraging any child or children to do so; shall be deemed an idle and disorderly person within the true meaning of this Act.[5]
>
> …
>
> Every person wandering abroad and lodging in any barn or outhouse, or in any deserted or unoccupied building, or in the open air, or under a tent, or in a cart or wagon … and not giving a good account of himself or herself … shall be deemed a rogue and a vagabond.[6]

Supported by major charities and voluntary and professional organisations,[7] as well as members of the House of Commons and the House of Lords,[8] EVA evolved

---

[2] ibid, 182–85.

[3] See, eg, *Hansard* HC Deb 151, col 457 (20 April 1989) and 157, col 195 (17 July 1989).

[4] Matthias Kelly, EVA co-founder, interview by author, September 1998.

[5] Vagrancy Act 1824, s 3.

[6] ibid, s 4.

[7] EVA members included the Housing Campaign for Single People (CHAR), the British Medical Association, the Children's Society, Crisis, the Law Society, the National Association of Probation Officers (NAPO), the Inner London Probation Service and the Save the Children Fund. See EVA 21, 24, 12.

[8] Supporters included MPs Jeremy Corbyn, Llin Golding, Pat Wall and David Nellist, plus Lord Henderson of Brompton, Lord Alexander of Weedon, Lord Stallard and Lord Meston. See EVA 14, 12. The Liberal Democrats called for repeal of the Vagrancy Act at their 1990 conference; Liberal Democrats, *Federal Conference Report, Blackpool, 16–20 September, 1990* (1990) 3.

into a sustained lobby that over the next two years was able to create significant pressure on the government to justify the retention of Vagrancy Act offences, particularly that of begging.[9] Notably, the leader of the opposition, Neil Kinnock, stated: 'As I am sure you are aware, the *Labour Party* fully supports the repeal of what you rightly call an archaic piece of legislation which simply exacerbates the problems faced by many homeless people.'[10] In arguing for repeal of the 1824 Act, EVA pointed to Tory policies such as discharging the mentally ill for 'care in the community' and restrictive changes to the social security system as causes of the increase in the numbers sleeping and begging on the street.[11]

As part of EVA, the National Association of Probation Officers (NAPO) engaged in a media campaign against what they considered to be the 'disgraceful' use of the Vagrancy Act to punish the homeless on London streets.[12] Based on research in four of the 14 inner London magistrates' courts, NAPO pointed to an increase of at least 180 per cent in begging prosecutions. 'Probation officers working with the homeless,' stated the association, 'have observed that prosecutions tend to occur in groups, suggesting periodic swoops by the police.'[13] In response to a parliamentary question from an EVA supporter, the Home Office admitted that the Metropolitan Police had mounted Operations Burlington and Taurus during 1990–91.[14] Indeed, such police operations (including Operation Meyer) were initiated in 1988 and were specifically tasked with policing the homeless population of Charing Cross.[15] NAPO'S concerns were well founded: between 1988 and 1990, the number of convictions for begging trebled, from 490 to 1,450.[16] The impression that the police had begun cracking down on the homeless population was widespread among the volunteer community in London.[17] 'It is difficult,' commented an official from the Westminster Diocese Social and Pastoral Action Group, 'to see police action as other than a "cleaning up" operation, a response to

---

[9] I acknowledge the assistance of Ruth Bush of Bush Parliamentary, who facilitated access to the EVA campaign papers, and Matthias Kelly, co-founder of EVA, for his permission to examine and quote freely from them.

[10] EVA 22, my emphasis.

[11] In particular, EVA noted the barring of 16- and 17-year-olds from making claims; the fact that income support and housing benefits were no longer paid in advance, 'leading to the Catch 22 situation that without benefit money no deposit can be paid to secure accommodation and without accommodation no claim can be made'; the escalating cost of accommodation; and the government's new strategy of offering hostel places to those considered to be 'roofless'. See EVA 14: 1. For a review of the legislative changes in this period in relation to housing, see I Loveland, *Housing Homeless Persons* (Oxford, Clarendon Press, 1995).

[12] National Association of Probation Officers [NAPO], 'Dramatic Rise in Vagrancy Prosecutions', press release, 14 May 1990.

[13] ibid.

[14] *Hansard* HC Deb 199, col 21 (27 November 1991).

[15] Metropolitan Police Service [London], 'Homelessness: The Charing Cross Homeless Unit', written by sergeant in the Charing Cross Homeless Unit, 6 June 1997, 1.

[16] Home Office, *Criminal Justice Statistics, England and Wales, 1976–1977*, vol 1, Supplementary Tables, 1976–1977.

[17] Kelly, interview.

public unease at an embarrassing spectacle, while its root cause continues to be ignored.'[18]

EVA engaged in a wide variety of activist techniques; it generated coverage in the mainstream media,[19] initiated letter-writing campaigns among its members[20] and met with unimpressed Home Office officials to state its case.[21] EVA's main tool of reform, however, was the introduction of a private member's bill in the House of Lords. The Crime of Vagrancy Abolition Bill (1990) was introduced by Lord Stallard with all-party support. The bill proposed to repeal both sections 3 (begging) and 4 (rough sleeping) of the Act while retaining the 'indecent exposure' offence, which was still occasionally used by police forces.[22]

With supporters in the House of Lords generating publicity and campaigning privately, the Tory government responded to EVA that it had no intention of decriminalising begging and sleeping rough. The government advanced two tangential arguments in support of retaining those offences. The first was that begging remained a serious issue of public order and protection that deserved to be the subject of criminal law. In a letter to EVA's founders, the Home Secretary, David Waddington, wrote:

> I understand and share your concern about the homeless, but I do not think the solution is to repeal the Vagrancy Act. The basic purpose of vagrancy laws is to preserve public order and decency and to protect individuals from offence or injury … I understand in general, the police arrest [for begging] only where there is some element of threatening or intimidating behaviour. The Government believes that the protection the Vagrancy Act 1824 continues to offer society is necessary. We have no plans to repeal sections 3 and 4, as amended.[23]

This rationale for the continued criminalisation of begging and sleeping rough, based on the justification of protecting the public from 'threatening or intimidating behaviour', was reinforced to EVA supporter Labour MP Llin Golding by Home Office Minister John Patten, who stated that 'the purpose of criminal law as far as begging and sleeping rough are concerned is to preserve public order and decency and to protect the individual from offence or injury.'[24] This was further reinforced by the Parliamentary Undersecretary of State for Health (Lords):

> The basic purpose of the vagrancy laws is to protect individuals from offence or injury. They … offer a necessary measure of protection to society. The government understands

---

[18] EVA 7: 2.

[19] N Cohen, 'Vagrancy Act Dismays Reformers', *The Independent*, 26 October 1990, 5; J Carvel, 'Fourfold Rise in Arrest of Homeless under Vagrancy Law', *The Guardian*, 14 May 1990, 1; EVA 24, 16, 18, 19.

[20] EVA 12.

[21] EVA 4.

[22] The bill received its first reading on 8 November and second reading on 11 December 1990, was dispensed with at the committee stage on 24 January 1991, and passed its third reading on 5 February 1991.

[23] EVA 1.

[24] EVA 5.

and shares the concerns about the problems of homelessness but it does not believe that the solution is to repeal the vagrancy laws.[25]

In justifying protection of the public as a reason for retaining the 'collecting alms' offences (section 3), the Home Office argued that if left 'unchecked', begging 'can lead to no-go areas for the public and therefore to more serious crime'[26] and can create an 'aura of distress for others who use the streets'.[27] As an information officer from the homeless campaign group Crisis commented, this evocation of 'no-go' areas and 'aura of distress' revealed a fundamental contradiction in the government's position on begging and sleeping rough: it claimed that begging and sleeping rough were social problems[28] while at the same time insisting they were also 'law and order' matters that required police action.[29] The evocation of a crime-control slippery slope – one that dramatises an appeal to the 'broken windows' theory – was vividly evoked by a Metropolitan Police commander who, in responding to a motion by the Association of London Authorities that the Vagrancy Act be repealed, stated:

> There is also an argument put forward by criminologists that to allow 'nuisance' offences such as begging to continue unchecked, ultimately results in a 'degenerative cycle' in a particular area. People no longer pass regularly through the area and more serious crime begins to flourish. Furthermore not all persons begging are in genuine need (one person arrested recently had over £300 in his possession).[30]

And while the co-founder of EVA believed that some senior police officers were privately supportive of the repeal campaign, the police did nothing to counter frequent Home Office suggestions that the police themselves desired retention of their Vagrancy Act powers.[31]

The second plank in the Home Office's defence of the Vagrancy Act was the argument that, while still needed for public protection, the Act had nonetheless been sufficiently moderated by amendments over the years, with many of its archaic powers removed or blunted. Most notably, the Home Office pointed to the Vagrancy Act 1935, whereby prosecutions for sleeping rough could be brought only against someone who had refused a place of shelter to which he had been directed and which was 'reasonably accessible'.[32] This requirement had radically reduced the number of rough-sleeping prosecutions in the postwar years and has rendered the rough-sleeping section unenforceable for the past 30 years. The impetus for the 1935 amendment was public outrage over the death of Thomas Parker in Winson

---

[25] EVA 17.

[26] EVA 8: 1.

[27] ibid, 3.

[28] A view clearly stated in the Home Office Select Committee's 1980–81 report. See *Third Report from the Home Affairs Committee, Session 1980–81: Vagrancy Offences* (London, HMSO, 1981), 20, 25; EVA 10: 2.

[29] EVA 15: 3.

[30] EVA 9: 3.

[31] Kelly, interview.

[32] EVA 1, 2.

Green Prison in June 1933. The case was noted in a briefing note in the preserved papers of the 1976 Working Party on Vagrancy and Street Offences:

> Parker was an ex-guardsman who had been to Tamworth in search of work, and having been found sleeping out and without money, he was arrested and sentenced to fourteen days' imprisonment with hard labour. The man however had a nervous disorder and suffered from claustrophobia. He created a disturbance in the prison and died later as a result of injuries received while on his way to the punishment cell.[33]

The case led to 'public opinion [being] stirred', and the bill amending the Act passed through Parliament without opposition. Quite notably in relation to the circumstances of Parker's death, the words 'not having any visible means of subsistence' were also repealed. In their response to EVA, Home Office officials were correct in suggesting that the rough-sleeping section had practically fallen out of formal use because of the 1935 Act, although as EVA pointed out, this did not mean that the section was not being used informally to 'move on' those who lived and slept on the streets.[34]

In responding to the allegation that the Vagrancy Act was being used indiscriminately to sweep the streets and carry out arrests, Home Office Minister John Patten stated that begging and sleeping rough were not arrestable offences under section 24 of the Police and Criminal Evidence Act 1984 (PACE). However, Patten wrote, 'there is a general power of arrest in section 25 of the Act if the suspect's name and address are not known or the address given is doubtful, in which case it would be impossible to serve a summons.'[35] This position appeared to confirm EVA's contention that people who begged were subject to arrest because of their status: 'it is not possible to serve a summons upon the homeless [so] they are always dealt with by way of arrest.'[36] Patten also claimed that 'there is no specific power of arrest attached to the 1824 Act,' an assertion that is correct only in the sense that there is no *specific* power; there remains a general power of arrest in the Act which police officers can use. As we shall see, EVA's concerns about the power of 'any person' to arrest 'vagrants' were fully justified.

In response to EVA's accusation that the Act was being used to target peaceful beggars, the Home Secretary commented that he understood that, 'in general, the police only arrest where there is some element of threatening or intimidating behaviour.'[37] EVA correctly noted, however, that nowhere in sections 3 and 4

[33] HMSO, (1972d) Working Party on Vagrancy and Street Offences Memorandum on 'Sleeping Out'. CRI 655/3/13/7/1972-1975. 2.

[34] EVA 25.

[35] EVA 2. Section 25 of PACE at the time read as follows: '(1) Where a constable has reasonable grounds for suspecting that any offence which is not an arrestable offence has been committed or attempted, or is being committed or attempted, he may arrest the relevant person if it appears to him that service of a summons is impracticable or inappropriate. ... (3) The general arrest conditions are (a) that the name of the relevant person is unknown to, and cannot be readily ascertained by, the constable; (b) that the constable has reasonable grounds for doubting whether a name furnished by the relevant person as his name is his real name; (c) (i) the relevant person has failed to furnish a satisfactory address for service; or (ii) the constable has reasonable grounds for doubting whether an address furnished by the relevant person is a satisfactory address for service.'

[36] EVA 25: 3.

[37] EVA 1.

are the words *threatening* or *intimidating* used, and if indeed this behaviour were present, the police would be obliged to prosecute under section 5 of the Public Order Act 1986.[38] Indeed, anticipating the criticism that abolition of the Vagrancy Act would somehow leave holes in general criminal law, EVA produced a detailed 'Schedule of Alternative Offences' which listed current legislation that could be applied to occurrences that might conceivably be covered by the Act.[39]

Throughout their defence of the begging and sleeping-rough sections, Home Office officials repeatedly appealed to the findings of the 1980–81 Home Affairs Committee.[40] The conclusion of the Committee that 'laws against begging and sleeping rough should remain on the statute book at least for the time being'[41] glossed over the findings of the 1976 working party that recommended that begging should remain a criminal offence only to the extent that it was 'persistent'.

The Home Office maintained what EVA reformers called a 'head in the sand' attitude about the everyday realities of the Vagrancy Act,[42] and attempts to repeal the begging and sleeping-rough sections ultimately failed. Most notably, Lord Stallard's repeal bill was opposed by the Tories in the Commons and was 'talked off the table'.[43] A subsequent Commons private member's bill (put forward by Tory backbencher Ken Hargreaves) also failed,[44] as did an early day motion.[45] EVA was successful, however, in lobbying for an amendment to the Criminal

[38] EVA 25: 5.

[39] EVA argued that the remaining offences in ss 3 and 4 could be addressed through other current legislation:

s 3 ('causing or procuring or encouraging a child to beg') by s 4 of the Children and Young Persons Act 1933; s 4 ('indecent exposure by a man') by s 28 of the Town Police Clauses 1847 and as common law nuisance – EVA retained this offence in its abolition bill, being sensitive to arguments that it would be seen to weaken legal protection for women and children; 'exposing wounds and deformities' by s 17 of the Public Health (Control of Diseases) Act 1984; 'obtaining donations under false pretences' by s 15 of the Theft Act 1968; and 'being on enclosed premises for an unlawful purpose' – at common law the owner can eject using reasonable force without a court order – by s 7 of the Criminal Law Act 1977. More generally, EVA pointed to a wide range of legislation that could be used to address threatening, abusive or insulting behaviour or words (such as the Public Order Act 1986) which were often attributed to so-called 'aggressive beggars'. In addition, attention was drawn to several sections of the Theft Act 1968 that involved menacing conduct (s 14), obtaining property by deception (s 14) and the use of shabby clothes which could be used in the course of or in connection with any cheat as defined in s 15 (s 25). See EVA 26.

[40] Home Office, *Third Report*.

[41] EVA 3: 2, 1.

[42] EVA 10: 1.

[43] Kelly, interview.

[44] On the Vagrancy Amendment Bill, see *Hansard* HC Deb 193, cols 862–66 and 923–24 (25 June 1991); 193, col 1304 (28 June 1991); 194, col 620 (5 July 1991).

[45] EVA (13). Early Day Motion No 931 read: 'The House identifies Sections 3 and 4 of the Vagrancy Act 1924 [*sic*] as an anomaly whereby people unable to survive without recourse to peaceful begging may become liable to criminal prosecution; recognises that adequate criminal sanctions are available against begging accompanied by an [*sic*] form of threat or public disturbance whatsoever; draws attention to the high level of cross party concern about this matter in another place; and calls upon Her Majesty's Government to repeal this redundant legislation.'

Justice Act 1991, which restricted the powers of the court to imposing a fine on those convicted of begging and sleeping rough.[46] The co-founder of EVA considered this change 'a significant advance' because it 'indicated clearly Parliament's desire to see, at the very least, a diminution in criminal sanctions against those who slept rough or begged.'[47] This trend towards less punitive sanctions was consistent with the amendment to the Criminal Justice Act 1982 which legislated that begging and sleeping rough were no longer imprisonable offences,[48] a reform initiated on the recommendations of the 1980–81 home affairs committee.[49]

In arguing for repeal of the begging offence, EVA does not appear to have pressed the case of *R v Dalton*,[50] which has important implications for policing of the begging offence.[51] Charged with begging or collecting alms, the defendant was seen by a policeman stopping cars and asking for money; after several attempts he appeared to receive something from one of the drivers. It was established that at the time of the offence the defendant was well dressed, was employed as an electrician and had travelled to London from Carlisle by train, for which he had a return ticket. Defence counsel argued that there was simply 'no case to answer', because section 3 was directed against people with a particular 'habit or mode of life'. Referring to *Pointon v Hill*[52] and *Mathers v Penfold*,[53] the court agreed with the defence and held that:

> It was therefore necessary to show that the defendant had definitely come to the conclusion that he did not wish to work and that he had adopted the calling of a beggar. Proof of the begging on an isolated occasion, without more, was insufficient to raise a prima facie case.[54]

A decade before the EVA campaign, the courts had reaffirmed the offence of begging as a 'character crime' in that the person had to adopt the 'calling of a beggar'. Surprisingly, the *Dalton* decision did not appear to be raised as an issue in the EVA debate, despite the evidential burden the decision placed on the police. EVA continued more modest lobbying after its Criminal Justice Act victory. With the re-election of the Tory government in 1993, the group felt that it had achieved all it could, and disbanded.[55]

---

[46] Criminal Justice Act 1991, s 26(5). See M Wasik and R Taylor, *Blackstone's Guide to the Criminal Justice Act, 1991* (London, Blackstone, 1991) 82.

[47] Kelly, interview.

[48] EVA 3: 1.

[49] Home Office, *Third Report*.

[50] CLR 375, 1982.

[51] N Corre, 'A Proposal for Reform of the Law of Begging' (1984) *Criminal Law Review*, 750–53.

[52] 12 QB 306 (1884). The case involved striking miners who were convicted of begging after conducting a house-to-house collection. The conviction was quashed, as the court held that the statute was directed against those who had a 'particular habit and mode of life' which did not include simply soliciting subscriptions.

[53] 1 KB 513 (1914). Again this case involved the conviction of a man on strike who sold tickets on behalf of his union. Drawing on *Pointon v Hill* (1884), the stipendiary magistrate dismissed the case.

[54] *R v Dalton* (1982).

[55] Kelly, interview.

II. 'Homeless Encounter' Policing: Charing Cross and Manchester Homeless Units

The Metropolitan Police Service's Charing Cross Homeless Unit was the first and, along with a smaller unit in Manchester, the only unit during the early years of New Labour that was dedicated specifically to policing the 'homeless community' visibly living and sleeping on the street. The Unit was established in February 1993 as a continuation of Operations Burlington, Meyer and Taurus, which so alarmed EVA reformers.[56] The six-officer Homeless Unit – consisting of five constables and a sergeant – considered those living on the street to be a specific population that must be policed in a specialised way. It acknowledged that 'the majority of the homeless are law abiding' and that the homeless are themselves the subjects of crime, the most notorious being the activity of 'taxing', which involves acts of extortion and street robbery. This notion of a population that required protection was outweighed by a concern that, 'as with any other community, there are those [among the homeless] that break the law.'[57]

The primary form of crime committed by the homeless was that of begging, which, if not stopped – in an echo of Home Office arguments during the EVA debate – could lead to aggression and violence. 'There is no doubt,' the Unit stated, 'that if this offence is allowed to go unchallenged far more serious matters arise: simple begging escalates through to aggressive begging, threatening behaviour, assaults and robbery.'[58] This conflation of begging with harmful criminal behaviour is illustrated by the view that many people who are homeless and begging are felons on the run from the law who need to be sussed out. The Unit drew attention to the fact that it frequently pursued requests from other forces for missing persons, as well as to its success rate in discovery and arrest on outstanding warrants for serious criminal offences:

> Many rough sleepers came to London to seek anonymity, because of its size and the number of people, they feel they can disappear. Regular foot patrolling in both uniform and plain clothes and a constant and diligent approach of speaking with the homeless has resulted in the discovery and subsequent arrest of many persons wanted on warrant. The offences involved have been of the most serious nature and have related to all parts of the UK.[59]

Along with this depiction of an underbelly of mendicant life that hides serious criminals was a more practical concern with what a vocal local business community thought of the sight of people who begged and were homeless.[60] 'The overwhelming opinion,' stated the Unit, 'of the residents, traders and business

---

[56] Metropolitan Police Service, 'Homelessness', 1.
[57] Metropolitan Police Service, 'Homelessness', 2; 'Power of Arrest', in-house memorandum, 1998.
[58] Metropolitan Police Service, 'Homelessness', 2.
[59] ibid, 3.
[60] Metropolitan Police Service, 'Power of Arrest'.

people of Charing Cross is that begging has to be controlled. Without the policy that we operate there would be an inundation of complaints.'[61]

The sergeant who headed the Unit characterised its work as striking a balance between what it viewed as the interests of rough-sleepers and those of the business community, using the following example.[62] Especially during the summer months, a large rough-sleeping population congregated behind the famous Savoy Hotel. The Homeless Unit resisted requests from the Savoy to simply 'move on' the rough-sleepers. Instead the police approached Westminster Council to discuss their presence; the Council in turn arranged to have a mechanised streetsweeper, equipped with disinfectant, come along very early in the morning, rouse those sleeping rough, and clean the pavement on which they had bedded down. The Homeless Unit emphasised that this scheme apparently satisfied everyone: it allowed the rough-sleepers to use the pavement and have a 'clean place to sleep' and it satisfied the Savoy's management, who at the start of each business day would have the rough-sleepers removed and the area 'disinfected'.[63]

The Unit carried out regular head counts of the homeless and estimated that about 50 per cent of the rough-sleepers in London were located within its division.[64] Of special interest was the Strand, which the unit suggested was popular for several reasons: the area is a '24-hour' street with well-lit shop frontages and busy pedestrian traffic, and it has shop entrances set back from the public footpath. 'The homeless know they can bed down in these areas,' the Unit suggested, 'without causing obstruction to the highway, and are confident they will not be moved on as they are on private property.'[65]

The Charing Cross unit had a specific policy for dealing with people who collected alms. When people begging were first encountered on the street by an officer of the Homeless Unit, they were warned, their details were noted, and they were given advice on where accommodation and assistance could be found. This advice was given in the form of an A4-size piece of paper handed to the offender. The information handout listed hostels for men, women and young people and advised that hostels were 'often full, or may have restrictions on who they can accept, so phone to check'.[66] If the same person was again encountered begging, the individual was arrested and a formal caution usually issued. On a third occasion the individual was arrested and a charge of begging was laid under section 3 of the Vagrancy Act. The Metropolitan Police Service has not made detailed statistics available; however, for the eight-month period from 1 January 1998 to

---

[61] Metropolitan Police Service, 'Homelessness', 2.

[62] Interview with sergeant, Charing Cross Homeless Unit, Metropolitan Police Service, August 1998.

[63] ibid.

[64] Metropolitan Police Service, 'What Is the Charing Cross Police Homeless Unit and What Services Can We Provide to the Homeless', written by sergeant, Charing Cross Homeless Unit, 1998.

[65] Metropolitan Police Service, 'Homelessness', 1.

[66] The lack of hostel accommodation rendered the sleeping-rough section inoperable, as the head of the Homeless Unit admitted to me; interview with sergeant.

25 August 1998, 598 warnings were given and 420 arrests were made, resulting in 152 cautions and 268 Vagrancy Act charges for begging.[67]

In May 1995, after two of their crime-control officers visited the London unit, the Greater Manchester Police set up a homeless unit modelled after that of Charing Cross.[68] While the Charing Cross unit was a continuation of previous operations dating back to 1988, the impetus for the Manchester unit appears to have been a more recent concern with general urban beautification, one that took on more importance after the rebuilding of the city core after the IRA bomb blast of 1996. The Manchester unit was made up of three officers – two constables and a sergeant – and followed the same warning–caution–charge protocol as the Charing Cross unit. Manchester developed handout cards which were launched on 11 December 1995, with the announcement that the city's 'street-people' would be 'given a helping hand' with the introduction of a referral scheme to 'help the homeless find food and shelter in the city centre'.[69] The referral cards were produced with the 'help and support' of the Manchester Chamber of Commerce and Industry[70] (signified by its logo printed on the card), which in a press release launching the programme stated:

> While having sympathy for these people who are homeless and resort to begging, many members of the Chamber feel that the abundance of beggars has a bad effect on the city's reputation and hinders the efforts of those trying to promote Manchester as the provincial centre of commerce, industry, trade and leisure. It can also be intimidating to visitors to the city centre.[71]

These cards would, according to the police, provide assistance to the 'truly needy' and 'genuinely homeless' while facilitating 'a strong law and order approach', which was needed 'to deal with aggressive and professional beggars'.[72] As in the case of diverted-giving programmes, the message was clear: given a referral card, the 'real' beggars would have somewhere to go to receive help, while those left on the street – the 'aggressive' and 'professional' beggars – could be subject to police intervention. In addition, a 'guide card' was produced for the police to carry, 'giving a more comprehensive list of referral agencies and a synopsis of the laws relating to vagrancy'. Notably, the card issued to officers explicitly instructs on the requirements of PACE – that an arrest can be carried out only if the person does not have a serviceable address at which to receive a summons – and a paragraph explaining the evidential burden placed on each constable by *R v Dalton*.

What is most notable about both of these specialised operations is the creative ways in which each unit configured their arrest powers in relation to people

---

[67] ibid.

[68] Interview with two constables, Homeless Unit, Greater Manchester Police, August 1998.

[69] Greater Manchester Police, 'Police Scheme to Help Homeless', news release PR/170, 8 December 1995, 1.

[70] ibid, 2.

[71] Manchester Chamber of Commerce and Industry [MCCI], 'Special Unit to Tackle Problem of Begging on Manchester's Streets', press release, 23 May 1995, 2.

[72] Greater Manchester Police, 'Police Scheme', 3.

who were begging. In Manchester the Homeless Unit initially used section 25 of PACE, which allows for the arrest of someone without an address. However, arresting beggars under PACE caused unit officers to run into trouble with some custody sergeants, who would obtain a service address from the offender and then insist that a summons be issued and the prisoner be released, as prescribed by PACE.[73] The result was that the beggar would not be held over in a police cell until they appeared in court. The Manchester police disliked this situation for two reasons. First, they considered the summons process hopelessly slow, and the summons was often ignored by the defendant. Second, the Homeless Unit felt it was important that the arrested beggar suffer the deterrent of a night in custody. Arrest and incarceration were necessary, explained one officer, because begging is 'something for nothing, no effort required, lots of return at the end of the day'.[74]

To solve this problem and ensure that the arrested beggar was incarcerated and not released on summons, the Manchester unit shifted its arrest powers to an authority that would have appalled EVA reformers: the 'preserved' archaic arrest provisions of section 6 of the Vagrancy Act 1824, which remarkably had remained intact for 174 years. As discussed in chapter two, this section reads:

> It shall be lawful for any person whatsoever to apprehend any person who shall be found offending against this Act, and forthwith to take and convey him or her before some justice of the peace, to be dealt with in such a manner as is herein-before directed, or to deliver him or her to any constable or other peace officer of the place where he or she shall have been apprehended, so to be taken and conveyed aforesaid.

For the Manchester unit, the apparent reason for using this archaic power was to avoid the arrest provisions laid down by PACE – that after giving a serviceable address the person is to be released – a requirement which the police felt would prevent them from being 'effective' against beggars and incarcerating them as a deterrent.[75]

The Charing Cross Homeless Unit also carried out arrests using this archaic 1824 power. In contrast with Manchester, where the power was evoked to hold offenders overnight in a police cell as a deterrent, the Charing Cross unit used it to effect its own form of deterrent: simply arresting beggars off the street and then immediately bailing out the offenders at the police station after they were charged. Given that section 25 of PACE allows only for the arrest of someone without a service address, the widespread bailing of prisoners with a serviceable address would call into question the reason for the original arrest. As the unit sergeant commented, for a PACE section 25 arrest, an officer 'cannot justify asking custody officers for bail'.[76] While the head of the Homeless Unit admitted that this

---

[73] Interview with two constables, Manchester. Many police officers dislike homeless people because they are 'dirty, smelly people', which does not make them very attractive prisoners to deal with.
[74] ibid.
[75] Interview with two constables; Greater Manchester Police, 'Vagrancy Act 1824'.
[76] Interview with sergeant, London.

tactic was 'controversial',[77] it was viewed as necessary to preserve the threat of arrest as a deterrent: 'We thought [in the context] of our begging policy [of bailing arrested beggars], perhaps we should be careful in placing a too-liberal interpretation on s 25.'[78]

Clearly, police worries over 'too liberal' an interpretation of section 25 did not dissuade them from being extremely generous in interpreting the archaic arrest powers of the 1824 Vagrancy Act. The Homeless Unit head sergeant rationalised this arrest policy in terms of the individual rights of those who beg: 'Why should the homeless not have access to bail?'[79] The Charing Cross unit, like that in Manchester, justified this arrest-and-bail tactic as the only 'deterrent' available to them.[80]

The use of the 1824 Vagrancy Act as a legitimate means to sidestep the requirements of PACE ignored the then Secretary of State's views on the use of powers that have been preserved in archaic statutes such as the Vagrancy Act. 'To avoid uncertainty and accusations of arbitrariness,' a circular states, 'police forces may consider it prudent to use these powers [where any citizen can arrest] only when the general arrest conditions in s 25 of PACE are also met.'[81] This advice, which would undermine the rationale for using the 1824 Act, was ignored by both units. In addition, in carrying out those arrests under the archaic power, officers often ignored the evidential burden prescribed by *R v Dalton* (1982).[82] To obtain this type of evidence would, according to the Charing Cross sergeant, 'complicate' the begging arrest-and-bail protocol.[83] And contrary to the characterisation by the Home Office to EVA that arrest powers would be used to protect the public from 'intimidating' or 'threatening' behaviour, both homeless units carried out arrests for any form of begging conduct – including those who passively sat on the pavement with a sign or cup in front of them.[84] In Manchester, the discrepancy is particularly visible when one considers the 'guidance card' issued to police officers, which is explicit on the requirements of PACE – that an arrest can be carried out only if the person does not have a serviceable address at which to receive a summons – and the evidential burden of *R v Dalton*.

It is notable that in both locations police collected some statistics with regard to the characteristics of those arrested, given how the 'deterrent' policies of both units were predicated on a view of begging that involved, as the Manchester officer

---

[77] ibid.

[78] ibid. The unit sergeant estimated that 'nine out of ten' offenders were bailed.

[79] ibid.

[80] ibid.

[81] Home Office, 'Police and Criminal Evidence Act 1984', circular 88/1985, 18 December 1985. The Unit was made aware of this provision through an internal memorandum prepared by the force's own research desk; interview with two constables, Manchester.

[82] Interview with sergeant, London; interview with two constables, Manchester.

[83] Interview with sergeant, London.

[84] ibid; interview with two constables, Manchester.

stated, 'something for nothing' and 'lots of return'. We might expect that their own information would support that apparent windfall nature of begging. However, the opposite was the case. In Manchester, the average amount found on a beggar at arrest was £6.08, and the majority of individuals had less than £10.[85] In Charing Cross, the records of the Homeless Unit in 1997, compiled as part of internal research of the unit, indicated that

> the majority of persons arrested for begging are male, of white European appearance, are aged between 16 [and] 30 and have previous convictions for a 'recordable' offence. Thirty-three per cent of all begging arrests are not homeless and about 95 per cent have less then £10 in their possession. The mean average [*sic*] is between £3 and £4.[86]

The data collected by both units betrays the judgement manifested in their deterrent policies, that people who are begging are not homeless and cadge great amounts of money. That opinion was evoked earlier by the commander of the Metropolitan Police who, in response to EVA, spoke of a beggar who was arrested with '£300 in his possession'. In carrying out a deterrence policy, the police, particularly in Manchester, were ignoring their own research, which suggested very little financial return for the beggar on the street.

III. The 'Forlorn Family' Look: Women Begging with Children in the London Underground

I now turn to a case that ignited considerable public controversy: women begging with children at Underground stations in the late 1990s. The London Underground occupies a notable place in the urban social imagination. Depicted in popular crime novels such as *King Solomon's Carpet*[87] and *Underground*[88] as a labyrinthine subterranean world populated by strangers and social outcasts, the Underground remains an archetypal space for experiencing the 'lonely crowd'. The Underground is policed by L Division of the British Transport Police,[89] and the everyday activities of commuters are governed primarily by a set of 32 by-laws.[90] A brief look at the main themes of these by-laws provides a useful

---

[85] Greater Manchester Police, 'City Centre Homeless and Begging Initiative, May 1995 to January 1997', including Appendix 1, 'Statistics Summary', and Appendix 2, 'Graphs and Charts' (1997), 2.

[86] Metropolitan Police Service, 'Homelessness', 2.

[87] B Vine, *King Solomon's Carpet* (London, Viking, 1991).

[88] T Hill, *Underground* (London, Faber, 1999).

[89] L Division has about 500 active officers and specialist squads to deal with graffiti and pickpockets (the 'dip squad').

[90] London Transport Executive Railways Bylaws, made under s 67 of the Transport Act 1962 – as amended by para 5(1) of Sch 3 to the Transport (London) Act 1969 and s 37 of the Transport Act 1981 – by the London Transport Executive and confirmed by the Secretary of State for Transport for regulating the use and working of and travel on their railways, the maintenance of order on their railways and railway premises and the conduct of all persons while on those premises.

impression of the peculiar nature of the Underground space, in which women begging with children became such visible targets.

Underground by-laws have four interrelated themes. The first is administration and policing of the paying of fares, implemented through the ticket, which is described in the by-laws as a 'document issued for the conveyance of any passenger'.[91] The by-laws outline conditions for dispensing, authorising and forfeiting tickets, for their control and integrity as a stable circulative form; thus the prohibition against behaviour which may 'alter, deface, mutilate, or destroy' tickets.[92]

The second theme revolves around management of a properly ticketed pedestrian traffic flow through the physical infrastructure of the Underground. These sections of the by-laws deal primarily with the acts of entering and exiting particular conveyance units, such as escalators, lifts and subway cars, as well as through spaces mediated or bifurcated by barricades and moving doors. Two by-law sections provide especially vivid examples of this intense management of pedestrian flow; both of them attempt to enforce an etiquette of turn-taking and patient politeness among strangers. The first one deals with entering conveyances that are simultaneously being used by exiting passengers:

> No person shall enter or attempt to enter any lift or vehicle through any door thereof until all persons who are leaving or are on the way to leave the lift or vehicle through such door shall have passed out of such door.[93]

And one deals with the act of 'queue jumping', which deserves to be quoted in full:

> The Executive may establish queues on the railway for the purpose of regulating the access to services and facilities ... and every person desirous of availing himself or herself of any such service or facility shall, upon notice or request by the Executive or an authorised person, take up position in the rear of one of such queues and move forward in an orderly and regular manner, and obey the reasonable instructions of an authorised person regulating such queues.[94]

The third theme involves regulation of orderly passenger conduct, expressed most generally in prohibitions against using language which is 'threatening, abusive, obscene or offensive' and behaving in a 'riotous, disorderly, indecent or offensive manner'.[95] Two specific sections deal with controlling potentially infectious or filthy passenger conditions; the first prohibits the presence of any person suffering from 'any infectious or contagious disease or disorder'[96] – reminiscent of

---

[91] ibid, s 1.
[92] ibid, s 6.
[93] ibid, s 10.
[94] ibid, s 28.
[95] ibid, s 17(1). Other, more specific sections include prohibitions against spitting (s 27[1]), littering (s 27[2]), graffiti (s 23), bookmaking and gambling (s 23) and various forms of vandalism (s 21).
[96] ibid, s 15.

Victorian concerns over cholera in Underground and train stations. The second section is no doubt directed at the presence of rough-sleepers and the homeless, prohibiting persons who are 'in an unfit and improper condition', including those 'whose dress or clothing is in a condition liable to soil or injure the linings or cushions of any carriage, or the dress or clothing of any passenger.'[97]

The fourth by-law theme involves controlling importuning conduct, including the activities of begging, busking, hawking and touting. Two general types of Underground begging are identified as being of concern to officials. The first involves static begging in tunnels and along platforms; described as 'vagrancy' and 'dirty, filthy and smelly', these beggar types often end up 'getting away', as the police do not want to take them into the station to process them.[98] Of more concern to Underground police is the activity of 'mobile begging', involving individuals who move through the trains importuning travellers person by person. As one officer describes them,

> a lot of people are sitting there in their own world, reading their book or their paper, and suddenly this person is very loud on the train, and they are thrusting their hand or a hat or a cup under their nose, and you feel intimidated, and because you're in such a closed [area] you feel guilty – you give.[99]

Mobile beggars are able to take advantage of a socially fragile space where individuals are engaged in acts of 'civil inattention'[100] such as newspaper reading or staring at posters or maps, politely ignoring others who are in close physical proximity. An especially popular place for carriage begging is on the westbound Piccadilly line, which heads out to Heathrow; the beggars aim 'at people leaving the country and going home, with spare change in their pocket, and put it in their hat because they don't need it anymore.'[101]

It is, however, the presence of women begging with children in the Underground that became a main enforcement concern of the authorities. The use of children to beg with has been a recurring theme in begging governance, most notably in panics throughout the nineteenth century over the kidnapping and maiming of children.[102] In the summer of 1996, personnel from a number of welfare and policing agencies met to consider the apparently increasing presence of women begging with children on Underground platforms. Officials noted that 'politically the issue is becoming more alive, with complaints from the public

---

[97] ibid, s 16.

[98] Interview with constable, British Transport Police, London Underground Area, February 1998.

[99] ibid.

[100] E Goffman, *Behaviour in Public Places: Notes on the Social Organization of Gatherings* (New York, Macmillan, 1963), 84.

[101] Interview with personal security manager, London Underground Limited, January 1998.

[102] N Rose, *Governing Freedom* (Cambridge, Cambridge University Press, 1998). This prohibition of begging was part of a much broader concern in child welfare legislation governing the prevention of cruelty to children, including exposure to 'moral dangers' such as alcohol, gambling, taking pawns, street hawking and forms of industrial employment.

increasing, including a High Court judge'.[103] Complaints had also been received, stated a Westminster Social Services co-ordinator,

> by the Director of Westminster Social Services and there have been reports in the *Evening Standard* of tourists finding children begging to be their most upsetting experience when visiting London. The matter has clearly built up a head of steam and could become a political issue in the lead up to a general election.[104]

In its first meeting, the working group characterised the problem as:

> children of pre-school age being used by their mothers to create the 'forlorn family' look and enhance the takings from begging. The children are also loaned around the extended family network and so the adult or young person accompanying them may be a distant relative or family friend. The children are often in the Tube stations for up to 5 to 6 hours per day, they have no play materials and spend hours sitting or 'lying' on their 'carers'' lap adopting a particularly passive and lifeless posture.[105]

Welfare officials noted that the children appeared to be harmed in three ways: by the lack of 'fresh air and exercise'; by the lack of stimulation for extended periods of time, 'which is unnatural for young children who are instinctively active'; and by 'induction into a life of begging and crime at an early age'.[106] In addition, there was a fear that they could injure themselves by falling down the stairs or escalators or onto the live rails, especially since, on a few occasions, children were seen wandering back and forth on the platforms collecting small change in plastic cups.[107] As the police constable involved in initiating the working group stated, 'one day, one of them will fall down at the escalator and suffer a terrible death, and they will fall on the track, because they run around, especially when they see police – they start running.'[108]

Clearly officials were aware of the possible liability and public relations issues the Underground would face if a child were to be seriously injured or killed.[109] In order to gauge the extent of this begging and decide on a course of action, the group decided to conduct what they called a 'short piece of research'. On 3, 4, 11 and 12 September 1996, police and Social Services teams approached and interviewed a total of 44 carer–children couples. Each survey was carried out by a social worker and a plainclothes police officer who together inquired as to the location and duration of the begging, the condition of the children and their relationship to the adult. Below is a sample of a completed survey form.

---

[103] Letter to constable, British Transport Police, from Child Protection Co-ordinator, Westminster Social Services, with reference to 'Children Begging on the Underground', 6 November 1996, 2.

[104] ibid, 1.

[105] British Transport Police, minutes of 'Meeting to Consider Children Begging on the Underground' at Westminster Social Services, 24 Greencoat Place, Victoria SW1, 1996; inverted commas in original.

[106] ibid, 2.

[107] Interview with personal security manager.

[108] Interview with constable.

[109] Interview with personal security manager.

British Transport Police Beggars Survey[110]

Date: 12/09

Time: 10.50 am

Station: OXO

Exact location (sketch plan): bottom of steps leading to Central Line

How long on Tube: 40 minutes

How long in position: 5 minutes

Carer's name: Lynn Rachael

Age: 16

Address: [London Council]

Relationship to child: aunt

Child's name: Mary Rachael

Age: 1 year, 11 months

Address: as above

Child's position (in relation to carer): on lap

Child's physical condition: rash under chin, says it's because she's teething and dribbles. Child yawning.

Child's dress: appropriate dress

Foodstuffs: yoghurt

When last in open air: [left blank]

Other comments: no buggy. No playthings. Mary has been on the system with at least 2 carers on each of the 4 days of the survey.

Person compiling: PC 0000

Agency: police

Table 1 Women/girls seen begging with children on the London Underground on 3rd, 6th, 11th and 12th September 1996 (British Transport Police)

No.	Time and Station	Social Worker Remark
1	11.55 am Piccadilly Circus	Child on carer's lap. He had bags under his eyes and was tired. Clean dress. No Toys – no buggy.
2	Noon Piccadilly Circus	Child on blanket by the side of carer. Physical condition appeared fine. Dress clean. Buggy filthy. Claims [name] was her social worker.

(continued)

---

[110] British Transport Police, 'Beggars Survey', 12 September 1996. Pseudonyms have been used to mask the identities of subjects.

Table 1 *(Continued)*

No.	Time and Station	Social Worker Remark
3	12.25 pm Oxford Circus	Child on carer's lap. Grubby clothes. Bruise on left eye, mark on nose and scratch on forehead. No toys – no buggy.
4	12.40 pm Oxford Circus	Carer gave age as 17. Child on feet, didn't speak. Clean. Quite forlorn. Glazed expression. Fringe in eyes. Same address as carer. No toys – no buggy. Carer said that child cannot be understood when she speaks.
5	1 pm Oxford Circus	Child had very dirty face. Very large child – looked older than 2 years of age. No toys – clean buggy.
6	1.45 pm Oxford Circus	Child on carer's lap. Child alert, grubby clothing and appearance. Carer would appreciate help from social services. Agreed to SSD writing her.
7	2.15 pm Holborn	Child relatively clean. No toys, no buggy. Does not know the name of the site where she lives.
8	2.15 pm Holborn	Child on blanket by carer. Carer was about to change child's messy nappy as we appeared. Child relatively clean. Buggy filthy. Carer says she avoids social workers.
9	2.30 pm Holborn	Child standing. Had scratch on forehead and cheek, forlorn look, dark rings around eyes, sore looking eye, tired.
10	2.30 pm Holborn	Child looked very forlorn. Tired looking eyes, dirty hands, possible eczema, dry and very red cheeks. Grubby.
11	3.10 pm Oxford Circus	Child was on carer's lap. Child had scratch on forehead, bags under her eyes, marks on nose and bruise on left eye. No toys. No Buggy.
12	10.30 am Oxford Circus	Child, very large, was on carer's lap. He had blonde hair, and appeared healthy. Relatively clean. Child had some toys. No buggy.
13	11 am Holborn	Child dirty.
14	11.10 am Leicester	Child on carer's lap. Tired appearance, scratch on face. Grubby. No Toys. No change of nappy.
15	– Holborn	Sitting next to to carer on the ground. Child had scab on face. Grubby. Appeared very tired.
16	11.25 am Russell Square	Child on carer's lap. Child well dressed and had healthy complexion. Child had pen and pad to draw.
17	11.45 am Holborn	Child on carer's lap. Small bruises and scratches on child's face. Very dirty clothing, no socks, very poor appearance.
18	11.45 am Holborn	Child on carer's lap. Child small build, bags under her eyes, pale complexion, brown hair, tired but relatively lively. Dirty face and hands.

(continued)

Table 1 *(Continued)*

No.	Time and Station	Social Worker Remark
19	12.40 pm Oxford Circus	Child on carer's lap. Child was reasonably clean and appropriately dressed. Health visitor [name] in [location].
20	2.15 pm Oxford Circus	Child on carer's lap. Child bright and lively. Dirty clothes.
21	2.20 pm Oxford Circus	Child on carer's lap. Seemed bright and alert. Wearing shorts and a T-shirt. Bruises to legs, small mark scratch on the back of the neck.
22	2.50 pm Piccadilly Circus	Child on carer's lap. Child alert and clean.
23	3 pm Piccadilly Circus	Child on carer's lap. Child was wearing dirty clothes. Marks to right side of face. Appearance okay. Speaks well.
24	10.55 am Oxford Circus	Child asthmatic, bit grubby and pale looking. Carer wants child to go to nursery when aged 4. Carer claims benefit.
25	11.05 am Tottenham Court Road	Begging on her own. Looked health[y]. Clean. Attended [name] school.
26	11.20 am Leicester Square	Child looked healthy but dirty. Child's mother lives somewhere in Hackney. Child living at carer's address – her grandmother's.
27	11.35 am Holborn	Child had very bad eczema on both cheeks which looked untreated and cut on left eyebrow and graze below left eye. Small cut under nose. Dirty. Quiet and withdrawn.
28	11.45 am Holborn	Child has eczema on mouth and chin – very dirty and does not attend school.
29	12.20 pm Green Park	Child appeared healthy – big for age. Clean.
30	1.15 pm Oxford Circus	Child had dirty face and small graze to forehead. Appeared healthy.
31	1.25 pm Oxford Circus	Child looked healthy, but very dirty.
32	2 pm Russell Square	Dirty. Both carer and child smelly. Child attends [name] school.
33	2.36 pm Holborn	Child looked healthy but very sleepy and lethargic.
34	10.50 am Oxford Circus	Child had a rash under the chin. Carer said it was due to teething and dribbling. Child tired. No toys. No buggy. Child's mother [name]
35	10.55 am Oxford Circus	Dirty, unwashed. Completely unworried being interviewed by the police.

(continued)

Table 1 *(Continued)*

No.	Time and Station	Social Worker Remark
36	10.55 am Oxford Circus	Unclean otherwise appeared okay. Carer said that the mother knew where the child was.
37	11 am Oxford Circus	Child's parents reside at caravan site in Ireland.
38	11 am Oxford Circus	Child has blonde hair, bags under her eyes and pale complexion. Carer sister of [name]. They do not live together. Child is carer's brother's child – she doesn't know her brother's address.
39	11.15 am Oxford Circus	Child dirty but otherwise apparently okay.
40	Noon Leicester Square	Child asleep on carer's lap. Child woken, but immediately fell into a deep sleep again. No toys.
41	1.15 pm Leicester Square	Child's hair very unclean. Dirty face and clothing. No toys. No buggy.
42	1.35 pm Embankment	Child had pale complexion and dirty face.
43	1.35 pm Embankment	Child had dirty face and hair. Grubby appearance.
44	1.45 pm Holborn	[name] had cut below left eye. Carer on previous day was advised that the child should see a doctor. Not done. Dirty clothes, unwashed appearance.
	Comments	On each occasion the carer was asked to take the child home and then leave the Underground. Invariably they returned. We have not recorded every time we saw them begging. It can be seen that the child is often with a different carer. The relationship of child to carer, names, addresses and dates of birth have not been verified, and are the details supplied by the carers. All were Irish. Many of the carers were unable to read or write.

The survey results were summarised by a Westminster child protection co-ordinator as illustrated in Table 1. The observations recorded for 'child's position' and 'physical condition' are remarkable for their detail and speak to the extent to which the police and social workers were attempting to find clues about child-abuse risk in the state of the children's dress, cleanliness, demeanour, skin condition and facial expression.[111,112]

In summarising the results of the survey, the child protection co-ordinator reported to the working group that the problem consisted of 'a limited number

[111] The 44 recorded interviews involved 25 separate children, many of whom were seen begging more than once, often with different carers. The average reported age of the children was 3.1 years.
[112] Letter from Westminster Social Services. Five of the children were under one year old.

of Irish travelling families who use children of predominately pre-school age to assist in begging from tourists between the hours of 10.00 am and 3.30 pm.'[113] The co-ordinator noted that the children were kept in the Underground for five to six hours at a time, were generally described as being in a 'grubby and dirty' condition, and were 'passive and withdrawn', with 'neither toys or stimulating activities to engage them'.[114] The implication of the social services analysis was that the women had intentionally manufactured a deprived, 'forlorn waif' look for their children to increase begging takings. As the co-ordinator commented,

> Clearly a well dressed, clean, happy child is not such an asset for begging as one who is a forlorn waif and in need of a good meal, but there are child concerns in keeping young children for such long periods of time in depressing, dirty, and under-stimulating environments for the explicit purpose of supplementing the families' income to the tune of £30 a day.[115]

Nevertheless, the preschool children used for begging, while not being cared for in the most ideal way, did not appear to be neglected to an extent that would constitute child abuse. Most children had some form of toys and food, were adequately dressed and showed no visible signs of physical abuse.[116] The presence of scratches and rashes could easily be explained by the carers.[117] While the practice of begging is 'undesirable and abusive to the needs of the children', commented the report, there were no grounds for intervention. The situation was, according to the officials, best dealt with as a 'children-in-need' rather than a 'children protection' matter,[118] a crucial distinction in the reformist Children Act 1989.[119] The conditions observed did not constitute a situation where there were grounds – the causing of 'significant harm' – for child protection intervention in the form of child-assessment or emergency protection orders.[120] In the context of the women begging with children, 'The thresholds for [child protection] intervention are much higher than the public would generally be aware', the child protection co-ordinator noted.[121] The social workers' refusal to consider the begging to be a form of child abuse was a constant source of annoyance for Underground police officials.[122]

---

[113] ibid, 1.
[114] ibid.
[115] ibid, 2.
[116] Interview with constable.
[117] ibid.
[118] Westminster (1996: 2).
[119] In the reformist 1989 Act, the notion of 'children in need' was introduced in an attempt to strike a better balance between legalistic child protection measures and family support services. For a review of the policy research which informed the notion of children in need, see HMSO (1995). Section 17(1) of the Act defines children in need: 'a child shall be taken to be in need if – (a) he is unlikely to achieve or maintain, or to have the opportunity of achieving or maintaining, a reasonable standard of health or development without the provision for him of services by a local authority under this Part; (b) his health or development is likely to be significantly impaired, without the provision for him of such services.'
[120] HMSO (1995: 23).
[121] Letter from Westminster Social Services, 2.
[122] British Transport Police, operation report, 19 January 1998; interview with personal security manager.

Nevertheless, the child protection co-ordinator noted that begging with children was not only illegal under section 4(1) of the Children and Young Persons Act 1933 but was also against the spirit of the Children Act 1989. Westminster Social Services suggested that the group should adopt three tactics in dealing with women begging with children. The first tactic would involve 'dissuading families from using children' to beg with and would involve local authorities working 'through their contacts' with the travelling community to emphasise the 'unacceptable' nature of begging. The proposal noted that the Irish travelling community viewed begging as 'inappropriate' childcare and did not consider it a 'cultural' aspect of their community.[123]

The second proposal was that the parents or carers should be prosecuted 'as soon as possible'.[124] Arrested women would be taken to Euston or Victoria Station, and those with no 'genuine address' would be held in custody overnight and bailed to appear in court the following day. The purpose of prosecuting would be to dissuade begging by

> presenting the courts with a policy of intervention and making them aware of the child care concerns. To date courts have shown little interest and have let the offenders off with a small fine and the Police have resorted to cautioning. The objective would be to encourage the court to fine the carer the amount of money taken from them at the point of arrest. Begging would hopefully become unprofitable.[125]

The third tactic, closely related to the second, was to ensure that children were returned to a family member as soon as possible after the arrest. 'It is not intended that small children be kept in police stations for any unnecessary length of time.'[126]

Several problems were identified by the working group in terms of arresting and prosecuting the women. Consistent identification of the families proved difficult because of the perceived 'borrowing' of children by aunts, sisters and friends.[127] The anti-authority views of the adults were also cited as a problem, and mention was made of the fact that members of the travelling community were often thought to lie about their identity and address.[128] The central problem of arresting these women, however, was care of the children while the carer was being processed:

> If the child is with his/her mother at the time then they would be held in a detention room at the police station until the process of charging the mother is completed. This would take most of the day and cut across the early late shift divided at 2pm-ish. If the child is not with his/her mother then the 'carer' would be separated from the child and charged. The child would inevitably become distressed and require a great deal of

---

[123] Letter from Westminster Social Services, 2; British Transport Police, 'Travellers Survey: Children Being Used for Begging', minutes of meeting at 55 The Broadway, London SW1, 2 September 1996.
[124] Letter from Westminster Social Services, 2.
[125] ibid.
[126] ibid.
[127] British Transport Police, 'Children Begging on the Underground', minutes of meeting held at 55 The Broadway, St. James' Park Tube Station, London SW1, 5 December 1996; interview with constable.
[128] Interview with constable.

care and looking after. Clearly the amount of time, effort and money put into using the criminal justice system to deal with these problems does not pay dividends.[129]

Despite the fact that using the justice system did not 'pay dividends' with these sorts of problems, and despite noting that previous attempts at moving on the families had failed because of 'lack of cohesion amongst the various agencies',[130] Social Services supported the idea of a dedicated police operation. Between 6 and 9 May 1997 the police launched an operation that targeted 'Irish women' begging with children, on the Underground, code-named Operation Phoebe.[131] Utilising plainclothes sweeps involving about 20 officers, including two-member custody teams, 'Phoebe One' resulted in 13 women being charged under section 4(1) of the Children and Young Persons Act 1933, which reads:

> If any person causes or procures any child or young person under the age of 16 years or, having custody, charge, or care of such a child or young person, allows him to be in any street, premises, or place for the purpose of begging or receiving alms, or of inducing the giving of alms (whether or not there is any pretence of singing, playing, performing, offering anything for sale, or otherwise) he shall, on summary conviction, be liable to a fine ... or alternatively ... or in addition thereto, to imprisonment for any term not exceeding three months.

Because this was a 'recordable' offence under the 1933 Act, the women were photographed and fingerprinted and their identities were listed in the London Transport Police's computerised intelligence database, known as PINS. The women were then immediately bailed and summoned to appear in four different courts.[132] The court disposals were as follows:

- eight did not attend court and bench warrants were issued;
- one was deferred to a youth court; and
- four were found guilty, of which:
  - one was fined £100 for begging, £25 for fare evasion and £2 for compensation;
  - one was found guilty and given a conditional discharge;
  - one was fined £50; and
  - one was fined £30, plus £15 costs.

Arising from frustration with the women who failed to attend court, a second operation ('Phoebe Two') was carried out in October 1997; it involved executing bench warrants at the residences of the women. An intelligence officer created 'target profiles' using details collected in the first operation.[133] The operation targeted 12 women and resulted in the arrest of five. The operation was an attempt,

[129] Letter from Westminster Social Services, 2.
[130] ibid.
[131] Most police operation names are taken from pre-generated lists with encyclopaedic themes. This operation's name was taken from a list with the theme of British warships.
[132] British Transport Police, internal memorandum, 27 June 1997.
[133] British Transport Police, London Underground 'Pickpocket Target Profile', 1996.

according to the police, to show the women that 'we're not going to give up' just because they did not show up for court.[134]

While information on the full extent of the Phoebe operations is incomplete, it appears that six took place between May 1997 and December 1998. Field reports for two of the operations provide an indication of their dedicated nature. 'Phoebe Four' was carried out on 3 and 4 December 1997 and involved 23 police officers, including two sergeants who headed the custody teams. The operation resulted in the arrest of six 'itinerant female beggars with children' and the reporting of two more, a result which led the reporting constable to comment that it was 'disappointing for the amount of resources used'.[135] Of the six women arrested, one was found guilty and given a seven-day custodial sentence, one was given a 12-month probation order and four failed to attend – two were later arrested under executed warrants.

'Phoebe Five' was carried out on 26 February 1998 and involved 16 constables, three sergeants and one inspector. In addition, an inspector, a custody sergeant, a gaoler and an intelligence officer were on duty at the Albany Street custody facility where the operation was based. The result of this operation was the arrest of four women begging with children. The reporting constable's comments on this operation succinctly illustrate the failure of the Phoebe operations in terms of targeting these women with formal legal processes:

> This latest operation seems to prove that the use of legislation open to Police Officers is not working. Sentences are not heavy enough or broken conditions are not being dealt with by magistrates' courts. It appears to prove that almost a year after Phoebe was introduced, itinerant women with young children *are still* on the Underground with police action having very little success. What else can we do?[136]

As is often the case when the failure of law and regulation is clear, officials responded with more aggressive regulation through a series of dedicated operations. They did this even though police action seemed to have little deterrent effect, the reported women routinely avoided showing up for court, and, while the operation was couched as helping children in need, there was no apparent benefit to the children. From 1 May 1995 to 31 December 1998, 305 offenders were arrested and reported under section 4 for begging with children, only 44 of whom were prosecuted. The small number of actual prosecutions resulting from these arrests is notable. 'The proof is not always made out in this offence,' commented an inspector in the Criminal Justice Division, 'and is reduced to begging (s 3, Vagrancy Act 1824).'[137] Indeed, during the same period, 481 offenders were prosecuted for begging under the Vagrancy Act.[138] This suggests that police

[134] Interview with constable.
[135] British Transport Police, operation report, 19 January 1998.
[136] British Transport Police, operation report, 12 March 1998, 2; emphasis in original.
[137] Letter to author from inspector, Criminal Justice Unit, British Transport Police, London Underground Area, 27 May 1999.
[138] ibid.

were initially using their arrest authority under the Children and Young Persons Act 1989 to arrest the women off the street, then later reducing the charge to begging under the Vagrancy Act 1824. As of April 1999, Operation Phoebe had been expanded to include the Metropolitan Police, to target 'refugees' begging on trains.[139]

Several observations can be made about the particularly gendered and racialised character of this operation. Perhaps the most notable aspect is the extent to which officials attempted to practise a social-work physiognomy on the women begging with children in their effort to detect child abuse. The signs of child abuse which the social workers looked for (see Table 1) were located in the appearance of the child and the relation of the child's body to that of the woman carer. Indeed, the clues that officials focused on in judging the children to be objects of a 'forlorn waif' look – the child's gaze, signs of cleanliness and purity, the position on the carer's lap – are all central components of an iconic Western image of motherhood, that of the Madonna and Child. The social-work remarks can be read as an anti-Madonna inventory of 'bad motherhood', where the love between mother and child – a maternal gift relationship – has been breached by the deceit and mendacity of the mother in exploiting her child's innocence.

Perhaps the most powerful aspect of the mother-and-child icon is that it presents the intimate bond between mother and child as 'natural' and not culturally constructed.[140] In constituting the women begging with children as simply committing a mendacious act that was abusive, officials seemed incapable of conceptualising the presence of these women and children within a larger landscape of economic hardship or cultural isolation. It is notable that there appeared to be no consideration by officials that the women and children might actually be as they appeared – that they might in fact be indigent, desperate and truly in need of money. The officials seemed to assume that the 'forlorn family' look was completely manufactured by the women carers.[141] The possibility that the women and children were, for example, victims of exploitative family relations was not taken seriously by the police.[142] The main goal of the operation was to push them back into the private sphere of family relations, where they would presumably belong. Indeed, there seemed to be absolutely no consideration that such displacement could potentially be harmful to the children.

For the women begging with children, this displacement takes place within an economy of personal family relations – the 'natural' location of maternal

---

[139] Interviews with constable, February 1998, April 1999.

[140] M Sturken and L Cartwright, *Practices of Looking: An Introduction to Visual Culture* (New York, Oxford University Press, 2001), 37.

[141] British Transport Police, 'Meeting to Consider Children Begging'.

[142] ibid. I thank Thomas Acton, Professor of Romani Studies at the University of Greenwich, for this suggestion. See T Acton, 'Modernisation, Moral Panics and the Gypsies' (1994) *Sociology Review* 4, on the 'moral panics' surrounding 'gypsies' in modern life. For a review of the discriminatory character of criminal justice legislation in relation to travellers, see L Clements and S Campbell, 'The Criminal Justice and Public Order Act and Its Implications for Travellers' in T Acton (ed), *Gypsy Politics and Traveller Identity* (Hertfordshire, University of Hertfordshire Press, 1997).

welfare – where the children are seen by welfare officials to circulate – to be 'loaned' and 'passed around' – within a community of private relations. Yet it is exactly this dual space of public and private care and giving that seems to have failed many of these women and their children in the first place. The work of Lauren Berlant is relevant here. She argues that, in a conception of citizenship located in a view of victimised children, there has been a triumph of the 'intimate sphere' of personal relations over that of public life.[143] A central consequence of this intimate public sphere is that citizenship is infantilised to the extent that one's civic participation involves rescuing children from 'predators' or 'bad mothers'. We see here a policing operation that clearly resonates with Berlant's analysis, with its punitive focus on 'bad mothers' who would exploit their children to produce a 'forlorn waif' look. Certainly, while welfare officials invoked the spirit of the Children Act in rationalising police action, this law also places a statutory responsibility on Westminster Council to assist families with 'children in need'. It is not clear to what extent officials, in arresting the women away from their children, acted to discharge that responsibility, as there is no evidence in the context of the police operation that Social Services made use of their assistance powers as part of the operation.

It is important to note that the 1989 Act was widely considered to emphasise moving away from coercive legal instruments (such as child protection orders) towards provision of family support services – a shift that the notion of children in need symbolises. Yet we have seen how, from the perspective of social services, this notion was used to legitimise an extremely blunt and coercive course of legal action in which prosecution of the women was viewed as a way of 'presenting the courts with a policy of intervention'.[144] What we see in all three of these cases is a process that in the end re-inscribes the raison d'etre of vagrancy law codified in the categories of the 1824 Act – that of the status offence of being an idle and disorderly person. The fact that the majority of these women were convicted for begging as 'vagrants', rather than for offences under child protection legislation, illustrates how the operation was directed at punishing women who were seen to be 'bad mothers' rather than being centred in a social welfare context of assisting children. The punitive character of the operation that resulted in many of these women being convicted as vagrants reveals two of the most racist and discriminatory uses of vagrancy law: the singling out and targeting of 'immoral women' and of 'gypsies'.

These three police operations – all specialised to make the welfare of street people a priority – confirm that EVA's criticisms were not only correct but probably understated, on three counts: (1) that beggars were being arrested only for 'threatening or intimidating behaviour' was simply not true; (2) the arrest of

---

[143] L Berlant, *The Queen of America Goes to Washington City: Essays on Sex and Citizenship* (Durham, NC, Duke University Press, 1997), 45.
[144] Letter from Westminster Social Services, 2.

beggars was capricious and penal in the way archaic arrest powers were mobilised; and (3) the evidential burden of *R v Dalton* was taken into little account. The actual status of being visibly homeless and asking for money was manipulated as a discretionary resource to ensure that the end result would be arrest or incarceration as a punishment or deterrent. Most notably, despite the diminution of arrest powers and punishments over the previous decades, the Vagrancy Act 1824 remained a powerful tool to police those who begged on the street. It is this legal landscape that would be reassembled, starting in 2003, propelled by a movement that warned how kindness to people begging on the street could kill them.

5

Kindness Kills:
Begging, Drugs and Death

Giving money to people begging helps kill them.

Louise Casey[1]

A new interest in 'Truth' does not come from a new vision, but from the same old vision applying itself to new visible objects that mobilize space and time differently.

Bruno Latour[2]

How did Winchester's experiment in diverted giving instigate a much wider gift-crime movement that would enable historic changes to vagrancy law? Two distinct stages can be identified. The first is the wave of diverted-giving schemes from late 1995 to 2000, with the Winchester model migrating to a handful of locations, dovetailing with a new emphasis on local solutions to fight antisocial behaviour, and gaining mobility within the channels of the emerging Town Centre Management (TCM) movement. These early schemes evoked a welfarist mentality in urging people not to give money to those begging, who were viewed to be a general nuisance who would 'drink' their money. In 2000, a second wave of diverted giving initiated a much more severe moral instruction to the public: that to give to a beggar is to be complicit in drug addiction and death. This 'death turn' in diverted-giving logic was set in place by the Rough Sleepers Unit (RSU) in 2000 with its national Change a Life campaign, and would cascade into major urban centres, setting in place a wider field of gift-crime regulation. By 2003, the putative connection between begging and drug addiction had become a dominant theme of how people begging should be understood, one that would propel historic reforms to vagrancy law, most notably in the connection between 'persistent begging' and drug treatment.

---

[1] L Casey, Director, Rough Sleepers Unit, to Dr Suzanne Fitzpatrick, 30 October 2000, 2.
[2] B Latour, 'Visualization and Cognition: Thinking with Eyes and Hands' (1986) *Knowledge and Society: Studies in the Sociology of Culture Past and Present* 6, 12.

I. The Migration of Diverted Giving

The rise of the TCM movement in the late 1990s and its influence on the character of public spaces has been one of the most important developments in city-centre regulation. Over the past two decades, most major British towns and cities have hired a professional town-centre manager, and diverted giving was often one of a clutch of practices promoted and implemented by local multi-agency partnerships.

The first example of the promotion of diverted giving by the TCM movement was a 'good practices' note written by the Winchester estates manager, published in the Association of Town Centre Management (ATCM) newsletter, which publicised the apparent success of this new scheme. The article notes that both begging and homelessness can have a 'negative effect on a city's image' and recommends a number of practices that, along with diverted giving, are now widespread, including alcohol by-laws, CCTV, radio links (between stores with CCTV), codes of practice for street entertainers, co-ordinated use of street furniture, and the pedestrianisation of city cores.[3]

Local crime-and-disorder partnerships (mandated by the 1998 Crime and Disorder Act) became closely integrated with TCM strategies for retail safety and security. The early work of officials in Winchester pioneered this 'partnership' approach, with the perceived success of Make It Count used by the city in its application for funds to establish a public–private network of CCTV cameras in the pedestrianised city core. In the opening paragraphs of Winchester's submission for funding to the 1997 Home Office CCTV Challenge Competition, the city engineer wrote:

> Whilst the city appears to be prosperous it suffers from high levels of unsociable behaviour ... begging is a particular problem which is being tackled in a number of ways. A recent campaign to encourage the public to give to local charities rather than direct to beggars has attracted national attention.[4]

An important feature of the subsequently funded system was the way Marks & Spencer's private cameras were integrated into the publicly funded and monitored CCTV system. In Figure 7 (page 51), a CCTV camera mounted on the corner of the Marks & Spencer building can be seen across the pedestrianised High Street through the window behind Sainsbury's diverted-giving box. This is a striking example of a major goal of the TCM movement: to colonise public space as an adjunct of private retail commerce, using an array of subtle control measures that target both the physical and emotional order of pedestrians.

[3] ATCM, *Year Book, 1997* (Cheshire, Macmillan, 1997).
[4] Winchester City Engineer, 'Home Office Challenge 1996 CCTV Bid', Winchester, 1996.

The major accomplishment of the Winchester experiment was how officials grappled with the question, how can public feelings at the sight of someone begging be rendered into a technical problem that could be intervened in? Make It Count enabled Winchester officials to become technicians of public emotion, setting in place 'feeling rules'[5] by which the public could 'give' to those begging in a way that did not directly give to them at all. And officials knew they had to be very careful in asserting a moral prescription about what to do when a beggar is encountered, given that public attitudes towards those who beg are marked by deep ambivalence.[6] The work of these officials and the subsequent diverted-giving migration are vivid examples of a 'socio-technical network' – a complex of alliances, rationalities, knowledges and technical practices that enables actors to regulate people and things, often in mundane or unobserved ways.

Two central concepts of socio-technical networks are visible in the workings of the Winchester experiment. The first is that of translation, defined by Callon and Law as

> a process in which sets of relations between projects, interests, goals, and naturally occurring entities – objects which might otherwise be quite separate from one another – are proposed and brought into being.[7]

In Winchester, city officials aspired to construct a stable and durable relationship between the sight, feelings and actions of the passers-by and an officially sanctioned form of charity. In other words, Winchester translators worked to forge a direct relation between the giving hand of the passer-by and a distant and worthy recipient who would be the object of diverted-giving charity. And the obstacle to this relation was the very real presence of the beggar, who distracted the passer-by and called into question official charity efforts. A vital tool of translators is 'investments of form', which is characterised as

> work undertaken by a translator to convert objects that are numerous, heterogeneous, and manipulable only with difficulty into a smaller number of more easily controlled and more heterogeneous entities ... nonetheless sufficiently representative to manipulate the translated object as well.[8]

The two key investments of form utilised by the Winchester translators – ones that could open up a channel through which pocket change could be diverted – were diverted-giving boxes and posters. As I discuss in chapter two, both the boxes and

---

[5] See AR Hochschild, *The Managed Heart: Commercialization of Human Feeling* (Berkeley, University of California Press, 2012).

[6] Adler, Bromley and Rosie found that of those who encountered beggars, 50 per cent said they never gave while 45 per cent said they gave sometimes; only 5 per cent gave on a routine basis. M Adler, C Bromley and M Rosie, 'Begging as a Challenge to the Welfare State' in R Jowell et al (eds), *British Social Attitudes Survey: The 17th Report* (London, Sage, 2000) 209–37.

[7] M Callon and J Law (1989), 'On the Construction of Socio-technical Networks: Content and Context Revisited' in *Knowledge and Society: Studies in the Sociology of Science Past and Present* Vol 8, 57–83 at 59.

[8] ibid, 64.

posters were customised to create a channel of pocket-change management that could withstand the apparent impulse to give to someone begging. At the same time, the main translated target – the beggar on the street – could still be manipulated, in a more mundane but powerful way, by being informally 'moved on' by the police. An important aspect of this channel for diverted pocket change is how the boxes were able to 'accumulate space and time', enabling a chain of invisible hands acting to divert the money.

The translation expertise that emerged in Winchester spread into the wider city-centre management network through a dossier put together by the city's estates manager and circulated to other sites. The dossier included copies of the 'good practices' note, the poster and a picture of the Tuskguard box in Marks & Spencer (labelled 'example of collection box' and sometimes accompanied by the original Tuskguard technical drawings). This traffic in diverted-giving paperwork was accompanied by human actors who circulated through Winchester and other cities, managing alliances and sharpening their translation skills.

Here is a brief summary of how translation expertise was networked in the first six Winchester-inspired schemes:

- *Taunton*: After visiting Winchester and examining the scheme, city councillors from Taunton informed their city-centre manager that the Winchester scheme 'seemed to work'.[9] Taunton hired a local manufacturer to produce six charity boxes, closely based on the Tuskguard model used in Winchester, and installed three of them.[10]

- *Stoke-on-Trent*: The Stoke-on-Trent scheme 'evolved out of a diverted-giving scheme identified at Winchester from the Association of Town Centre Management Good Practice Guide'. It involved additional information from Winchester, including faxed copies of diagrams of the original Tuskguard diverted-giving box.

- *Bath*: In September 1996, at its City Environment Improvement Team meetings, the City of Bath began to actively examine documents touting the success of the Winchester scheme.[11] A police representative tabled a Winchester 'Make It Count' poster in support of the programme, and it was noted in the meeting minutes that Marks & Spencer had 'funded the production of secure collection boxes' in that city.[12] 'Focus boxes' were installed by Tuskguard at nine 'focus collection points', including the police station and Bath Abbey.

- *Cambridge*: In a visit to Winchester on 28 January 1997, Cambridge city-centre managers met with city officials and the police to collect detailed

---

[9] Interview with City Centre manager, Taunton, October 1998.
[10] The three boxes were located at the municipal building, the post office and a city-centre retailer. The box at the municipal building raised only £58.70 over seven months.
[11] *ibid.*
[12] Bath, Minutes of meeting, City Environmental Improvement Team, 3 September 1996.

information on the scheme, in the hope of starting one in their pedestrianised city centre.[13]

- *Yeovil*: Working on information received from Winchester by a former mayor, Yeovil Town Council initiated a diverted-giving scheme in May 1997.[14]

- *Oxford*: In explaining the origins of the Oxford scheme in 1998, the Oxford University marshal cited the Winchester project as a success. He had also visited the diverted-giving scheme in Bristol to collect information and visit participating retailers.[15]

This sphere of circulating actors, texts and visualisms enabled alliances between individuals, objects and ideas in different cities and allowed actors to mobilise specific local resources.[16] One important insight of socio-technical network theory is that *actors* is understood to include non-human objects in terms of how translation occurs. Indeed, the Tuskguard-designed diverted-giving boxes undertook to achieve a key translation in many of the first wave of diverted-giving schemes. The diverted-giving boxes in the private spaces of retailers acted as proxies to replace the encounter between the beggar and people on the street. In the words of Latour, the boxes acted as a 'location [that] can accumulate other places far away in space and time, and present them synoptically to the eye'.[17]

By the summer of 1998, the 'Winchester model' of diverted giving had gained enough visibility as a town-centre management success story that Tuskguard, the company that Marks & Spencer had hired to design the cylindrical box, began to independently market the charity boxes to city councils and retailers as a tool to reduce begging. As a company that specialised in retail crime-proofing, Tuskguard promoted the boxes as but one of a range of 'security solutions' to 'site harden' retail premises and physically protect clients' property. In promotional material specifically developed to introduce the boxes to city-centre officials, Tuskguard made it clear that the Winchester scheme had acted as the prototype, with Marks & Spencer playing a leading role: 'The original concept was initiated by Marks & Spencer in conjunction with other high street traders, the city council and Tuskguard in the Winchester area'.[18] Stating that it was proud to be part of the diverted-giving 'success story', Tuskguard explained to potential customers:

> The aim was to reduce begging in front of high street premises and generally throughout shopping centres and communal areas. It gives pedestrians the opportunity to make a donation to organisations and authorities that would aid the needs of those within

---

[13] Interview with assistant city-centre manager, Cambridge, October 1997.

[14] Letter to author from town clerk, Yeovil, enclosing 'Helping Hands Scheme', 28 January 1998.

[15] Interview with Ted Roberts, university marshal, Oxford University, August 1998.

[16] Not surprisingly, some of the information that circulated was inaccurate, partly because of faulty details in the ATCM note. For example, in a meeting with the Hampshire police, Cambridge officials were advised that the programme had reduced the 15 to 20 regular beggars to four or five, as local beggars had 'changed their lifestyle ... or moved elsewhere'.

[17] Latour, 'Visualization and Cognition', 11.

[18] Letter to author from managing director, Tuskguard Ltd, with reference 'Donation Boxes', enclosing marketing materials including 'Premises Protection' graphic, 13 August 1998.

the local area that require support. It has proved very successful in that 1) it discourages begging and raises awareness of pedestrians to the issues and 2) gives people the opportunity to donate money freely without the feelings of guilt or intimidation.[19]

In marketing this 'guilt-free' form of giving at a distance to the beggar that is free of intimidation, Tuskguard noted that the design and placement of the box could be modified on site by Tuskguard personnel to accommodate specific interiors. A prominent advantage of these boxes, noted to potential retail customers, was that they could be presented as part of a wider community scheme ostensibly not directly connected to the security interests of the retailers. As Tuskguard noted to potential customers in evoking the success of the Winchester scheme, 'uniformity of the product throughout an area appears to be part of the success, thus taking away any inferred connection that the scheme is linked to any particular store or retailer'.[20] This desirable feature, which masks the true retail-oriented intentions of diverted giving – to get rid of 'undesirables' through a construction of public caring and compassion – is a central effect of translation practices, where the initial origin or circumstances of a process are cloaked and obscured. As will become clear, black-boxing became even more prominent in the wider network that would forge hard linkages between begging, giving and drug addiction.

By 1999, 'diverted' and 'alternative' giving projects based on the Winchester model had been established in seven other locations.[21] Many of the schemes used the Tuskguard collection box and adapted the language, rationale and iconography of Winchester's 'Make It Count'. They also exhibited the versatility of local actors in adapting elements of the Winchester experiment to their own distinct sites.

Perhaps the most ambitious attempt in the first wave of Winchester-based schemes occurred in Oxford, where a diverse group – university students, the local night shelter and city councillors – came together to form the Oxford Poverty Action Trust (OxPAT). The main driving force behind OxPAT was Oxford University's marshal, who acted as head of the university's security services. The marshal took part in the City Forum on Anti-Social Behaviour and was one of the university's members of the Oxford City Centre Management Working Party. As noted above, in explaining the origins of the Oxford scheme, the university marshal cited the Winchester project and also made a fact-finding visit to examine Bristol's approach.[22] The marshal saw diverted giving as a way to target professional beggars by giving the public an alternative:

> When I pass someone begging, well, am I giving them money to feed a drug habit? Am I giving them money to support an alcohol habit? Am I giving money so he can buy a bottle of paracetamol so he can go and top himself? You just don't know, do you?[23]

[19] ibid.
[20] ibid.
[21] Bath, Cambridge, Yeovil, Taunton, Bristol, Cambridge, and Stoke-on-Trent.
[22] Interview with Ted Roberts.
[23] ibid.

OxPAT is unique in that it remains the only diverted-giving scheme that has registered itself as an official charity. The group does not carry out direct street collections, but it does engage in other fundraising activities. After more than a year of lobbying for the programme by the marshal and the city-centre manager, the scheme was launched in December 1998, with boxes located in Marks & Spencer, Blackwell's bookshop and the Westgate Shopping Centre. In addition, up to 38 smaller plastic counter-type boxes were eventually placed around the city (including at 13 Oxford colleges) when it became clear that no more than four locations could be found for the larger Tuskguard boxes. Private sponsors donated £2,500 to launch the scheme, including Oxford University Press, which donated £800 in services to print the posters.[24] The scheme was launched with the support of the Bishop of Oxford, who posed for a photo opportunity as he unveiled the box at the Westgate Shopping Centre.[25]

The poster for the OxPAT scheme (Figure 12) is a realistic and literal rendering of the intention of diverted giving to capture the compassion – and the pocket change – of the passer-by. With the St Giles' Church bell-tower in the background, a well-dressed pedestrian, his briefcase beside him, is sorting loose change in the palm of his right hand while a beggar sits impassively, coins sprinkled between his feet and his begging sign. 'There is another way you can help,' the imagined passer-by is told. Even the small OxPAT logo visualises diversion: a person sitting cross-legged holding the OxPAT name, stylised as a sort of funnel that will divert *munero* from *mendico*.

The City of Bath, which had recently appointed a city-centre manager, involved a more diverse range of actors that would prove harder to bring together in organising the mechanics of diverted giving. While the scheme found favour with the police, the chamber of commerce and selected retailers, the local night shelter and the *Big Issue* remained opposed to the scheme. The *Big Issue* questioned how the money would be used to help people 'in need' and felt that the 'collection boxes would take away people's means of feeding themselves and that there was the possibility of petty crime'.[26]

The City of Bath Environment Improvement Team (CEIT) stressed that it was important the scheme not be presented as 'anti begging' and that diverted giving alone would not 'solve begging'. The committee felt the scheme would alleviate two problems:

(1) The public donating to 'beggars' who in fact are not homeless, and are allegedly funding drug and drink habits from their takings.
(2) The sheer numbers of beggars on the streets – this scheme will reduce numbers and reduce the impact of beggars on the city centre environment.[27]

[24] ibid.
[25] *Oxford University Gazette*, 'New Move to Help City's Homeless', 17 December 1998, 512.
[26] Bath, Minutes of meeting, City Environmental Improvement Team, 3 September 1996.
[27] ibid.

Figure 12 Poster for the Oxford Poverty Action Trust (OxPAT) programme, Oxford 1998 (photo by author)

Bath's assistant city-centre manager was caught in the middle of this disagreement between the *Big Issue* and the Julian Night Shelter and other city retailers and officials. The scheme appeared stalled, most notably because of lack of money to cover start-up costs. However, the local Liberal Democrat MP, Don Foster, secured a £2,000 donation from businessman Malcolm Pearce, owner of the Bristol Rugby Club and chairman of Lordswood Dairy.[28] The local authority contributed another £1,000 towards start-up costs. With some reluctance the assistant city-centre manager launched the 'Focus' scheme in October 1998, without the support of any major volunteer or charity organisations such as the Julian Night Shelter or the regional *Big Issue* office, which was just yards away from the city-centre manager's office. Boxes were installed by Tuskguard at nine collection points, including the police station and Bath Abbey. The Abbey's participation was seen to be a coup for the programme; the assistant city-centre manager felt that its participation provided a 'certain legitimacy that perhaps it wouldn't have had if it was just a bunch of businesses [that had] got together'.[29]

A major problem for the Bath scheme was how the council could not point directly to charities that would benefit from public donations. The assistant city-centre manager admitted that this would 'make things difficult' and that asking people to give to 'an unspecified cause' would be problematic for marketing of the scheme.[30] The lack of support from charities also presented a second major problem for Bath's assistant city-centre manager: deciding how the money should be allocated. The Julian Night Shelter argued that the scheme might compromise outreach work, a position eventually supported by the local newspaper, which editorialised against diverted giving.[31] The City did not have firm plans for distributing the money, or even criteria that might be used to decide on recipients. As the assistant manager suggested,

> If somebody came as an individual with the backing of an organisation such as the *Big Issue* or the Genesis Trust and said, 'I need a six-month rail pass because I've got a new job for the first time in ten years, to go to Bristol', that's something we'd look extremely favourably at. But [not] with individuals coming along saying, 'I need a thousand pounds because my house was repossessed'.[32]

The poster developed for Bath's Focus scheme is an awkward collage of diverted-giving tropes (Figure 13). As it urges pedestrians to 'FOCUS your assistance – make sure your donation really counts', a *munero* hand poised to drop a coin is revealed in the O of 'FOCUS' through the lens of a magnifying glass – a Sherlock Holmes – type clue as to what to do when encountering a beggar. Two *mendico* hands reach from the background to the 'How You Can Help' text that offers instructions to the public. The Lordswood Dairy logo is prominently displayed, presumably in recognition of Malcolm Pearce's £2,000 donation to the scheme.

---

[28] Interviews with assistant city-centre manager, Bath, October 1998 and April 1999.
[29] ibid (1998).
[30] ibid.
[31] ibid.
[32] ibid.

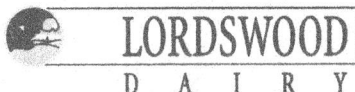

The plight of the Homeless in Bath is a concern to both our residents and visitors. The Focus Scheme has been established as a result, and involved multi-agency discussions between The Council, Police, Homeless Groups, and Resident and Trader Associations.

The Aims of The Scheme

To assist in addressing the causes of homelessness in Bath City Centre.
To raise new, additional revenue which can be redistributed via Homelessness, Drug and Alcohol Charities to assist the needs of vulnerable people.

How You Can Help

We ask you to place your change directly in one of the FOCUS Collection Boxes situated throughout the City Centre.

Every penny of funds collected through the FOCUS Scheme will be held in a Charitable Fund, to which all local Homelessness and Drug and Alcohol charities can apply for financial assistance.

FOCUS your assistance - MAKE SURE YOUR DONATION REALLY COUNTS...

Collection Boxes are located at:

Bath Abbey, Abbey Churchyard
Boots The Chemist, Southgate
W.H. Smiths, Union Street
Midland Bank, Milsom Street
Midland Bank, Southgate

Marks & Spencer, Stall Street
Bath Police Station, Manvers Street
Iceland, Ham Gardens
Bottoms Up, Westgate Street

The FOCUS Scheme has been jointly established by:
Bath & North East Somerset Council
The Avon & Somerset Constabulary
Bath Abbey
The Bath Chamber of Commerce
The Abbey Green & York Street Trader and Residents Association

LORDSWOOD
D A I R Y

Figure 13 Poster for the 'Focus' scheme, City of Bath 1998 (photo by author)

In November 1999, Stoke-on-Trent launched its own Make It Count scheme, which 'evolved out of [the] diverted-giving scheme identified at Winchester from the Association of Town Centre Management Good Practice Guide'. As the marketing material for the scheme states, 'It is a good thing that you want to do something but giving directly to a beggar will only worsen the situation – hold on to that thought and take your donation to one of the many collecting boxes throughout the city.' The poster developed for the scheme is a more stylised, cartoon-like version of the Winchester visual, with coins awkwardly positioned between *munero* and *mendico*.

Utilising Winchester-inspired tropes and themes, Stoke-on-Trent initiated a major shift in how officials configured the goals of diverted giving. Stoke-on-Trent's was the first scheme to characterise people begging as drug addicts, and to caution that giving to people begging would fuel addiction. While the official publicity for the Stoke-on-Trent scheme followed Winchester in presenting a welfarist (but paradoxical) message of helping those in need, the rationale for the Stoke-on-Trent scheme had a much sharper moral edge. The Make It Count working party, which included the city-centre manager, a local police commander and retailers such as Marks & Spencer, identified the problem as:

> ... the majority of beggars have major drug dependency problems. ... the five or six regular beggars [at that time] disguised the fact that there are dozens of rough sleepers and hundreds of homeless people in Stoke-on-Trent – most of whom do not beg.[33]

Attached to this begging–drugs linkage was the explicit view that real, genuinely homeless people do not beg. 'We also hoped to lift the public's awareness that Begging and Homelessness are not directly linked and that supporting begging often feeds drug and alcohol misuse.'[34] A press conference at Marks & Spencer launched the scheme on 17 November 1999, at a cost of £2,600. 'Are there any negative aspects to the scheme?' the local working party asked rhetorically in briefing notes prepared for the press. 'Yes, it will reduce a funding stream to drug dealers. Other than that we have not found any negatives.'[35] Officials projected that they could generate between £3,000 and £5,000 a year from the scheme, based on wildly inaccurate information that the Winchester operation was bringing in £14,000 per year.[36] But, like Winchester, there was no substantial follow-up or evaluation, with officials soon lamenting that the scheme lost momentum after three months and appeared to stagnate.[37] Make It Count was nevertheless viewed as a success and received attention and recognition from the Home Office. North Warwickshire MP Mike O'Brien, a Home Office minister, gave 'high profile and effusive support' for the scheme and was kept briefed by Stoke-on-Trent officials.[38]

---

[33] Stoke-on-Trent, 5 November 1999, 1.

[34] ibid, 6; capitals in original.

[35] Stoke-on-Trent (1999), 'Make it Count Project Summary/Revised Action Plan/Additional Background Briefing Notes' (Stoke-on-Trent City Centre Management) 3.

[36] Staffordshire Police (Nigel Manning) (2000), 'Make-It-Count Scheme: Partnership Response to Begging in Stoke-on-Trent City Centre', *Problem Solving Quarterly: Newsletter of the Police Executive Research Forum* Vol 13, No 3, 5.

[37] Staffordshire Police, 'Make-It-Count-Scheme' 7.

[38] Stoke-on-Trent, 'Make it Count Project Summary', 3.

The scheme was subsequently lauded by Home Secretary Jack Straw as a 'national exemplar' and went on to win the Staffordshire Police Problem Solving Award.[39]

II. Kindness, Drugs and Death

In an opinion piece for *The Guardian* published about a year later, on 10 October 2000, the Rough Sleepers Unit (RSU) director, Louise Casey, asked the public: 'So what do you do?' when faced with a beggar on the street 'with their hands out begging for money'. 'Walk on by, stop and talk, give some money or buy some food?'[40] The answer, Casey argued, was that people should not take the 'easy option' and 'should think twice about giving handouts on the street' to make sure that 'the pound given will not go towards the fiver needed for the next heroin hit'. To help the public face this risk of indiscriminate giving, the RSU was going to launch a national 'public awareness scheme' which would help alleviate the risk of giving money to a drug addict who was not even homeless: As Casey stated,

> The public face a real dilemma in this situation. Is this person [begging] homeless, in desperate need and begging simply to get by? Or do they have somewhere to live? Are they claiming benefits and begging for drink or drugs? No one really knows the answer and no one will ever really know. What we do know is that there are more people out on the streets during the day than there are sleeping rough overnight.[41]

And while Casey and the RSU did not apparently know the answers, she did comfortably cite the police in Nottingham, who 'believe that up to 90% of people who beg are doing so to sustain drug addictions', and in Brighton, where 'almost half of those begging have told the police that they use their income to sustain an addiction to heroin'.[42] Alarmed by Casey's lackadaisical attitude about what is known about those who beg, and the potentially harmful consequences of a national 'diverted-giving' campaign, 60 social policy experts responded with an open letter to the Prime Minister. The academics, including Hartley Dean, Ruth Lister and Suzanne Fitzpatrick, argued that diverted-giving schemes did not work, that a diverted-giving emphasis would lead to an increase in policing and the use of the vagrancy law, and that 'withholding income from people who beg will not help those with drug and alcohol problems to overcome them'.[43] The academics also warned that those who beg do so as an alternative to crime. As Hartley Dean stated in a *Guardian* interview, 'There is persuasive evidence that some at least of those begging would resort to criminal activities. You don't

---

[39] Staffordshire Police, 'Make-It-Count-Scheme', 8.
[40] L Casey, 'Brother, Spare the Dime', *The Guardian*, 10 October 2000, 20.
[41] ibid.
[42] ibid.
[43] L Casey (2000), letter from L Casey, Rough Sleepers Unit, to S Fitzpatrick, 30 October 2000.

have to be Einstein to work that out.'[44] Their letter also expressed worry about the simplistic mindset exhibited by Casey and the RSU, whereby public support for voluntary agencies and giving to people begging were framed as 'mutually exclusive alternatives'.

In a response dated 30 October 2000 to Suzanne Fitzpatrick (who organised the protest letter), Louise Casey chastised the academics for expressing their views publicly, as 'many of the points you raise … are based on misinformation and misunderstanding'. She added:

> Whether the public gives directly to people who beg on the street is a matter for them. We are not encouraging the public to give to charities in order that their money goes on '*deserving cases*'. We are encouraging them to help in ways that will change people's lives and not help them buy their next supply of drugs.[45]

Casey characterised concern about increased policing and Vagrancy Act use as 'completely untrue and scaremongering', stating that 'it is entirely down to local communities, working in partnership with the police, to develop effective community safety plans'. She defended diverted-giving schemes as 'one element of a range of responses open to local authorities', and cited how John Bird set up the *Big Issue* as an 'alternative to the public to give to people begging'.[46] On the criticism that the RSU viewed giving to charities and giving to those begging as mutually exclusive alternatives, Casey responded 'we are not', only to starkly describe the issue in exactly that way: 'One way gives homeless people a chance to rebuild their lives. The other way, giving money to people begging, helps kill them.'[47]

One week later, on 6 November 2000, a dramatic shift took place that would initiate the second wave of diverted giving and give gift-crime policing a national stage. The RSU launched its national diverted-giving campaign, 'Change a Life'. Utilising many of the tropes of the first diverted-giving wave, 'Change a Life' presented itself as a national solution to the moral dilemma of the beggar's hand. As the RSU explained in its main promotional pamphlet, *The Facts of Change a Life*,

> Few human beings can walk past their fellow man in the street and not be moved by a desire to help. Many members of the public give money directly to the people on the street. Although this is always an individual's choice, it can stop people getting the help they really need to change their lives and tackle the problems that are keeping them in a dangerous situation.[48]

---

[44] J Vasgar and K Scott (2000), 'Crime Risk of Anti-begging Policy', *The Guardian*, 31 October.
[45] Casey (2000) 2. Italics in original.
[46] ibid.
[47] ibid.
[48] DETR [Department of Environment, Transport and Regions], *The Facts of Change a Life* (London, DETR, 2000) 6, 2.

Figure 14 Image for the Rough Sleepers Unit (RSU) 'Change a Life' campaign 2000 (photo by author)

While Winchester-inspired schemes paid detailed attention to the immediate diversion of pocket change (and the relief of one's feelings) in the space of small and often pedestrianised city centres, Change a Life relied on much more distant and mediated channels to divert pocket change. The national scheme urged the public to wait until they got home to relieve their charitable impulses, urging the public to give in one of three ways. The first was the 'gift of time', through which people could volunteer their skills or provide professional expertise: 'It may be anything from serving meals in a day centre to driving a mini-bus.'[49] The second was the donation of 'surplus goods, equipment or other items that might help a homeless person or charity'. 'You'd be surprised,' the Change a Life literature stated, 'to hear that many charities need, for example, suits for former rough sleepers to wear.'[50] The third was giving 'via a phone line' or 'a website'[51] enabling 'every penny of your donation' to go directly to charities such as Crisis, Centrepoint, Homeless Direct and the Salvation Army, all of which agreed to participate in the scheme.

[49] DETR, *The Facts of Change a Life*, 6.
[50] ibid, 1.
[51] ibid, 6.

The RSU mounted an unprecedented national advertising campaign in England to market the scheme, with advertising on tube tickets and in newspapers and with posters and campaign leaflets. Its main publicity tool was the six-page pamphlet titled 'The Facts of Change a Life', which explained 'the right help given the right way'.[52] The main image to advertise the scheme (see Figure 14) shows a man on sitting on the pavement, holding a piece of cardboard with a handwritten (and thus personal) plea that hides his face: 'If you really want to help me, call Change a Life.' The image used by the RSU contains a muddled and paradoxical message that would be the hallmark of diverted-giving schemes and the wider field of gift-crime regulation. The beggar himself tells the public not to give to him, with a message written on his own sign, suggesting that he is indeed homeless and worthy of help. This despite the fact that the legitimacy of beggars as worthy rough-sleepers was called into doubt by Casey herself in her opinion piece. This paradox is made even further visible in the connotation that rough-sleepers need help as a vulnerable population *because they are in fact begging*.

During the 1997 election campaign, when asked if he gave to those begging, Tony Blair replied that he did not give but would buy a *Big Issue* or contribute to other charities. Four years later, Prime Minister Tony Blair would endorse the spirit of the new national diverted-giving scheme with comments that he had given earlier that year to the Active Communities Convention, included in the RSU Change a Life publicity pamphlet:

> Most of us have given money to charity, or bought a copy of the *Big Issue*. But in one sense that is the easy part. Giving time is harder. Yet in many ways far more rewarding. And everyone – however rich or poor – has time to give.[53]

In the context of his previous statement three years earlier on how he did not give to those begging, it is notable that instead of speaking of his own charitable preferences, Blair used the collective *we* to represent a national consciousness about the plight of the unfortunate – one that could now be relieved through a national act of compassionate citizenship. Blair evokes a notably strange notion of time and giving: that somehow poor people have as much time to give as rich people. This seems to be a conception of time that has no connection with labour, coin or status; the idea is that, as the saying goes, time is money. This is peculiar indeed, given the prominent role that time plays in ongoing debates about how efficiently and adequately the public is being served by government, for example, when it concerns waiting times for medical procedures or train connections. Even more paradoxically, in promoting a scheme that urges against giving 'something for nothing' to the beggar, the notion of time evoked relies on exactly that idea – that time, and the things of value that consume time, is really nothing

---

[52] ibid, 3.
[53] ibid.

(everyone apparently has it) and can be given freely. No real sacrifice or resources are needed for this form of giving.

While the first wave of Winchester-inspired diverted-giving programmes evoked only general notions of social harm in their portrayals of 'aggressive begging' and beggars who 'drank their money', they lacked a strong moral reason for not giving to beggars. In a shift of emphasis that first appeared in the Stoke-on-Trent scheme, the giving hand and pocket change of the public could now be made complicit in the suffering and disorder of drug addiction. As the RSU states in its pamphlet, 'when a member of the public gives money to someone begging on the streets, it is likely that it is trapping someone in drug addiction'. Or as Louise Casey lectured the social policy experts in her response to their letter, the scheme 'gives homeless people a chance to rebuild their lives. The other way, giving money to people begging helps kill them'.[54] In support of this new emphasis on drug addiction, the RSU cited a 'large-scale independent study' it had commissioned, one that would guide its response to those who begged and would 'form the basis of discussions between Government, the statutory sectors and the voluntary sector on what services are needed to help those that beg'.[55]

The RSU's finding, one noted prominently in their promotional four-page pamphlet that accompanied the launch, 'The Facts of Change a Life', is that this research 'shows that 86 per cent of beggars are currently using drugs'. Drugs used at least once a week by people begging include heroin (49 per cent), crack (35 per cent) and cocaine (18 per cent).[56] The phrase '86 per cent of beggars are currently using drugs' was the key evidence cited by the RSU that giving money to people begging puts them in a 'dangerous situation'. The RSU also noted that 'about half [52 per cent of the respondents] drank alcohol' and that three-quarters had some other source of income other than begging, including benefits (69 per cent) and *Big Issue* selling (19 per cent).[57] Notably, the RSU indicated that half (49 per cent) of those begging were sleeping rough and another 33 per cent were staying in hostels or night shelters.[58] The fact that half of those begging also slept rough directly contradicts Casey's insinuation weeks earlier that those begging were not rough-sleepers because 'there are more people out on the streets during the day than there are sleeping rough overnight'.[59]

The independent research that the RSU had commissioned, titled *Looking for Change: The Role and Impact of Begging on the Lives of People Who Beg*, was conducted by four academics at the University of Luton and formally released by the RSU in May 2001, six months after the Change a Life initiative was launched.[60]

---

[54] ibid.

[55] ibid, 4.

[56] ibid, 6.

[57] ibid, 5.

[58] ibid, 6.

[59] L Casey, 'Brother, Spare the Dime', 20.

[60] S Jowett, G Banks, A Brown and G Goodall, *Looking for Change: The Role and Impact of Begging on the Lives of People Who Beg* (London, RSU, 2001).

Looking for Change remains one of the most comprehensive studies undertaken in England on those who beg. The findings confirm that most people begging are among the most vulnerable and victimised of the population of rough-sleepers.[61] Focusing in particular on the 'finances' of street life, the survey involved 260 respondents who begged in five cities in England: London, Bristol, Manchester, Leeds and Brighton (all of which would have a diverted-giving scheme in place).[62] Interviews with professionals such as police officers and hostel, drop-in centre and outreach workers were also conducted.

The RSU campaign statement that '86 per cent of beggars are currently using drugs' would become a slogan in the years to come, a byword that all beggars are drug-addled frauds and simultaneously depicting the act of giving to them as a gift crime complicit in drug addiction, serious crime and death. However, a close examination of *Looking for Change* reveals a picture of the 'lives of those who beg' that is startlingly different from the presentation of the RSU, in terms of both the character of the drug use and how people begging spent the money given to them by the public.

In carrying out their analysis of the survey answers regarding drug use, the authors delineated the responses to questions about 'current drug abuse' among those who begged in two categories: 'problem drug abuse' and 'any other drug abuse', based on classifications by the Drug Prevention Advisory Service (DPAS) of the Home Office. The DPAS research, which assessed intervention programmes that would result in processes for treatment, noted that while 'hard and fast definitions are impossible', it is nonetheless useful to differentiate between casual/controlled use and 'problematic use', which the researchers characterise thus:

> We take problematic drug use to be that which involves dependency, regular excessive use, or use which creates serious health risks. Those users who we regard as problematic typically consume large amounts of heroin, crack, or amphetamine, usually as part of a pattern of poly-drug use; they generally show signs of dependency; their drug use poses risks to themselves and others; and they are often extensively involved in crime to support their drug use.[63]

The definition of 'problem drug use' – characterised by signs of dependence, risk of harm and involvement in crime – very broadly covers what most people would likely associate with having a 'drug problem' that might threaten the user and the community. The impression promoted by the RSU was that 86 per cent of people who begged could be categorised as such, and that all of this drug use involved the 'Class A' drugs crack, heroin and cocaine, ones most associated with crime, trafficking, and overdose deaths.[64] However, the authors of *Looking for Change*

---

[61] ibid, 6.
[62] ibid, 5.
[63] M Edmunds, M Hough, PJ Turnbull and T May, *Doing Justice to Treatment: Referring Offenders to Drug Services* (London, Home Office, 1999) 8.
[64] ibid.

state that 'over half report a significant drug problem (57 percent) according to the definition of [DPAS]'.[65] So while the RSU's 'facts' insisted that 86 per cent of beggars were currently using drugs, only 57 per cent of them were doing so in a way that the Home Office itself viewed as problematic. Of course this level of drug use is deeply troubling, a reminder of the desperate circumstances that those who beg and sleep rough are in and the urgent need for access to medical care and addiction services. Nevertheless, the figure for problematic use was just over half (57 per cent), not 86 per cent, a figure high enough to cast all people begging as dangerous consumers of Class A drugs such as crack, heroin and cocaine.

A further reading of the commissioned research makes visible a much more grievous misrepresentation by the RSU of 'the lives of those who beg' based on the authority of independent social science research. The crucial connection that underpinned the campaign – that the money given to those begging would 'trap someone in a drug addiction' – was that all money received by beggars was used exclusively to buy drugs, and that begging money was their only source of income for drug purchases. Nothing is said in 'The Facts of Change a Life' about how much money received from the public was actually spent on drugs, or on non-drug items. However, the *Looking for Change* researchers did investigate the 'spending priorities' of beggars with regard to the money they received from the public, in terms of both the types of items bought and what they spent most of their money on. On both measures, the majority of money received from begging was spent not on drugs but rather on food.

Respondents reported that 86 per cent of the items bought with their begged money was food, while drugs stood at 58 per cent; 45 per cent said that food was the item they spent the most on, versus 37 per cent spent on drugs.[66] The report also documented that young people are particularly vulnerable in terms of relying on begged money for their food supply. The research indicated a 5 per cent increase in the use of cadged money to obtain food from when they first started begging, and those under 19 were also more inclined to beg for food than those in older age groups.[67] Further complicating the gift-crime message of the RSU are the findings that one-quarter of the people begging relied exclusively on begged change as their sole source of income. As the authors state, this group that got most or all of their income from begging appeared to be the most vulnerable, with 70 per cent of them being rough-sleepers.[68]

[65] ibid, 24–25. 'Non-problematic' drugs included LSD, hallucinogens, glues or solvents and cannabis.
[66] Jowett et al, *Looking for Change*. 20; 6% said they spent most of their money on tobacco, 5% on shoes and clothes, 14% on alcohol and 3% on accommodation.
[67] ibid, 11.
[68] ibid, 16.

One is given pause to reflect on the mendacity of the RSU in misrepresenting the 'lives of those who beg'. The real empirical truth of the Change a Life research is that the figure of the beggar that advertised the scheme (see Figure 14) – one who makes a personal plea to the public not to give him money – is in fact declining pocket change that will help him buy food rather than drugs, and that this need for food money is even greater if the person begging is a young person or a rough-sleeper. Hartley Dean has noted the trend towards the 'selective interpretation' of social science evidence, where the 'government has a tendency to interpret social science evidence so as to infer support for pre-established policy priorities'.[69] Indeed, academics today expect that their work will be vulnerable to some level of political spin. In the case of the RSU and Change a Life, however, the RSU went much further than spinning a message. There was active misrepresentation about the 'lives of those who beg', an intentional false impression given to the public on a major issue of public interest and government policy: why people beg and what they do with begged money. If the RSU had honestly depicted how people begging used their money – those begging used cadged money slightly more often to buy food than to buy drugs – could they even have launched the Change a Life scheme? It is difficult to see how this would have been politically possible. To still recommend not giving to those begging when half the time the money would have been used to buy food would have been viewed as abjectly cruel. Indeed, such accurate reporting of their own research would have probably confirmed to some people that the risk of giving money to those begging was worth it in terms of helping them. To portray the actual truth about giving money to people begging on the street would first and foremost destroy the 'death turn' connection that makes the public directly complicit in drug addiction and overdoses. In fact, being truthful about what those who beg do with their money would have confirmed that begging is a desperate survival activity that overlaps with the causes, deprivations and suffering of rough sleeping and homelessness.

The Change a Life initiative was depicted in the media as an embarrassment to the government. Like other diverted-giving efforts, Change a Life was economically nonsensical, and there is no evidence that it changed giving patterns or the frequency of people begging, or resulted in any tangible benefits for those on the street. After running for 16 months (until March 2002), Change a Life raised only £13,937.98.[70] The cost for advertising the scheme to the public was an astonishing £240,000[71] – in other words, for every £20 spent on advertising the campaign,

---

[69] H Dean, *Social Policy Review* 12, H Dean, R Sykes and R Woods (ed), (Newcastle, Social Policy Association, 2000) 45.

[70] P Edwards and K Elliott, *Change a Life End of Campaign Report* (London, Broadcasting Support Services, April 2002), 8.

[71] Personal communication, Rough Sleepers Initiative, 2004.

£1 was raised. As with almost all other diverted-giving schemes, no final audit or accounting was carried out. The only follow-up was a report done by Broadcasting Support Services, which offered a 'statistical breakdown of the enquiries received' and noted that 457,078 hours of 'time donations' had been made.[72] The report is devoid of any information to make sense of what this figure means.

It is useful at this point to revisit the opinion piece that Louise Casey wrote to launch the Change a Life scheme, and specifically her public statement with regard to what is known about people begging on the street:

> Is this person [begging] homeless, in desperate need and begging simply to get by? Or do they have somewhere to live? Are they claiming benefits and begging for drink or drugs? No one really knows the answer and no one will ever really know. What we do know is that there are more people out on the streets during the day than there are sleeping rough overnight.[73]

Her comments can be read as baffling, even bizarre, given that she, as head of the RSU, claims a state of perpetual ignorance about the lives of those who beg ('no one will ever really know') when the RSU itself had commissioned extensive research that answered these questions, research which had been completed for the Change a Life launch weeks later. Did she read her own commissioned research? At the same time, she seems to know enough ('what we do know') to raise doubts that those begging are not also rough-sleepers, because there are more on the streets than are sleeping rough overnight.[74] Indeed, her comments, and the level of misrepresentation that the RSU carried out, are not just morally unconscionable but profoundly unethical: a betrayal of the hardship and suffering experienced by every single vulnerable person who participated in the Change a Life research. The full Change a Life report, which included the finding that those begging spend more of their cadged money on food than on drugs, was quietly made available six months later.

Backed now by the prominence of a national RSU diverted-giving programme and independent research showing that '86 per cent of people begging currently use drugs', both a second wave of diverted giving and a wider gift-crime movement were formed.[75] The complicated relationship between begging and sleeping rough would

---

[72] Edwards and Elliot, *End of Campaign Report*, 6.

[73] L Casey, 'Brother, Spare the Dime', 2.

[74] ibid.

[75] At about this time, a surprising intervention would take place: Sir John Bird, the founder of *Big Issue*, published an incendiary essay for Politeia. Bird articulates an extremely crude 'law and order' view to 'clear the streets' of rough sleepers and people begging. For Bird, we are 'muddled because we lack the will', and that we should end our 'retreat from the streets' by returning to the all-out enforcement of vagrancy law. Most of his argument is so confusing and badly informed that it is hard to make sense of or take seriously. It is simply inexplicable that he could call for a police action that would surely target many of his own *Big Issue* vendors and clients. J Bird, *Retreat from the Streets* (London, Politeia, 2002).

be – as visualised by the money-man icon – diminished to a narrow and punitive truth: beggars are drug addicts who are not homeless. Gift-crime approaches
saw explicit expression in Home Office – initiated antisocial behaviour 2004 Action
Plan trailblazers in Brighton, Bristol, Leeds, Camden and the City of Westminster.
Diverted-giving schemes would be included in Home Office anti-social behaviour
'tool-kits' as a model for cities to emulate.

In Leeds, for example, West Yorkshire Police initiated an operation to tackle
'begging and rough sleeping' (linked to Class A drug abuse), an effort that would
utilise the Vagrancy Act and involve police community safety officers (PCSOs)
and a diverted-giving 'Change for the Better Scheme'.[76] In Bristol, the diverted-
giving project was relaunched in 2002 as a project of their Rough Sleepers
Initiative, one that would tackle the daily problem of beggars on Bristol's streets,
arguing that '[t]he vast majority of beggars have drug abuse related problems
and the money they get from well-meaning citizens very often goes to buy
drugs. Very few beggars – less than 10 per cent – are genuinely homeless.'[77]
In December 2002, the City of Nottingham announced a major TCM initiative
aimed at 'curbing street begging, drug and alcohol use' in the city centre. Evoking the damage done to the tourist economy by begging, and the need to protect
'well-intentioned people' who might give to beggars, the city launched the 'Make
It Count' diverted-giving scheme. Funded by the Communities Against Drugs
Fund, the scheme was presented as central to a 'crime and disorder reduction partnership'. The diverted-giving scheme was re-branded the next year as
'Respect for Nottingham', with posters (see Figure 15) that conflated begging,
rough sleeping and drug trafficking.

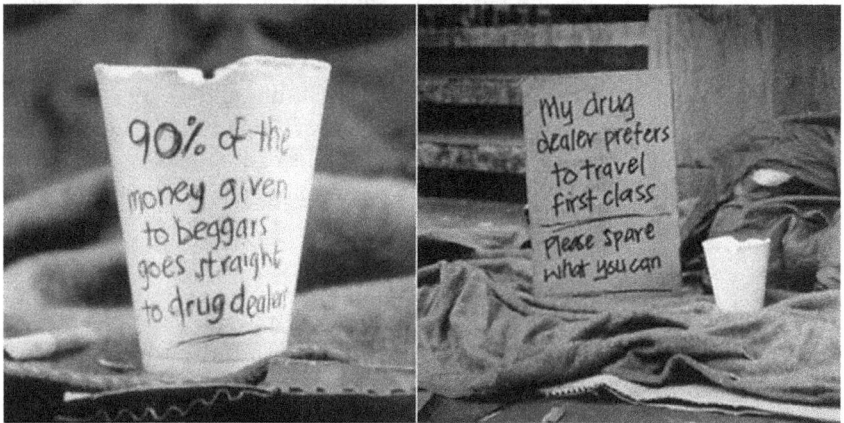

Figure 15 Posters for Nottingham's 'Count Me In' programme, 2003 (photos by author)

---

[76] Leeds Council, 2004.
[77] Bristol City Council, 2002.

How (or if) the Home Office linked diverted-giving schemes to receiving funds for community partnerships is unclear. Certainly from April 2003, 'drug action teams' were required to 'integrate with, or work more closely' with 'crime and disorder partnerships', resulting in combined 'drug and crime teams'.[78] In Manchester, one of the sites where the Change a Life research was conducted, the 'Change for the Better' scheme was launched, urging the public to 'please give to the box and not to the beggar'. The city-centre management company that oversaw the scheme stated:

> £10 can buy a beggar a bag of heroin – or it could buy them food that could last them for days. Often beggars will spend money you give them to fuel their addiction instead of on food, so your money is being spent on buying drugs to keep them in a habit that may kill them.

The four posters used to market the scheme made the following claims in exhorting the public to be tight-fisted:

> THEY'RE A BEGGAR FOR IT. Over 70% of street beggars already receive state benefit.
>
> HUNGRY OR HIGH? 90% of street beggars do it to sustain drug use.
>
> IT BEGGARS BELIEF. The majority of street beggars don't sleep rough.
>
> FOOD OR FIX? Would you give a beggar a pound for a fix?[79]

Absent in this campaign is any mention that in fact the majority of those begging in Manchester do sleep rough, and that people begging there spend more money on food than on drugs. The demonisation of those begging as drug-addicted frauds would find a powerful visual expression in the Your Kindness Can Kill schemes. Launched in 2003 by Thames Reach, the money-man image in particular (see Figure 1) would become an icon of diverted giving and gift-crime regulation. As one charity-sector observer noted in 2008, the money-man figure had 'seeped into the national consciousness'.[80] Of the 31 diverted-giving schemes today, at least 15 of them use the money-man icon and Kindness Kills slogan, which Thames Reach has made available for other jurisdictions to copy. Jeremy Swain, the chief executive of Thames Reach, has been an enthusiastic defender of the Kindness Kills approach for the past 15 years.[81] The money-man icon provided a powerful visual that sharpened the moral urgency of the 'death turn' initiated by the RSU. The Your Kindness Can Kill campaign characterised a refinement in the second wave of diverted giving, where the actual 'diverted' or 'alternative' giving mechanism of the scheme faded into the background. There has been no concerted effort by Thames Reach to set up a specific channel to collect funds that might

---

[78] Home Office, *Drugs Use and Begging: A Practice Guide* (London, HMSO, 2004) 15.

[79] Manchester City Council, 'Change for the Better', diverted giving posters 2003.

[80] New Philanthropy Capital, *Thames Reach, Analyst: Eleanor Stringer* (New Philanthropy Capital, London, 2008), 5.

[81] J Swain, 'Giving Money to the Homeless Isn't Generous – It Can Condemn Them to Death' (2017) *New Statesman America* 3 November.

be given to those begging, other than more generally promoting giving to recognised charities, including Thames Reach itself. This is no doubt as much a practical feature as anything. As with Change a Life, it would have been extremely difficult to set up and manage a network of diverted-giving boxes in the heterogeneous space of London. Thames Reach actively promoted the muddled message of gift-crime regulation, with the goal of 'ending street homelessness' by urging the public not to give to those begging, even though those begging are paradoxically depicted by Thames Reach as not being homeless.

III. Idle and Disorderly:
The Resuscitation of Vagrancy Law

The most permanent consequences of the wider field of gift-crime regulation that formed after the RSU Change a Life scheme are the reforms to the power and reach of the Vagrancy Act 1824. The reforms initiated in 2003 are a direct consequence of how those begging had become viewed within the narrowly defined disorder of drug addiction. These reforms represent a remarkable shift that occurred between 1997 and 2003. While Tony Blair in 1997 could comfortably reveal his charitable character by stating that he did not give to those begging, the reality was that it would have been politically fraught, if not impossible, for Blair to go further and suggest rearming vagrancy law. Begging was still widely viewed as an activity that overlapped with rough sleeping and social and economic deprivation. Indeed, the early Winchester-inspired schemes assumed that many of those begging were in fact homeless, and a worthy object of social services for rough-sleepers. Not to link begging and rough sleeping would have destroyed the charitable ethos of the Winchester project. By late 2003, that social welfare trope had been discarded, leaving a crass and punitive view of those who beg as fakes who deceive the public.

Now reoriented as a problem of drug addiction, the offence of begging could resuscitate the archaic character of the Vagrancy Act. These reforms are even more remarkable considering that, as I discuss in chapter four, the trend had been one of diminishing vagrancy law powers and punishment. One can glean an initial appetite for some type of vagrancy law reform in the 2002 consultation paper *Living Places – Powers, Rights and Responsibilities: A Review of the Legislation Framework*. The paper addresses issues that were 'associated with achieving cleaner and safer public spaces and local environments'.[82] The issue of begging comes under a review of the 'overhaul of powers to deal with persons in the streets'. 'For Begging the usual penalty is a fine or a night in the cells,' the paper notes, evoking use of the Vagrancy Act by the homeless units in Charing Cross and Manchester, 'which does little to stop the underlying reasons for the person begging (such as drug misuse),

---

[82] DEFRA [Department for Environment, Food and Rural Affairs], *Living Places – Powers, Rights and Responsibilities: A Review of the Legislation Framework* (London, DEFRA, 2002) 1.

and in some cases can lead to further begging in order to pay the fine.'[83] The paper adds that begging in a public place is illegal under section 3 of the Act and that rough sleeping is an offence under section 4, but, following the 1935 Act, someone sleeping rough may be prosecuted only if 'he or she has previously been directed to a reasonably accessible place of shelter and failed to apply for or refused accommodation there.'[84]

Two suggested changes were put forward: (1) to 'update language of the Vagrancy Act 1824 and Pedlars Act 1871', and (2) 'New powers for Magistrates to deal with repeat offenders such as the establishment of "begging courts" so that Magistrates see repeat offenders and understand the wider context of begging (fear of crime, street crime, drug dealing, homelessness etc.).'[85] The paper notes that the 'possible limits and drawbacks' of these options might include 'public anxiety when arresting apparently vulnerable beggars.'[86] In its response to the consultation paper, the homelessness charity Crisis pointed out its concern that there was already legislation in place to deal with serious offences by homeless people, and that a great emphasis on enforcement might 'have the effect of exacerbating the problems faced by some of the most vulnerable people in our society.'[87] It is notable that the idea of 'begging courts', which was never explored further, had a welfarist concern that was out of step with gift-crime regulation. Indeed the proposed purpose of the courts, to understand 'the wider context of begging', which would include 'homelessness', is anathema to the narrow and punitive view of begging that characterises the second wave of diverted giving.

It would be the 2003 white paper 'Respect and Responsibility: Taking a Stand Against Anti-social Behaviour' that would initiate historic vagrancy law reforms. Striking an almost retributive tone, with a populist appeal for local solutions, the government urged communities to 'tackle' and 'stamp out' crime and disorder. 'Our aim is a "something for something" society,' Home Secretary David Blunkett states in the preface, 'where we treat one another with respect and where we all share responsibility for taking a stand against what is unacceptable.'[88] Located in an ethos of a 'something for something' society, the disorder of drug-addicted beggars, compounded by the giving hands of the public, could now be formally addressed in criminal law. As the white paper states,

> There are places for rough sleepers to sleep at night, there is support and treatment available for their health needs and drug habits, and there are benefits available to pay for food and rent. The reality is that the majority of people who beg are doing so to sustain a drug habit, and are often caught up in much more serious crime. When

---

[83] ibid, 45.

[84] ibid.

[85] ibid.

[86] ibid, 47.

[87] Crisis, Response to DEFRA, *Living Places* Consultative Paper (Crisis, London, 2002) 2.

[88] HMSO, *Respect and Responsibility: Taking a Stand Against Anti-social Behaviour* (London, HMSO, 2003) 3.

members of the public give them money on the street it does not help them deal with their problems.[89]

The white paper consolidates three assertions initiated in the Change a Life 'death turn', ones that would underpin legal reforms: (1) beggars are drug addicts who spend their begging money on drugs; (2) beggars are not rough sleepers; and (3) the public giving money to those who beg are complicit in the disorder and death of drug addicts. In emphasising begging as a drug problem that needs to be 'tackled', the white paper highlighted the Bristol 'Street Wise' diverted-giving campaign, in which police made more than 300 arrests and found that '100% of beggars have a dependency on Class A drugs'.[90] Two reforms were announced in the 2003 white paper: making begging a recordable offence, and a 'new power' to deal with 'persistent begging' that would enable drug treatment. What followed over the next two years was a complex series of legal manoeuvres that would have been politically and legally fraught only a few years earlier.

The first reform was that begging would be made a recordable offence, enabling a wide system of intelligence through police databases, including the taking of photographs and fingerprints.[91] Up until that point, Vagrancy Act offenders were relatively invisible in terms of having a criminal record. The only way in which constabularies had any records of their contacts with those begging was if they had detailed their activities with vagrancy offenders themselves on a local database. This lack of intelligence about those begging can be seen in the activities of the homeless units in Manchester and Charing Cross that I discuss in chapter four. In each case, the homeless units set up their own in-house databases to track contacts, cautions and charges involving those who begged; this allowed them to carry out their own protocols in terms of warnings, and also to make sure, in theory, that they were conforming to the evidential burden of *R v Dalton*: that for a 'collecting alms' offence (section 3) to be committed, the begging activity must occur on more than an 'isolated occasion'.

Begging as a recordable offence would mean that begging offenders would have the details of their offences available on the Police National Computer (PNC). This would provide local officers with real-time intelligence data in encounters with people begging and sleeping rough on the street. This change also meant that offenders had a criminal conviction which would now be attached to their

---

[89] DEFRA, *Living Places*, 47.

[90] ibid. It is unknown how at this time the police measured 'dependency' on Class A drugs for those whom they arrested. I deal with the reliability of such statistics in the concluding chapter.

[91] Begging and persistent begging were made recordable offences with effect from 1 December 2003, when they were added to the Schedule to the National Police Records (Recordable Offences) Regulations 2000 by virtue of the National Police Records (Recordable Offences) (Amendment) Regulations 2003 (SI 2003/2823). The references to s 3 (begging) and s 4 (persistent begging) of the Vagrancy Act 1824 in the Schedule to the Criminal Justice and Court Services Act 2000 (as amended) are consistent with that.

record. As Crisis commented, 'we are concerned that making begging a recordable offence will burden an already vulnerable people with a criminal record creating a further obstacle to their reintegration into mainstream society'.[92] Making begging a recordable offence also had the likely advantage in 2003 for local officials in compiling evidence of past offences that could be included for applications for ASBOs (and their predecessors, PSPOs).

The importance of making begging a recordable offence becomes clear when one considers the second reform announced in the white paper, that a 'new power' would be introduced to 'deal more effectively with persistent beggars', and that after three or more convictions, community sentences could be imposed, including those for drug treatment. As David Blunkett stated, 'such a change would tackle the nuisance and intimidation' that those begging cause for 'those going about their lawful business'.[93] There are two parts to this new power: a new offence of 'persistent begging', and the making of the offences of both begging and persistent begging 'trigger offences' that would enable drug testing and counselling on arrest. How did the offence of 'persistent begging' come into being? One must pause here and review both s 3 and s 4 of the Vagrancy Act 1824 to understand the peculiar nature of this reform.

Section 3 provides that:

> Every person wandering abroad, or placing himself or herself in any public place, street, highway, court, or passage, to beg or gather alms, or causing or procuring any child or children to do so; shall be deemed an idle or disorderly person within the true intent and meaning of this Act.

Section 3 is a prohibition against any sort of begging, including simply asking for money on the pavement; there is no requirement that the begging be aggressive or a nuisance. It is basically a criminal prohibition on asking for anything, in any way, from a passer-by. And the case of *R v Dalton* establishes that begging 'on an isolated occasion' is not sufficient for an offence to be committed. An officer must have proof of begging on more than one occasion to make out an offence.

Section 4 provides that:

> Every person committing any of the offences herein-before mentioned, after having been convicted as an idle and disorderly person; ... shall be deemed a rogue and vagabond ... every person wandering abroad and lodging in any barn or outhouse, or in any deserted or unoccupied building, or in the open air, or under a tent, or in any cart or wagon.

The rough-sleeping offence had become for the most part inoperable since the early 1980s because of the evidential burden placed on the police by the 1935 Act,

---

[92] Crisis, *Begging and Anti-social Behaviour: Crisis' Response to the White Paper Respect and Responsibility – Taking a Stand Against Anti-social Behaviour* (London, Crisis, 2003) 6.
[93] DEFRA, *Living Places*, 47.

most notably that the offence could be enforced only if free and adequate shelter space was available.[94]

The creation of a new offence of persistent begging required no textual amendments to the offence itself, because it was *already present in the sentencing grades* of the Act. The new offence of persistent begging relied on the archaic language and structure of an 1824 Act that had not been repealed, language that enabled the marking of status offences that was so central to organising archaic forms of punishment. Anyone convicted under section 3 shall be deemed an 'idle and disorderly person', and anyone who has been convicted *again* as an idle and disorderly person shall be deemed a 'rogue and vagabond' under section 4. The ingredient of persistence then flows from the sentencing grades. Thus, the offence of 'persistent begging' or 'begging on more than one occasion' (section 4) is begging after being convicted once and having the status of an idle and disorderly person. This creates a confusing legal oddity, as the word *persistent* is not present anywhere in section 3 or section 4. The categories of 'idle and disorderly' and 'rogue and vagabond' were introduced as sentencing grades in 1713.[95] These categories that punished vagrant bodies for 300 years still have a vital role to play in early twenty-first-century England for poor people on the street.

In 2010, minor reforms to the Act were carried out to address anomalies having to do with sentencing. A central consequence of this was that initially persistent begging was an offence under section 4. This has to do with the provisions of section 70 of the Criminal Justice Act 1991 that were in place, which abolished imprisonment (at the urging of the 1981 Home Affairs Committee). With its repeal, the Crown Prosecution Service started to record persistent begging under section 3, starting from 2010/11. The penalty for both the current offences of begging (s 3) and persistent begging (s 4) is a fine not exceeding Level 3 on the standard scale (£1,000).

How does this new offence of persistent begging, one that would 'deal more effectively with persistent beggars', act as a mechanism to provide mandatory drug treatment through community sentences? The answer is that begging (section 3) and persistent begging (section 4) are made 'trigger offences'. Trigger offences are criminal offences that are viewed as closely linked to crime generated by Class A drug use, and usually involve acquisitive and minor property crime. Those arrested for trigger offences are drug-tested, photographed and fingerprinted. Mandatory drug counselling is also given to those arrested.

How did the two begging offences become trigger offences, along with theft, shoplifting and handling stolen goods? The addition of trigger offences is made by delegated legislation using a statutory instrument. A draft of the statutory instrument containing the order must be laid before and approved by a resolution in each

---

[94] This section also includes the offence of 'being in an enclosed premises', which is still enforced today.
[95] 12 Anne c.23.

house of Parliament. What evidence was accepted in the Commons and the Lords that would make begging and persistent begging into trigger offences?

In the House of Commons the issue was debated for 30 minutes, with Edward Heath chairing the committee. In supporting the draft, Heath noted: 'In Leeds in the past 12 months, 47 beggars have died of heroin overdoses. In Brighton two years ago, the death of 49 beggars from overdoses led to its anti-begging campaign.'[96] While these are dramatic and troubling statements, the figures appear to be unsubstantiated. There are no records to indicate that those numbers of 'beggars' died in Bristol and Leeds. What the figures may indicate are all the overdose deaths recorded in the cities during those years. To conflate all overdose deaths with the deaths of 'beggars from overdoses' would be a fantastic instance of how the 'death turn' was now depicting all drug deaths as being directly related to begging. In addition, Mr Heath approvingly quoted Andy Hayman of the Association of Chiefs of Police: 'ACPO fully support the extension of trivial offences to include handling stolen goods, attempted acquisitive crime and begging ... It is right to focus testing on those suspected of the crimes most closely linked to the use of Class A drugs.'[97]

In the House of Lords, the evidence presented was no less derivative of the main themes of gift-crime regulation, in particular the view that begging had no relation to rough sleeping and was only a function of the drug addicts needing money for their next fix. In supporting the draft, Lord Goldsmith inaccurately cited the findings of the Change a Life research:

> So far as begging is concerned, the evidence is strong. A research study found that 86 per cent of beggars were currently using drugs. The study, which covered five major towns and cities, estimated that 75–90 per cent of beggars used class A drugs, primarily heroin, and for many of those the routine of begging sufficient cash to fund the habit was a total pre-occupation.[98]

He also pointed out that the Home Secretary claimed, on the Home Office website, that 'We know that more than 85 per cent of beggars have a drugs or alcohol addiction and are begging to fund their habits.'[99]

As I have discussed, the study found that the figure for problematic Class A drug use was in fact 57 per cent, and begging to fund drug purchases was not a 'total pre-occupation' – those begging were at least as preoccupied with obtaining food to eat as they were drugs. The discussion and evidence presented in both houses were made in complete ignorance of the main conclusion of the Change a Life research: that begging is carried out by vulnerable people, the majority of whom

---

[96] *Hansard*, HC Session 2003–04, First Standing Committee on Delegated Legislation (Debates) col 4 (Monday 21 June 2004).

[97] ibid, col 8.

[98] *Hansard*, L Criminal Justice and Court Services Act 2000 (Amendment) Order 204 (Debates) col 907.

[99] ibid, col 905.

are rough sleeping or marginally housed. This comfortable lack of curiosity by the House of Lords members about how begging is fundamentally different from acquisitive offences is revealing. Begging is similar to shoplifting, for example, only if one assumes that money given to the beggar by the public is ill-gotten. Understood as a trigger offence, those who give money to people begging are victims of gift theft.

There is a perverse aspect to making begging a trigger offence associated with low-level property crime. Some scholars have argued that the increased policing and criminalisation of people who beg will result in displacement: that those begging as a street survival activity will turn to petty property crimes out of desperation. Would making begging a trigger offence lead to an increase in other trigger offences that actually involve the minor deprivation of property from others? The answer is unclear, but the fact that the question never occurred in the House of Lords deliberations reveals how begging is no longer widely viewed as an activity associated with rough sleeping and wider economic and social deprivation.

A third set of reforms was to accompany the making of begging a trigger offence. The reforms were accompanied by changes that would revise the powers of arrest and detainment for both police constables and police civilians. First, the 'any person' arrest power that had been preserved in the original 1824 Act (section 6) – and relied upon by officers of the Manchester and Charing Cross homeless units (against the advice of section 25 of PACE) – was finally repealed in 2005 and replaced with a conditional power of arrest.[100] The change was long overdue. As I discuss in chapter one, that power was used extensively by private anti-mendicant agents and local council officials throughout the nineteenth century to target a range of disorderly characters. And as I have documented in chapter four, the power could still be used by police homeless units to authorise their own local conception of deterrence (through arrest or a night in the cells). The Home Office rightly repealed one of the most capricious police powers, one that had for centuries been used to target poor and disorderly people.

However, while the 1824 Act's 'any person' arrest power was repealed, a new set of powers was given to police community support officers (PCSOs) and other accredited persons in relation to trigger offences, including 'persistent begging'. While PCSOs are not given powers of arrest in relation to begging and persistent begging, they can nonetheless be given the power to 'require a person to stop committing' these offences. If a person refuses to comply, the PCSO can detain the person for up to 30 minutes or, if the person agrees, he or she can accompany the officer to the police station. It is a criminal offence for the person to make off after the PCSO has informed him that he is detained, and the officer has the

---

[100] Section 6 was repealed (1 January 2006) by the Serious Organised Crime and Police Act 2005 (c 15), s 178(8), Sch 7 para 2, Sch 17 pt 2; SI 2005/3495, Art 2(1)(m)(u). This repeal encompassed the third and most serious sentencing grade of the Act, that of being an 'incorrigible rogue'. See page 19.

right to use 'reasonable force' to detain that person. On balance, the reforms to the arrest powers of the Act represented an increase in the ability of the police to target begging, particularly in an informal way. The repeal of the preserved power of arrest was an improvement to the extent that it would stop the sort of rogue behaviour that occurred in Manchester and Charing Cross, where officers should in any case have exercised, via s 6 of PACE, the conditional powers of arrest.

However, the new powers for PCSOs can be viewed as a modern update of the archaic 'any person' power used by private anti-mendicant and parish officers, under which civilians could detain someone who was begging and 'deliver them to a police constable' as section 6 required. These new powers suggest an unprecedented ability to use vagrancy law to stop and 'move along' anyone whom police civilians believe to be begging or sleeping rough. This is particularly problematic for two reasons: PCSOs are explicitly tasked to be sensitive to local conceptions of safety through city-centre management strategies and crime-and-disorder partnerships, which have, of course, been central supporters of diverted-giving schemes and gift-crime mentalities. Second, what constitutes begging can be wildly subjective – and can certainly, under the Vagrancy Act, include begging that is polite and peaceful. The ingredients of a begging offence, of being an 'idle and disorderly person', are left to the discretion of the officer, which is of course a feature of great utility in terms of enforcing a status offence.

The translation of all beggars into drug-addicted frauds who commit gift crimes with the public is given full and robust expression in the 2004 Home Office guidance publication *Drugs Use and Begging: A Practice Guide*.[101] This remarkable 54-page document illustrates the success of officials in uncoupling begging from the wider social context of rough sleeping and homelessness. Published for 'those who commission services for people with drug problems who beg and those working with them', and developed 'in recognition of the strong link between begging and drug use',[102] the guidance was the first major policy paper to consider the new 'persistent begging' offence. Not surprisingly, it cites 'Killing with Kindness'–styled diverted-giving schemes as a best practice to be emulated, a 'well planned and resourced alternative giving scheme' with a media strategy that includes 'updates and relaunches to keep in the public eye'.[103]

The guidance highlights several schemes as good examples. It cites the 'Killing with Kindness' campaign in Westminster and Camden, which involved Thames Reach and 'used hard-hitting images to inform the public that their contribution would almost certainly be used for Class A drugs and could lead to the death of the person begging';[104] Bristol's 'Don't Kill with Kindness' campaign, a 'hard-hitting poster and media campaign' along with a diverted-giving scheme;[105]

[101] Home Office, *Drugs Use and Begging: A Practice Guide* (London, Home Office, 2004).
[102] ibid, 5.
[103] ibid, 39.
[104] ibid, 46.
[105] ibid, 19.

Nottingham's diverted-giving scheme;[106] and Stoke-on-Trent's 'Make It Count', in which 'the public was made aware that the money they gave would be spent on drugs and would also support local drug dealers'.[107] In Liverpool, 'Operation Change' was established 'to discourage the public from giving their change to those who beg and instead support initiatives to help people to change'.[108] Bristol's 'Streetwise' alternative-giving scheme with collection boxes is cited as well,[109] as is Manchester's 'Count Me In' programme with its slogan 'Give to the box, not to the beggar'.[110]

The posters used for the Nottingham campaign (see Figure 15, page 130), cited as good practice by the Home Office guide, demonstrate how extreme gift-crime regulation had become: beggars were frauds and addicts, and giving to them supported local drug dealers. What is most notable about these images is that the person begging is not even depicted – not even his or her hands. After the 'death turn' initiated by the RSU, it is apparently enough to illustrate the squalor of sleeping rough to evoke criminality and mendacity.

The guidance has a ridiculous quality to it in how it uses the RSU's *Looking for Change* research report, but only in the most selective way to portray those begging as unworthy. The central conclusions of the report are ignored. Four dubious assertions stand out. The document notes that those who beg 'may be vulnerable to housing problems due to substance misuse, but there is little evidence to suggest that the majority who beg are rough sleeping'.[111] In fact, there is overwhelming evidence of a strong overlap between begging and sleeping rough. Looking for Change report itself states that 49 per cent of beggars did indeed sleep rough, while 33 per cent stayed in a hostel or night shelter.[112] Only 4 per cent reported staying in a 'bed and breakfast/temporary housing by council' or their own home.[113]

Second, the guidance notes a 'lack of awareness amongst the general public as to where the money they give to those who beg will go'[114] and 'a misconception that the money the public gives will go towards food or shelter, when the reality is that it is likely to be spent on alcohol or drugs.'[115] But this is no misconception: the majority of money was spent on food, in terms of both the percentage spent of cadged change and the number of items purchased.

Third, the guidance notes that 'By educating the public on the link between drug use and begging and offering alternatives for giving money as well as offering

106 ibid, 18.
107 ibid, 43.
108 ibid, 34.
109 ibid, 44.
110 ibid, 46.
111 ibid, 10.
112 Jowett et al, *Looking for Change*, 26.
113 ibid.
114 Home Office, *Drugs Use*, 10.
115 ibid, 19.

pathways that provide ways out of begging, the needs of both the public and those who beg to support drug use will be met.'[116] Yet there remains no evidence of how public education changes the nature of giving to people who beg. More strangely, how will not giving to people who are begging somehow 'meet the needs' of the drug user? And how exactly will the needs of the public be met?

Last, officials are encouraged to carry out 'Honest public awareness campaigns and alternatives to giving to drug users who beg'.[117] This strategy belies the mendacity that officials themselves have exercised in representing the lives of those who beg and the consequences of handing pocket change to someone on the pavement who is asking for help.

---

[116] ibid, 7.
[117] ibid, 42.

6

The Legal Beggar in Scotland

Street begging in Scotland is legal. In sharp contrast to their counterparts in England, officials in Scottish cities have been blocked by the Scottish government from having recourse to criminal law to police those who beg on the street. The Vagrancy Act 1824 (extended to Scotland in 1871) was repealed in 1982. The local burgh Acts in Scotland, which usually contained a begging section,[1] were repealed in 1991 as part of a reorganisation of local government law.[2] The lack of a criminal law against begging has infuriated some officials in major Scottish cities; for more than two decades they attempted to convince the Scottish government to reintroduce begging as a criminal offence. In 2005, for example, the Safer Aberdeen Task Group wrote to the Justice Department of the Scottish Executive, arguing that they should be granted permission to introduce a law to target begging. The request was based on an Aberdeen Community Services Committee report on street begging which recommended a partnership approach that included reintroduction of a by-law which 'would be used selectively to take action where other approaches are proving difficult'.[3]

One should not be surprised that, in conjunction with the establishment of a new criminal offence, the committee promoted an 'alternative giving' scheme, arguing that

> similar schemes are in operation elsewhere in the UK and provide an opportunity for members of the public to contribute to the welfare of street beggars without the risk of the money being spent by the individual on drink or drugs. There are examples of major high street retailers financing and operating giving boxes as part of their contribution to city centre safety.[4]

Despite their popularity in England, only one diverted-giving scheme has been established in Scotland – not surprisingly, given that a central component of the 'success' of diverted giving was aggressive policing efforts that relied on begging's being a criminal offence.

---

[1] The Edinburgh Corporation Order 1967, s 483(1) stated that 'a person shall not, in any public place or from door to door, beg or act in any way for the purpose of inducing the giving of alms'.

[2] Edinburgh, 'Proposed Bye-Law: Legal Issues', prepared by director of corporate services, 5EB03540, 21 May 1998, 3.

[3] Aberdeen City Council (2004) 'Street Begging Report', Report of the Community Services Committee, 14 September.

[4] ibid.

In responding to Aberdeen City Council, the Justice Department advised that, consistent with a past request, 'Scottish ministers would be unlikely to support the introduction of a bylaw on begging.'[5]

> Scottish Executive policy is … that in general, byelaws should not duplicate existing offence provisions. Aggressive begging is already addressed by common law (breach of the peace) and by statute (section 53 of the Civic Government Act and Anti-Social Behaviour etc [Scotland] Act 2004). In particular, the 2004 Act provides police and local authorities with a range of powers to deal with intimidating behaviour.[6]

The response goes on to highlight the resource of Scottish antisocial behaviour legislation and suggests that the measures being developed in Edinburgh might be a helpful guide to dealing with street begging.[7]

The fact that the Scottish Justice Department cited Edinburgh as an example of how to deal with street begging without recourse to criminal law is striking. In the summer of 1997 an extraordinary debate broke out in Edinburgh about re-criminalising people who begged on the street, igniting an acrimonious political battle between the local Tory establishment and the Labour-led council. The refusal of the then Scottish Office to recreate the criminal offence of begging in Edinburgh – a position that remains unchanged today – stands as a stunning contrast to the English case of continued use of the 1824 Vagrancy Act. Certainly calls to remove people who beg in Scottish cities have been no less shrill or prejudiced than in England, and the town-centre management movement – so central to the network to which diverted giving has migrated – has been as prominent in Scotland as in England. What has been different in Scotland is that, at the highest level of government, officials have refused to pander to a view that people who beg represent a serious crime-and-disorder menace that deserves criminal sanction. Indeed, the Scottish case could not offer a starker contrast to the reforms their English counterparts carried out in rearming the vagrancy law.

I. 'The Biggest Urinal in the United Kingdom'

The Edinburgh campaign to re-criminalise begging was ignited by media coverage in the summer of 1996 (about the same time as the Winchester experiment was being developed), when the *Scotsman* and the *Edinburgh Evening News* ran stories critical of the visibly indigent beggars and street drinkers on city-centre pavements. Citing the press coverage as evidence of a problem, Tory city councillor Lindsay Walls wrote to the Scottish Office urging reintroduction of vagrancy laws

---

[5] Letter from Anna Cossar, Policy Advisor, Justice Department, Criminal Law Division, Scottish Executive, to Councillor Martin Grieg, Safer Aberdeen Task Group, 10 January 2006, 1.

[6] ibid.

[7] ibid.

to deal with 'aggressive beggars'.[8] Referring to what he characterised as the 'very accurate reports' of the *Evening News* about the increasing problem of 'drunks and beggars', Councillor Walls argued that

> we simply cannot go on ignoring the feelings of a long suffering public who are threatened by the so-called 'beggars' in the streets of the Capital and beyond. Many of them are 'chancers', who are entitled to – and receive – enhanced benefits from the State.[9]

James Douglas-Hamilton, the minister of state responsible for criminal law in Scotland, responded to Councillor Walls by first pointing out that being 'drunk and incapable' was an offence under section 50 of the Civic Government (Scotland) Act 1982,[10] and that since 1993 provisions had been added to allow local councils to introduce city-centre by-laws to ban street drinking.[11] The specific issue of begging, Douglas-Hamilton commented, was more complex; there were 'moral and social, as well as legal issues to consider'.[12] The minister pointed out that those who did indeed 'extort money with menaces' were subject to the 'very flexible' common-law offence of 'breach of the peace', which addresses behaviour that threatens, intimidates or alarms.[13] In addition, people who beg under 'false or fraudulent pretence' could possibly be charged with the common-law offence of fraud.[14] Otherwise, he argued, those whose begging did not obstruct the highway or commit a breach of the peace or fraud at common law were not in fact committing any criminal offence. 'You urge the reintroduction of the Vagrancy Acts', the minister wrote to Councillor Walls,

> by which I take it you mean the old local offences of the burgh acts which made it an offence to beg. I am not persuaded that this is justifiable. No one would argue that begging is welcomed. But to rule that beggars should be treated as criminals, even where their behaviour does nothing to cause alarm, would categorise those who may be genuinely deserving of charity in a way which many people would find it difficult to agree to.[15]

The acknowledgement by a minister of state that at least some of the people who beg on the street are in genuine need, that often their behaviour is not alarming,

---

[8] Letter from Minister of State James Douglas-Hamilton, Scottish Office, to JL Walls, Councillor, City of Edinburgh, RB24086, 29 August 1996, 1.

[9] ibid.

[10] s 50(1) reads: 'Any person who, while not in the care or protection of a suitable person, is, in a public place, drunk and incapable of taking care of himself shall be guilty of an offence and liable, on summary conviction, to a fine not exceeding £50.'

[11] The model by-law was approved after pilot projects in Dundee, Motherwell and Galashiels. The most notable deployment of this by-law has been in Glasgow. Scottish Office, Douglas-Hamilton to Walls, 1.

[12] ibid.

[13] ibid, 1–2.

[14] 'That route may not often be taken,' comments the minister, 'but it remains a longstop, and the possibility that it may be resorted to does, I think, have an effect in curbing the more blatant claims of some of those who do beg'; ibid, 2.

[15] ibid.

and that many people would find criminal sanctions disagreeable stands as a remarkable contrast to the often hysterical characterisation of begging by English officials – as a fraud carried out by drug addicts that would result in crime and death. Undeterred by the response from the Scottish Office, Councillor Walls tabled a council motion that the city agree in principle to establish a by-law to prohibit 'any person in any public place begging ... within 15 metres of a cash dispensing facility'.[16] The council agreed in principle to study the possibility of a 'cash machine' by-law, but the issue of begging appeared to fade away as the summer ended.

The issue of the legal beggar on Edinburgh streets resurfaced in the summer of 1997. While the refusal of the Scottish Office to allow a criminal law against begging made any further promotion redundant, proponents of re-criminalisation pushed forward; perhaps they sensed an emotive issue that could harass the Labour-led council, which had been invigorated by the dramatic win of New Labour in the 1997 general election. Over the next few months the *Evening News* and the *Scotsman* (edited by Andrew Neil) launched a sustained campaign to re-criminalise begging through the enactment of a local by-law.[17] This form of 'aggressive reporting', as it was described by the co-ordinator of Edinburgh's Streetwork project,[18] reached a climax in August, when Andrew Neil, addressing the Edinburgh Book Festival, remarked that 'beggars are turning Scotland's capital into the biggest urinal in the United Kingdom'.[19] Advocates for the homeless such as the *Big Issue* and Streetwork were alarmed at the hostile press coverage. 'We are very concerned,' wrote Mel Young, the director of the *Big Issue*, to the Labour Group leader, 'that the council is being forced to react to this coverage in a very right wing and reactionary way.'[20]

The *Evening News* published its own anti-begging by-law and faxed it to the Labour council leader.[21] The media coverage became frenzied – 'Begging Battle

[16] Letter from JL Walls, Councillor, City of Edinburgh, to Rt Hon Michael Forsyth, Minister of State, Scottish Office, 24 July 1996, 2. Councillor Walls attributed the idea of a cash-machine by-law to a similar ordinance in New York City which the *Evening News* had brought to his attention; ibid, 1.

[17] eg, J McBeth, 'Capital's Beggars Needy or Greedy?' *The Scotsman*, 23 June 1997, 22. In a commentary, Andrew Neil suggested that 'Paris, Stockholm and other major capitals have the same afflictions but they do not allow their social drop-outs to desecrate their city centres. It is inconceivable, for example, that the French would allow the Louvre to be treated as an outdoor toilet, which is what we have allowed our magnificent Royal Scottish Academy to become'. A Neil, 'Scapegoats for Squalor', *The Scotsman*, 28 June 1997, A16.

[18] S Hendry, '"We've Got as Much Right as You to Sit on Streets": Beggars Hit Back at News Plan', *Evening News*, 10 September 1997, 6.

[19] D Lister, 'Beggars "Ruining Edinburgh,"' *The Independent*, 12 August 1997, 3.

[20] Letter from M Young, Director, *Big Issue* Scotland, to Keith Geddes, Labour Group leader, Edinburgh City Council, 30 July 1997.

[21] The *Evening News* by-law reads: 'City of Edinburgh By-law (Aggressive Begging): (1) A Person shall not, in any public place or from door to door, beg or act in any way for the purpose of inducing the donation of money, food, or drink. Nothing in this subsection shall make it an offence to take part in any collection licensed or authorised. (2) Any police officer may arrest without warrant any person whom he has reasonable cause to suspect of having committed an offence against this section.' N Morrison, 'City of Edinburgh Byelaw' *Evening News*, 29 August 1997, 2.

Victory in Sight', reported the *Evening News*[22] – as the Council announced that it would meet in chambers on 9 September 1997 to debate a by-law. Three individuals who actively begged on city streets formed a 'right to beg peacefully' committee and faxed the Council, asking permission to present themselves as a deputation.[23] The three beggars, known as Santa, Ricky and Jimmy, arrived at the chambers for 'tea and sympathy', as the *Scotsman* reported, and spoke against the by-law, as did a local advocate for the homeless, Tam Hendry.[24] A planned 'right to beg peacefully' street protest was cancelled after the death of Diana, Princess of Wales, an event which all but stopped the relentless media coverage of the begging issue.

The Council refused to recommend enactment of a no-begging by-law and, with support from the Liberal Democrats, pushed through a motion which instructed the Urban Regeneration Subcommittee of the Council's Policy and Resources Committee to study begging as part of the wider issue of 'social exclusion'.[25] This channelling of the anti-begging campaign into the larger rubric of social exclusion was congruent with the early ethos of Tony Blair's 'New Deal' of welfare reforms, a major aspect of which was setting up the Cabinet Office – level Social Exclusion Unit. The anti-begging campaigners heaped scorn on formation of the new committee. Councillor Walls called it 'another delaying tactic'[26] and the *Evening News* called it a 'deranged notion'.[27] The *Scotsman* 'outed' Labour and New Democrat councillors who had voted for establishment of the committee, making public their names, addresses and home telephone numbers.[28] The issue of re-criminalising begging was effectively sidelined for the next seven months, until the Policy and Resources Committee released its report.

II. Drafting a Begging By-law

Titled *Managing Edinburgh's City Centre*, the Committee's report was released on 28 May 1998. It is noted in its opening paragraphs that much of Edinburgh's city centre was designated a World Heritage Site by UNESCO in 1996, a distinction that recognises its 'outstanding, universal value and ranks Edinburgh in the same

---

[22] *Evening News* (Edinburgh), 'Begging Battle Victory in Sight', *Evening News*, 29 August 1997, 1.

[23] P Laing, 'Beggars Send Their Demands by Fax: Hi-Tech Battle against Ban Bid', *Daily Record*, 8 September 1997, 17.

[24] Hendry, '"We've Got as Much Right"'.

[25] Edinburgh, 'Begging and Homelessness', Appendix 6 to Strategic Policy 0092/SP/IF (1998).

[26] Letter to author from JL Walls, 7 November 1997.

[27] *Evening News*, 'City Study into the Obvious Beggars Belief', *Evening News*, 22 September 1997, 2.

[28] *Scotsman*, 'Zero Tolerance for Council Failures', editorial, 10 September 1997, 11, and 'Councillors Who Back Motion', 10 September 1997, 3; C Holme, 'Councillors "Outed" over Beggars', *The Herald*, 11 September 1997, 5. As the *Scotsman* editorial stated, 'the people of Edinburgh should make their views abundantly clear to sanctimonious councillors content to let other people suffer the consequences of their failures. We are happy to assist in any exercise in open government, and do so today by providing the addresses of those who forget that the public, too, has rights'; *Scotsman*, 'Zero Tolerance'.

status as the Taj Mahal and the Pyramids of Egypt'.[29] The Committee urges that action be taken to 'protect and improve the unique world heritage environment' and meet the 'demands for a higher quality of environment'.[30] Further, the report states:

> A healthy economic future is forecast for the city centre. It is proving flexible to chang-ing economic demands and major public sector intervention is not required. It is crucial to the city that the centre remains strong. If it fails to perform, the prospects for attract-ing inward investment and jobs, and for extending the benefits to the local economies throughout the city, are undermined. A number of problems do exist and three issues require immediate attention – antisocial behaviour associated with begging, accessibil-ity, and the traffic and design impacts of major new developments.[31]

Remarkably, the report views begging as the most important threat to protection of a 'healthy economic future'; the presence of beggars receives more attention than changes that were to take place with introduction of the new Scottish Parliament. It begins by noting that, in principle, enabling power for a by-law appeared to exist in a provision of the Local Government (Scotland) Act 1973.[32] Any proposed begging by-law would have to be 'promoted' to the secretary of state, who could hold a public inquiry into the matter before deciding if the by-law would be confirmed.[33]

Attached to the main report is a report by the director of corporate services on the legal issues of promotion of a begging by-law; it provides a remarkably thor-ough analysis of the 'possible contents' and consequences likely to face city officials in drafting and enacting such a by-law.[34] The legal analysis revolves around two possible versions of a by-law, Version A and Version B.

Version A is an attempt to reintroduce the burgh offence of 'collecting alms': 'Any person who in a public place begs or acts in any way for the purpose of inducing the giving of money or money's worth shall be guilty of an offence.'[35] Any gift, no matter how unlike money or how personal – perhaps a sandwich or a cigarette – could be translated into 'money's worth', a stable form that could be the object of a crime.

While Version A focuses on the gift-crime object – the thing potentially given and taken – Version B adds the conduct of aggression to the importunity:

> Any person who in any public place in the course of begging or acting in any way for the purpose of inducing the giving of money or money's worth behaves in a threatening

---

[29] Edinburgh, *Managing Edinburgh's City Centre*, strategic policy, 0092/SP/IF (1998), 5.
[30] ibid.
[31] ibid, 9.
[32] s 201 gives the Council powers to 'make byelaws for the good rule and government of the whole or any part of their area, as the case may be, and for the prevention and suppression of nuisances'; Edinburgh, 'Proposed Bye-Law', 3.
[33] ibid, 1–2.
[34] ibid.
[35] ibid, 3.

or aggressive way or adopts a threatening or aggressive manner shall be guilty of an offence.[36]

The vital ingredient of this offence is not just 'inducing the giving of money or money's worth' in itself, but the presence of a 'threatening or aggressive manner' that the beggar 'adopts'. This inclusion of an 'adopted' manner reproduces centuries-old concerns about begging as an act of theatrical mendacity and disguise, the feigning of an appearance of need that is not authentic.

The report discusses in some detail the significant obstacles facing promotion of either version of the by-law. Most generally, the secretary of state would have to be convinced of the necessity of creating a new criminal offence, especially after the old burgh laws had not been deemed significant enough to be preserved. Version B posed serious difficulties in this regard, most notably in that the activity of 'aggressive begging' could already – as was earlier pointed out by Minister Douglas-Hamilton to Councillor Walls – be dealt with as a common-law breach of the peace.

Edinburgh City Council's solicitor requested an informal opinion from the Scottish Office on the matter.[37] The reply is not surprising, given the Office's earlier response to Councillor Walls: 'The offence of breach of the peace does provide a means of addressing the problem of those who threaten, intimidate, alarm, and make a deliberate nuisance of themselves to the obvious annoyance of members of the public.'[38] In addition, the police opposed Version B of the by-law, also citing the fact that 'aggressive' forms of begging could be dealt with as breach of the peace under common law. The report noted that in prosecuting 'aggressive begging' offences, police officers would 'have to have evidence of aggressive or threatening behaviour in much the same way as they would to justify a charge of breach of peace'.[39]

The strongest blow against Version B was the 'clearly inimical' view taken by the authorities responsible for criminal prosecutions. Echoing the main argument that EVA had made to the Home Office in its efforts to repeal the English 1824 vagrancy law, the Scottish Lord Advocate's position was that current criminal law was adequate to deal with 'aggressive' begging.[40] Indeed, if aggressive begging was so similar to the offence of breach of the peace and was such a problem for pedestrians in the city centre, why did the police not use that power to crack down on so-called aggressive beggars? Breach of the peace is not included in the summary

---

[36] ibid, 4.

[37] Letter from Edward Bain, Council Solicitor, City of Edinburgh, to M Baxter, Home Department, Scottish Office, 15 December 1997.

[38] Letter from M Baxter, Home Department, Scottish Office, to Edward Bain, Council Solicitor, Edinburgh City Council, HPK00102.028, 4 February 1997.

[39] Edinburgh, 'Proposed Bye-Law', 7. The report adds: 'I am not certain whether case law precedent in relation to breach of peace could be cited in a prosecution for "aggressive begging" contrary to byelaws'; ibid, 5.

[40] ibid, 8; letter from Robert F Lees, Regional Procurator Fiscal, Lothian and Borders, to Edward Bain, Council Solicitor, Edinburgh City Council, RFL/DMLM/RPFF/18, 12 March 1998.

of crime statistics appended to the report, which on the whole documents a decrease in the level of reported crime in the city centre since 1991.[41] It does seem remarkable that, considering the constant, sustained emphasis on the problem of 'aggressive begging', the police were seemingly doing little to curtail that behaviour by using what they themselves admitted was effective criminal legislation. They did, however, express 'qualified support' for Version A of the by-law, which simply made collecting alms a criminal offence.[42]

However, just as Version B ('aggressive begging') was seen to reproduce current common-law powers, Version A constituted a gift crime that was extraordinarily vague and unclear. There is a requirement, as the report notes, that 'secondary' pieces of legislation (such as city by-laws) – which are not open to parliamentary scrutiny – should be 'certain in their terms'.[43] A by-law must clearly communicate 'what it requires or forbids to be done so that any person potentially affected is in no doubt as to what he or she is required to do or abstain from doing'.[44] The report notes that the Version A prohibition satisfies the 'certainty test' more than Version B.[45] Indeed, the vagueness inherent in Version B's notions of adoption of manner render that version weaker in this regard. The report suggests that Version A could be modified with a new ingredient:

> Any person who in a public place begs or acts in any way for the purpose of inducing the giving of money or money's worth, and fails to desist on being requested to do so by a Constable in uniform, shall be guilty of an offence.[46]

In order to increase the degree of certainty, the offence of inducing the giving of money or 'money's worth' is augmented by the act of failing to desist when told to by a uniformed constable. While the conduct of failing to desist is in itself clearer and more certain, the modified Version A still begs the certainty question: what type of conduct is one expected to desist from? The vagueness of a gift crime involving 'money or money's worth' is further emphasised in the discussion of how the modified Version A fails to draw a distinction between begging and busking. As the report states, Version A could be used to criminalise 'street performers who invite donations'.[47] It is certainly not surprising that the tenuous legal delineation between begging and busking gift encounters (as I discuss in chapter three) would be a troublesome complication for officials when crafting a new offence. Certainly the proposed offence of acting 'in any way for the purpose of inducing the giving of money or money's worth' draws absolutely no distinction between the two.

---

[41] Edinburgh, 'Crime and Incident Trends', app. 5 to *Managing Edinburgh's City Centre*, strategic policy, 0092/SP/IF (1998).
[42] Edinburgh, 'Proposed Bye-Law', 7.
[43] ibid, 5.
[44] ibid.
[45] ibid.
[46] ibid.
[47] ibid.

The legal report suggests that one way to construct a distinction between busking and visibly indigent begging would be to insert an exemption that no person who was a 'bona fide' performer should be considered to be begging. However, the report does not suggest how such *bona fides* would be established, although it does note (erroneously) that some English authorities had achieved formal control by licensing street performers; in fact no formal powers existed in England at the time for such a form of licensing. The use of codes of practice which seek to draw a distinction between '*bona fide* street performers and others' is also cited, although the city notes that such a practice 'would seem inevitably to turn to some extent on qualitative subjective judgement'.[48] The city solicitor was obviously well aware of the contradictions inherent in exempting street entertainers, as it is almost impossible to positively delineate busking from other forms of begging conduct. 'There is a clear risk', states the report, 'that such an exemption [for busking] would result in begging activities being continued to be conducted under the guise of street performers even by persons totally unskilled in any performing art'.[49]

Nevertheless, the report notes that, in supporting the modified Version A, the police favoured exemptions for busking and other activities which 'might be considered as begging under strict interpretation'.[50] Other than evoking the possibility of licensing buskers, the report makes no suggestion as to how such by-law exemptions or licensing schemes would be carried out.

The report raises a further, more prominent issue: civil liberties. In a letter to the Scottish Office (included in an annex to the document), the city solicitor states:

> I do, to some extent, apologise for raising this issue, but I am fairly convinced that if it is not canvassed by me at this stage, it is almost certain to be raised by bodies which hold an opinion that any byelaws associated with the prohibition or curtailment of begging are unacceptable from the unnecessary interference with civil liberties.[51]

Specifically, the solicitor was concerned that a by-law which criminalised begging per se could be challenged by judicial review in relation to the European Convention on Human Rights, with regard to two Convention articles. Article 10 enshrines a right of freedom of expression[52] and Article 14 states that the rights and freedoms

---

[48] ibid, 6.

[49] ibid.

[50] ibid, 7.

[51] Edinburgh, Letter from Edward Bain, Council Solicitor, to M Baxter, Home Department, Scottish Office, 15 December 1997.

[52] Art 10 reads: '(1) Everyone has the right to freedom of expression. This right shall include freedom to hold opinions and to receive and impart information and ideas without interference by public authority and regardless of frontiers. This Article shall not prevent states from requiring the licensing of broadcasting, television or cinema enterprises. (2) The exercise of these freedoms, since it carries with it duties and responsibilities, may be subject to such formalities, conditions, restrictions or penalties as are prescribed by law and are necessary in a democratic society, in the interests of national security, territorial integrity or public safety, for the prevention of disorder or crime, for the protection of health or morals, for the protection of the reputation or rights of others, for preventing the disclosure of information received in confidence, or for maintaining the authority and impartiality of the judiciary.'

set forth in the Convention should be secured without discrimination on various grounds, including status and property.[53] 'Since arguably any by-law,' the solicitor suggests,

> relating to begging might be regarded as focusing on persons who might be bereft of property or, alternatively, focusing on persons because of their particular 'status' there might also be an issue here of incompatibility between by-laws and the freedoms set out in the convention.[54]

Reminding the Council that it would be expected to take its own legal advice as part of the by-law promotion process, the Scottish Office responded:

> The only thoughts we have to offer at this point are that bylaws to prohibit begging, of a kind which would otherwise not involve an offence under criminal law, might, as you suggest, be challenged on the grounds they violated Article 14 or Article 10. There would seem to be a strong risk of violating Article 14 unless the bylaws distinguished between different groups, but if the bylaws prohibited the simple act of asking for alms, then there may be a significant risk of violating Article 10. Of course this is an informal view.[55]

Despite outlining the extensive difficulties involved in both versions, including the 'strong' and 'significant risk' of violating the European Convention, the overall report concluded by supporting promotion of a by-law to outlaw begging – much to the disappointment of the Labour Group, which had hoped that use of a by-law would finally be ruled out. It concluded that while legislation already existed to deal with street musicians who caused annoyance, there would be a need for a begging by-law 'to exempt other activities which might be loosely construed as begging'.[56] No suggestion was made as to how such an exemption for 'loosely construed' activities might be worded.

III. Diverted Giving: A Social Welfare Measure?

In the end, the main report recommends, in rather hesitant language, promotion of a by-law, stressing that a begging by-law 'should be viewed within the wider framework of city centre management and in the context of clearly defined policy', including the development of 'social welfare measures'.[57] This view is inimical to

---

[53] Art 14 reads: '(1) The enjoyment of the rights and freedoms set forth in this Convention shall be secured without discrimination on any ground such as sex, race, colour, language, religion, political or other opinion, national or social origin, association with a national minority, property, birth or other status.' See Gomien et al (1996) for a general discussion of the Convention articles.

[54] Edinburgh, letter from Edward Bain, Council Solicitor, to M Baxter, Home Department, Scottish Office, 15 December 1997.

[55] Scottish Office (1998).

[56] Edinburgh, 'Begging and Homelessness', 5.1.

[57] Edinburgh, *Managing Edinburgh's City Centre*, 13.

the observation made by the director of Corporate Services, who states in the legal report that

> the views expressed by the Lord Advocate, the Regional Procurator Fiscal and the Scottish Office suggest that any proposals to introduce byelaws which prohibit 'aggressive' begging will face acute difficulties in being confirmed by the Secretary of State.[58]

One should not be surprised, given our earlier analysis, that the major 'welfare' initiative which the report suggests might be introduced is implementation of a scheme based on the Make It Count pilot project in Winchester.[59] The report states that the Winchester scheme, 'in conjunction with more intensive policing of beggars and the introduction of closed circuit television (CCTV), has led to a considerable reduction in the number of beggars.'[60] In mimicry of the language used to promote the first wave of diverted-giving schemes in England, the Council indicates that the scheme would 'ensure that all money raised is spent on the basics of food, shelter and clothing, while at the same time removing any obligation that residents and visitors may feel to give money directly to street beggars.'[61]

In common with other cities that cited the Winchester project as a model, the report provides information about the apparent success of the diverted-giving operation that is inaccurate. It erroneously claims that the Winchester scheme raised £5,000 in the first six months from five boxes, that the number of boxes had since doubled to ten, and that the scheme was being actively managed by a 'joint agency group'.[62] And as a bizarre punitive twist in an appendix to the report, officials note that beggars should not really have access to a 'major social welfare measure'. 'It is important to note,' it comments, that the (future) 'Rough Sleepers Initiative [RSI] will not in itself address begging, *nor provide a service to beggars per se.*'[63] The report goes on to state why the planned RSI should not be available to beggars: 'as others who would otherwise be happy to seek the service under Rough Sleepers Initiative may be dissuaded from doing so if such services became labelled or understood to be a service for beggars.'[64] The logic at work here represents the central moral accomplishment of the first wave of diverted-giving schemes: to evoke beggars as a worthy object of alternative charitable giving while at the very same time excluding them as genuinely homeless individuals who could benefit from support. Even with little real chance that the by-law would be enacted, officials had already positioned people who begged outside the benefits of a programme to help rough-sleepers.

---

[58] Edinburgh, 'Proposed Bye-Law', 7.
[59] Edinburgh, 'Begging and Homelessness', 2.7.
[60] ibid.
[61] Edinburgh, *Managing Edinburgh's City Centre*, 14.
[62] Edinburgh, 'Begging and Homelessness', 2.7; *Managing Edinburgh's City Centre*, 15.
[63] ibid, 2.4, emphasis added.
[64] Edinburgh, 'Begging and Homelessness', 2.5.

Surprised by the tone of the report, which, according to one Labour official, exhibits an 'obsession' with begging, the Labour-led council declined to follow the recommendation to promote a by-law. It instead passed a motion to support a 'City Centre Summer Initiative' with a policing initiative which would target 'anti-social behaviour'.[65] The Council thus moved to block any further attempts to promote begging as a criminal offence by including the issue in a wider concern with 'antisocial behaviour', one which could be addressed through the new political emphasis on social exclusion.

In 2007 Aberdeen became the first Scottish city to introduce a diverted-giving scheme, called 'Give a Hand UP, Not a Hand OUT'. The cost of starting up the Winchester-inspired begging-box scheme was estimated at £4,000, with anticipation that the scheme would be funded through sponsorships.[66] 'While the money raised would be rather small,' an early planning document states, 'it does provide members of the public with a means of giving, secure in the knowledge that it will be used to assist individuals achieve alternative lifestyles.'[67] Officials in Aberdeen clearly hoped that an ostensibly successful diverted-giving scheme would provide political leverage with the Scottish government to get it to agree to a new criminal law against begging. In a letter to the Aberdeen community safety specialist who had yet again raised the issue of promoting a begging by-law, in January 2009 the Criminal Justice Directorate of the Criminal Law and Licensing Division stated:

> Turning to the principle of introducing a byelaw on street begging, it might be helpful if I restate the Scottish Government's position, as has already been indicated in correspondence with Aberdeen City Council. At present there are no byelaws banning begging in force anywhere in Scotland. We have long considered byelaws on begging to be unnecessary because the kind of behaviour that such proposals often seek to address should already be covered by the common law offence of breach of the peace, depending on the circumstances, or by measures under the Antisocial Behaviour etc. (Scotland) Act 2004. If the act of begging does not involve any alarming or distressing behaviour, such as might constitute breach of peace, then we do not consider that the behaviour should be criminalised.[68]

City officials in Scotland continue to press for a criminal by-law, and the Scottish government continues to indicate that it will not confirm a new criminal offence.

I conclude by making a few general observations about the differences between the English and Scottish cases. The most obvious point is that in Scotland, the lack of a criminal sanction renders the central purpose of diverted-giving schemes inoperable. It is not just a coincidence that the then Scottish Executive wisely declined to have the national Change a Life programme operate north

[65] Edinburgh, 'City Centre Inter-agency Stage 1', item 7.6, minutes of full City Council meeting, 28 May 1998.
[66] Aberdeen City Council (2004) 'Street Begging Report', Report of the Community Services Committee, 14 September, 2.
[67] ibid, 6.
[68] Letter to City of Aberdeen from Fraser Criminal Justice Directorate, Criminal Law and Licensing Division, Scotland, January 2009, 1–2.

of the English border, or that diverted-giving programmes, as a social welfare measure, have been started in only one city, and even then, only when explicitly tied to the hope of a new criminal law. The 'moral sorting' that diverted giving is credited with carrying out in English cities – that those left begging on the street are not really homeless and are deserving of police attention – only makes sense when there is a visible criminal sanction available. It seems likely that many of the actors one would expect to support diverted giving in Scotland (such as retailers) are in fact much less inclined to participate than their English counterparts, without some assurance of increased enforcement. Certainly, the fact that diverted giving itself is an inefficient (if not nonsensical) way to seriously raise funds for charity would only make it even less attractive to retailers who legitimately want to support a 'good cause'.

Deprived of a network of sites in Scotland, and without the visibility of a national stage and the support of some advocates for the homeless, diverted giving had little chance of becoming a 'gift crime' movement as it did in England. There seems little doubt that the explicit and principled stand of the Scottish government, one that involved a mixture of practical and legal reasons, has created a discourse about begging that is distinct from that in England, one that pushes hard to locate begging as a social rather than a crime-control problem.[69] One can see this in what Titmuss calls the 'moral vocabulary'[70] of how each government talks about its approach to begging. In the Scottish case, their response to calls for re-criminalisation is countered by a concern for human rights that take seriously the character of 'harm' that is involved. In addition to this, the moral issue of giving to someone begging is evoked, but only to the extent of suggesting that the public may have a right of choice to give, and that the public's reason for giving may not be unreasonable. In sum, this approach treats the public as thoughtful adults who can make choices about charity and make judgements about what 'harm' is. On the other hand, English officials, in articulating a gift-crime mentality, deploy explanations that are focused solely on the character of both those begging (drug-addicted frauds) and those who give to them (misguided and ill-informed). This individualisation of the causes of begging (and poverty) is made more acute by the fact that the mechanics of diverted giving tends over time to amplify the shrillest and most intolerant viewpoints. Any wider social, economic or moral considerations have been evacuated from gift-crime reasoning, narrowing the possible response to fear, suspicion, and a concern for enhanced policing. The result in England has been an intolerant policy that ignores empirical evidence and not only preserves but expands the role of criminal law. The result in Scotland has been a tolerant policy based on empirical evidence and the restrained use of criminal law.

---

[69] See Hermer, J and MacGregor, D, 'Urban Renaissance and the Contested Legality of Begging in Scotland' in Atkinson, R and Helms, G (eds), *Securing an Urban Renaissance: Crime, Community and British Urban Policy* (Bristol, Policy Press, 2007).

[70] Titmuss, RM, *The Gift Relationship: From Human Blood to Social Policy* (London, George Allen and Unwin, 1970) 230.

7

The Calling of a Beggar

In the end, if it is reciprocity that holds the mundane world together, it is beneficence that transcends this world and can make men weep the tears of reconciliation. If such prodigies of social interaction are rare, it is not for want of knowing how to produce them.

Alvin W Gouldner, 1972, 'The Importance of Something for Nothing'[1]

[P]ersistence in terms of numbers of recorded convictions cannot be taken as a measure of persistence in actual offending. The homeless poor may be persistently taken to court, and hence persistently returned to prison, because of a persistent failure to provide for them in any other way.

Suzan Fairhead, 1981, *Persistent Petty Offenders*[2]

In this final chapter I draw together some observations about gift-crime regulation, a powerful and peculiar movement that started from a provincial experiment by a few enthusiastic local officials who wanted to get begging people off their streets.

I begin by examining how citizens in Bristol and Nottingham challenged two of the most aggressive diverted-giving schemes in the context of 'truth in advertising'. The details of these adjudications carried out by the Advertising Standards Authority (ASA) provoke a number of wider observations about the mendacious character of diverted-giving schemes and the knowledge claims made in support of gift-crime regulation. Drawing on criminal justice statistics, I review century-long prosecution rates for begging and rough sleeping, along with rates of conviction for the begging offence from 1970 to 2004 and for begging and persistent begging from 2005 to 2015. Using court disposal data I establish that the new offence of persistent begging has no discernable connection to providing 'persistent beggars' with drug treatment through the use of community sentences. I observe that the persistent-begging offence is redundant and prone to confusion as to how it should be used. I examine the problematic notion of 'persistence' and suggest

[1] AW Gouldner, 'The Importance of Something for Nothing' in *For Sociology: Renewal and Critique in Sociology Today* (London, Allen Lane, 1973) 277.
[2] S Fairhead, *Persistent Petty Offenders* (London, Home Office, 1981) 2.

that it is intricately tied to the true meaning of the 1824 Act. The consequence is the policing and punishment of certain types of idle and disorderly people who are viewed to have taken on the 'calling of a beggar'.

I. Truth in Gift-Crime Prevention

In 2003, just before Christmas, a member of the public was walking in the heart of Nottingham when an unusual poster caught his eye at the intersection of Victoria Street and Bridlesmith Gate. As illustrated by Figure 15 (page 130), the city's diverted-giving campaign used two images designed to make passers-by hold on to their pocket change at the sight of someone begging. The first poster message, in the style of a beggar's writing on a coffee cup, warned: '90% of the money given to beggars goes straight to drug dealers.' The second warning again appropriated the voice of a beggar with a handwritten cardboard sign that read: 'My drug dealer prefers to travel first class – Please spare what you can.' Both visuals were stylistically similar to the cup and cardboard sign used by the Rough Sleepers Unit (RSU) in their Change a Life campaign, which had ended a year earlier. While the beggar himself is not depicted, both images prominently depict rumpled blankets and sleeping bags laid on cardboard on the pavement. Disturbed by the portrayal of people who beg as drug-addicted criminals, the passer-by was moved to complain to the ASA, a body charged with regulating 'truth in advertising'.

The passer-by, 'Citizen B',[3] promptly wrote to the ASA, arguing that the posters communicated 'a powerful factual statement, but one for which I believe there is no supporting evidence'.[4] Citizen B felt that, as the objective of the advertisement appeared to be the redirecting of financial donations, 'the matter is therefore not a trivial one'. In writing back to Citizen B, the ASA confirmed that the advertiser was Nottingham City Council and provided guidelines for submitting her complaint. A body whose mission it is to protect consumers from misleading and offensive advertising would adjudicate gift-crime claims that giving to those who begged would lead to drug abuse, overdose deaths and drug trafficking.

Since noting the first poster, Citizen B had discovered two other advertisements used to promote the 'Respect Nottingham' campaign on public billboards and on the council website, including one that linked begging to drug related gun crime. Citizen B made six specific complaints (3 posed as questions) to the ASA about the advertising campaign:

1.   The posters were offensive, because they demean the homeless and denied them the right to dignity.

---

[3] At the time, members of the public could complain anonymously to the ASA and have their identity protected in the adjudicative process. This was the case with this complaint in Nottingham, and I preserve their anonymity in this account with the pseudonym 'Citizen B'. I should note that, at their request, I advised Citizen B and submitted a brief to the ASA regarding the validity of their argument.

[4] Personal communication, Citizen B.

2. The posters were irresponsible, because they could encourage antisocial or violent behaviour towards beggars and the homeless.
3. The advertisements misleadingly implied that most beggars used illegal drugs.
4. Can the advertisers substantiate the claim that '90% of the money given to beggars goes straight to drug dealers' in poster [see Figure 15]?
5. Can the advertisers substantiate the link between begging, drug dealing and gun crime in the posters?
6. Can the claim 'respect for Nottingham', in the context of the poster, be considered offensive, because it implies beggars were not worthy of respect, beggars did not have respect for Nottingham and people who gave money to beggars did not respect Nottingham.[5]

In response to the complaint, Nottingham City Council turned to the agency that had produced the advertisements for it, SAM Design Consultant Ltd, for evidence of the claims made in the advertisements. This private firm responded with evidence which the council claimed was from police records, that 'over the course of two years, police records on arrests showed that 34 out of 37 beggars in Nottingham have been tested positive for Class A drugs'.[6]

On 22 September 2004, the ASA issued its adjudication, and to the disappointment of Citizen B, only one of the six complaints was withheld: the claim that 90 per cent of money given to beggars went to drug dealers.[7] The ASA instructed the council to withdraw that specific poster, and to not repeat the claim in further advertising. This decision in Nottingham was not without precedent.

On the way to work in Bristol in October 2003, Dr Adam Nieman saw an advertisement on the back of the bus in Hotwells which showed the face of a young man lying prostrate, his hair dishevelled, with a slight smile on his upturned face. Superimposed on the poster was the message 'Most beggars in Bristol are heroin addicts.'[8] The text below the image continued: 'Heroin kills. This could be the pound that kills him. Don't kill with kindness. Don't give money to beggars. Give your money to recognised homeless charities instead.'

Bristol's Your Kindness Can Kill campaign had been designated by the Home Office as a 'trailblazer for begging' scheme, along with those of Manchester, Brighton, Stoke-on-Trent, Camden and Westminster. The Bristol scheme had been noted as an exemplar in the 2003 white paper 'Respect and Responsibility' on how a local council can 'tackle begging in the city centre', where '100% of beggars have a dependency on Class A drugs'.[9]

An expert in the communication of scientific facts (much of his work involved designing science exhibits), Dr Nieman objected in particular to the factual

---

[5] ASA [Advertising Standards Authority], non-broadcast adjudication, Nottingham City Council t/a Respect for Nottingham, 22 September, 2004.
[6] Personal communication, Citizen B.
[7] Personal communication, Adam Nieman.
[8] ibid.
[9] ibid.

statement – one that underpins the 'your kindness will kill' logic – that the act of giving money to someone who was begging would kill him. He complained to the ASA on three points:

1.   The claim that 'most beggars are heroin addicts'.
2.   The implied causal link between donations to beggars and the death of heroin addicts.
3.   Whether the advertisement was offensive to homeless people.[10]

In their decision, the ASA upheld the second complaint, stating that the advertiser's assertion – that the majority of beggars are addicted to heroin and so, it would follow, that giving money to addicts would cause them to overdose – was made without evidence. 'It considered the claim was likely to mislead ... because the [Bristol] council was unable to show an established link between giving donations to beggars and the death of heroin addicts'.[11] The first and third complaints were not upheld, as the ASA accepted information from a database held by the Bristol Drug Action Team and police that had identified 285 beggars, 'of which 40 were "persistently begging"'. Of the total number of beggars identified, '95% were addicted to heroin'.[12]

The decision of the ASA to uphold the complaint that linked giving to beggars and overdose deaths was vilified by the Bristol City Council in a press release titled 'Advertising Standards Decision Attacked as Very Dangerous':

> The ASA was formed to protect the public from being ripped-off by lies about products and services. It isn't supposed to sabotage legitimate public information campaigns to cut drug related deaths and combat anti-social behaviour.[13]

The press release provides background information that repeats evidence the City Council presented to the ASA in support of its claim, including the fact that '86% admitted using drugs', as well as some general research claims on the hazards of heroin use. Despite its strong objections, the city could provide no evidence of any type that supported a link between giving to those who begged and overdose death. And consistent with the erasure of the hunger problem that people who beg face, there was no mention of the research finding that the majority of cadged money goes to buy food, even though Bristol was one of the five cities where the *Looking for Change* research was conducted. Interestingly, the claim cited in the 'Respect and Responsibility' white paper three years earlier in support of legal reforms to address 'persistent begging' – that '100% of beggars have a dependency on Class A drugs' in Bristol – was not repeated in any evidence that the council put forward to the ASA.

[10] ASA, non-broadcast adjudication, Bristol City Council, 25 February 2004.
[11] ibid.
[12] ibid.
[13] Bristol, 'Advertising Standards Decision Attacked as Very Dangerous', press release, 25 February 2004.

Dr Nieman responded to Bristol's criticism of the ASA decision by issuing his own press release. Quoting Bristol's corporate plan, which discusses 'reducing social and environmental nuisance', he argued that the campaign was not 'motivated by a genuine concern for beggars.' 'It looks to me', he writes,

> like the Council is trying to clear the streets of people it thinks are undesirable. I don't think they really care what happens to people who lose income from begging so long as they are [not] so visible. Beggars are citizens too, even those addicted to heroin. The Council is supposed [to] represent them along with everybody else, not treat them like Vermin to be eradicated.[14]

Back in Nottingham, Citizen B was unaware of the Bristol decision, despite the similarity between the complaints and the schemes themselves – both products of the socio-technical network generated by the Winchester experiment. Upset at the decision of the ASA and by the process itself, Citizen B decided to apply to appeal the decision to the ASA's independent reviewer. The argument for an appeal rested on two grounds: first, that the 'authoritative evidence' the ASA had accepted was in fact questionable, given that it had been supplied by the advertising firm employed by the council; and second, that the 'police statistics' quoted by the council were in fact wrong. Citizen B had done some detective work by contacting a local police official to inquire about the accuracy of the statistics on begging and drug use cited by Nottingham and the advertising firm, and the police official confirmed that the figures the council had quoted to defend the advertiser's claims were incorrect.

The independent reviewer of ASA adjudications, Sir John Caines, recommended that complaints 3 (about the statement that most beggars used illegal drugs) and 5 (the stated connection between begging, drug dealing and drug crime) could be reviewed on the grounds of 'new evidence'. Caines then conducted what amounted to his own investigation and confirmed to Citizen B that the original claim from police records – that 34 out of 37 beggars had tested positive for class A drugs – was not correct. In fact, of the 37 beggars 'known to police', 16 of them had tested positive for drugs, 12 were arrested but not tested, and seven were neither arrested nor tested. It is not clear how the testing was conducted or what drugs were tested for.[15] And, of course, this involved only beggars 'known to police', not the general population of people begging on the street at any given time.

Even though a central part of the council's original evidence 'from police records' had now been proved by Citizen B to be incorrect, Sir John Caines declined to uphold either complaint 3 or 5. A revised adjudication was issued on 23 March 2005. While acknowledging as 'incorrect' the initial information from

---

[14] A Nieman, press release, 25 February 2004.
[15] Personal communication, Citizen B. It is not clear what (if any) authority the police had to test beggars for drugs, or what protocol was followed, as this occurred before begging became a 'trigger offence' that made drug testing mandatory.

the police, the independent reviewer remained satisfied that the advertisers had been able to substantiate their claims. The refusal to uphold claim number 5 is particularly striking, given a complete lack of any plausible connection between giving to those begging and gun crime. Remarkably, the evidence that the ASA accepted from Nottingham Council consisted of a report from the chief constable that 'crack cocaine wars between drug dealers were fuelling a gun related crime wave in Nottingham' and the statistic that 'the police had made 740 arrests and seized 221 firearms and £2.5 million of crack cocaine and heroin since 2002'.[16]

One can only contrast this result with that of Bristol, where the council rejected an empirical linkage between 'donations to beggars and deaths by heroin'. Yet in Nottingham, the simply fantastic link between giving to people who begged and gun crime was accepted as valid without any plausible evidence whatsoever. Indeed, given what appears to be a lack of standards for what constitutes 'authoritative evidence' in adjudicating ASA complaints, it seems reasonable to suggest that the only reason complaint number 4 was upheld was because the advertisers used a specific, definitive figure of 90 per cent, instead of asserting a connection in more general and vague language.

The Nottingham evidence successfully cited by the city in response to the first complaint of Citizen B – that the posters 'demeaned the homeless and denied them their right to dignity' – is especially notable, considering the visual representations on the posters, which depict someone who also appears to be sleeping rough. The advertisers' argument, which the ASA accepted, was that the campaign was 'not about the homeless, but about those who beg', and they stated in their evidence that 'only a few beggars [on the street] were regarded by agencies as "street homeless"'. Why then, as Citizen B argued, did the posters suggest that those who begged were sleeping rough, by depicting blankets and sleeping bags? The advertisers explained that 'they had [also] used blankets and sleeping bags in the posters because beggars who were not homeless often used them to give the impression that they were sleeping rough in order to get money'.[17]

However, in providing evidence in relation to complaint number 3 – that the posters were misleading because they suggested that most beggars use drugs – the council cited information derived from a city survey which reported that of 92 rough sleepers in Nottingham, over half of them also begged on the streets.[18] Nottingham's own Rough Sleepers survey directly contradicted the city's claim that 'only a few' of those who begged were homeless. How the ASA could ignore such a blatant contradiction in the advertisers' evidence that the campaign was not about rough-sleepers, when in fact many of those begging did sleep rough, remains a matter of speculation.

That one of the most public forms of resistance to current campaigns against giving to those begging was carried out under the auspices of a body that regulates

[16] ibid. ASA (Advertising Standards Authority) Nottingham City Council t/a Respect for Nottingham, 23 March 2005.
[17] Personal communication, Citizen B.
[18] ibid.

'truth in advertising' for consumer products and services seems strangely appropriate. These adjudications are reminders of the centuries-old concern with detecting mendacity, fraud and disguise in the figure of the beggar, along with more recent concerns about the feelings of the passer-by at the sight of someone begging. Indeed, Citizen B in Nottingham and Dr Nieman in Bristol are examples today of what early-nineteenth-century beadles described as 'good natured people' who 'interest themselves' when a beggar is apprehended. Gift-crime regulation today has taken on the character of false advertising, of simulation that portrays visibly poor people as disguised frauds. Your Kindness Can Kill schemes in particular, with the crass and flippant use of the money-man icon, are a morally grotesque effort to diminish those begging as fellow human beings in distress. The very few evaluations of diverted-giving schemes carried out provoke the question of exactly what purpose they serve for people they present as helping. Evaluations of these schemes provide no meaningful or concrete follow-up in terms of being accountable for the claims that officials make – very much following the example of the RSU's Change a Life. For example, a 2013 evaluation report of a Your Kindness Can Kill campaign, carried out by Thames Reach and the City of London homelessness team, demonstrates how derivative these campaigns have become.[19] 'What exactly was being evaluated?', the report asks:

> Overall this is a very difficult campaign to evaluate the success of – begging will continue in the City and the people will continue to give. This is only one aspect of working with those who beg. With regard to the aim and objectives, this campaign was a success. It had a good balance between advertising and engaging with the public, whilst not being too resources intensive; for example, exploiting free advertising helped reduce the costs to enable expensive method [*sic*] of advertising on the Underground to be conducted.[20]

One apparent measure of official success is how cheaply the advertising could be carried out and the visibility and quality of the message to the public. 'The message and image on the posters are fine,' a City of London police constable was quoted in the evaluation, 'but some people didn't want to take a leaflet as they don't want to harm the environment'.[21] A year later the City of Westminster, as one of the Home Office begging trailblazers, issued a report about its approach to those begging on the street, which included help for beggars to 'change their disordered lifestyles' and assist those with 'chaotic lifestyles'.[22] They cited their 'Killing with Kindness' project as a success that would be continued because the scheme 'confirmed to the public that giving to beggars is counter-productive and provided clear statistical

---

[19] London, 'Evaluation of the Anti-Begging Campaign April May/2013', app A of 'Rough Sleepers Quarterly Update', Community and Children's Services, 2013. One exception is a relatively detailed evaluation done by Oxford City Council, commissioned by the Rough Sleeping and Single Homelessness team on their Your Kindness Could Kill campaign launched in 2012.

[20] ibid, 4.

[21] ibid.

[22] City of Westminster (2004) 2.

evidence that the majority of those arrested for persistent begging were users of crack cocaine and heroin'.[23] Yet there is no evidence whatsoever that it confirmed anything 'to the public' or had any impact in terms of people giving or not giving to those who begged.

The routine use of police statistics, like those cited in Westminster and Nottingham, in claiming the need for or success of diverted-giving schemes is a reminder that the police occupy an important space in the knowledge production about beggars and rough-sleepers, often in a way that portrays them as unworthy of public support as 'real' homeless people. In the Nottingham case, Citizen B managed to prove the advertiser and council wrong in their claim from police statistics that almost all beggars arrested tested positive for Class A drugs. Statistics cited from police arrest records and applied to represent all people begging on the street can be highly misleading. Even when accurately reported, it is important to note that these figures usually do not represent all those begging on the street on any given day: they are only a measure of those who have been (a) arrested by police *and* (b) given a drug test – and not all those arrested for begging are tested every time. And making these figures even less representative is the fact that the same person may be arrested and tested several times. Even worse, police reports using vague or highly subjective descriptions, such as beggars 'known to police', 'addicted to drugs' and 'from police records', are essentially useless in accurately reporting the drug use of those who beg and sleep rough on the street.

Police records can also be a very poor indicator of how many people begging sleep rough or are homeless. As I documented in chapter four, the questioning by police of a person arrested for begging – if they have a reliable 'home' address or 'serviceable address' – is done in direct relation to the decision of granting bail and administering a court appearance. Not having an address can mean that the person begging could be detained and held in custody. In other words, it is reasonable to suggest that a person would give a 'serviceable' address – even if they lived on the street or had unstable shelter – if they believed it meant that they would be released out of police custody. Thus the information the police obtain in their enforcement with someone begging most likely favours a higher reporting of 'beggars who have a home'. For example, in their discussion of the overlap between begging and rough sleeping in their review of the literature in 2018, Public Health England accepted evidence provided by Thames Reach that a large proportion of those who beg are not homeless. Specifically Thames Reach cited evidence that

> only 40% of people arrested for begging in a Metropolitan Police operation claimed to be Homeless … An operation in Birmingham in autumn 2013 showed that 6 out of 10 people arrested for begging had a home … most people begging have accommodation of sorts, either a hostel place or a flat or bed-sit.[24]

---

[23] ibid, 7.
[24] Public Health England, *Evidence Review*, 29.

Such second-hand accounts of housing status based on police arrest records – where an arrested person knows that his answer will shape the police response to him – should not be taken at face value.

A third related area of knowledge that is mobilised in favour of gift-crime regulation – sometimes by police but more often by local officials and observers – is that begging produces a financial 'bonanza'. Certainly stories of rich beggars making off in their Jaguars to have supper at their posh homes seem to be reliable weekend tabloid fare. As Erskine and McIntosh remind us, there is nothing new about these 'fraud and riches' stories about beggars, ones that tap into centuries-old worries about disguise and authenticity that I discuss in chapter one.[25] Researchers have suggested that with increased attention today to those begging in western European cities, 'the wildest claims about the nature, motivations and income of beggars are made'.[26] Claims that people begging make extravagant amounts take on a more urgent meaning today when that cadged money is perceived to be directly connected to drug addiction. Yields from begging are notoriously difficult to document: people tend to beg for short periods of time to acquire a fixed amount for a purchase, those begging can share or pool their resources, and begging itself is detested by many beggars as a humiliating and hazardous activity.

The available data nevertheless suggests that begging yields generally meagre amounts, and would certainly not qualify as 'easy money'. The Homeless Unit in Charing Cross in 1997 found that 95 per cent of those arrested had less than £10, and most had around between £3 and £4. In Manchester in 1996 the Homeless unit found that the average amount recovered on arrest was £6.08, with most of the people arrested having less than £10.[27] The RSU Change a Life report, which is probably the most comprehensive research done on finances from begging, reported that 59 per cent were getting more than £20 a day, and 12 per cent more than £50 a day. Fitzpatrick and Kennedy found that amounts ranged from £1 to £40 a day, with higher amounts dependent on one-off drops of £5 or £10 bills from the public.[28] Generally speaking the evidence suggests that those begging make relatively low amounts as part of a survival strategy to address immediate needs.

II. Criminal Justice Outcomes

I have argued that gift-crime regulation was the central driver of the set of reforms initiated in 2003, changes that assembled 'persistent begging' as an offence tied to drug treatment though community orders. As David Blunkett stated in the 2003 white paper, this new offence would protect the public from 'aggressive behaviour'

[25] A Erskine and I McIntosh (1999) 28–29.

[26] Adriaenssens, S and Hendrickx, J (2011) 'Street-level Informant Economic Activities: Estimating the Yield of Begging in Brussels' *Urban Studies* 48(1) 23–40. 23.

[27] These figures from police arrest records are probably prone to be underestimates, given that those begging may be likely to hide or pass on money to others if there is a threat of police intervention (see page 95).

[28] Jowett et al. *Looking for Change*. 16. S Fitzpatrick and C Kennedy, 'The Links Between Begging, Rough Sleeping and *The Big Issue* in Glasgow and Edinburgh' (York, Joseph Rowntree Foundation, 2000) 23.

while providing mandatory drug treatment. Did the new trigger offence of persistent begging lead to drug treatment through community sentences? An examination of select criminal justice statistics, including court disposals, for begging and persistent begging from 2005 to 2015 can provide a preliminary answer.

Figure 16 Average number of prosecutions in each year for five year periods, for rough sleeping (s 4) and begging (s 3), Vagrancy Act 1824, at all courts, England and Wales, 1900–1969

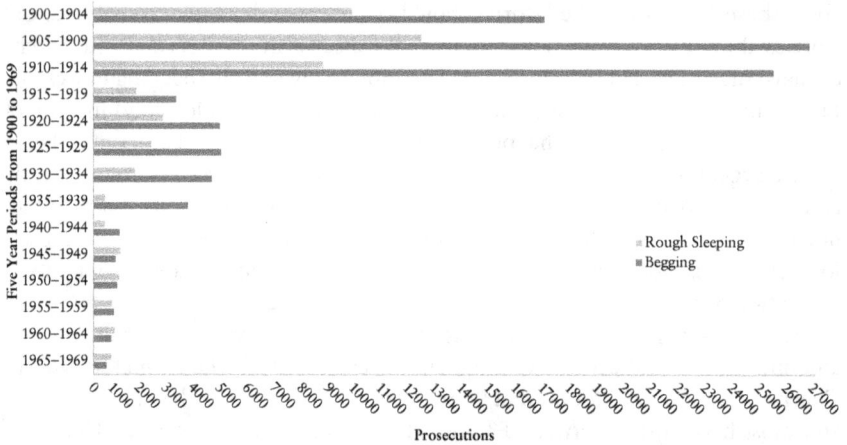

Source: Home Office 1972d Working Party on Vagrancy and Street Offences Memorandum on 'Sleeping Out' CRI 655/13/7 1972–1975 [Preserved Working Papers]. 2. Home Office 1972e Working Party on Vagrancy and Street Offences Memorandum on 'Begging' CRI 655/3/9/71 1971–1973 [Preserved Working Papers] 13.

First, though, it is useful to put this decade-long statistical picture in context, in terms of prosecution trends over the previous century for begging and rough sleeping and also for begging convictions from 1970 to 2015.

Figure 16 illustrates prosecutions, expressed in 5-year (mean) averages between 1900 and 1969, for both begging (section 3) and rough sleeping (section 4). I limit myself to three very general observations that touch upon points of my discussion. The first is to note the extraordinary level of enforcement in the pre-war years, when there were an average of 40,000 prosecutions *each year* for just begging and rough-sleeping offences under the 1824 Act. One sees here the formidable power and reach of the vagrancy law as part of a state project of policing undesirable and indigent characters.

Second, there is the question of the influence of the Vagrancy Act 1935. As I discussed in chapter four, the 1935 Act was a direct response to the death of ex-guardsman Thomas Parker, who died in an altercation in Winson Green prison in 1933. He had been serving a custodial sentence with hard labour for sleeping rough. The 1935 Act narrowed the rough-sleeping offence considerably, in that a conviction could be made only if the person had been directed by the police to a reasonably accessible (free) place of shelter and refused to take up that shelter. An internal memo of the preserved working papers of the 1976 Working Party on Vagrancy and Street Offences noted that 'there was a considerable drop in the number of prosecutions following the passing of the 1935 Act, and during the years of the Second World War, but a noticeable increase in prosecutions in the immediate post-war years.'[29]

Figure 17 Convictions for begging (s 3) 1970–2004, and begging (s 3) and persistent begging (s 4 and s 3) 2005–2015, Vagrancy Act 1824, at all Courts, England and Wales

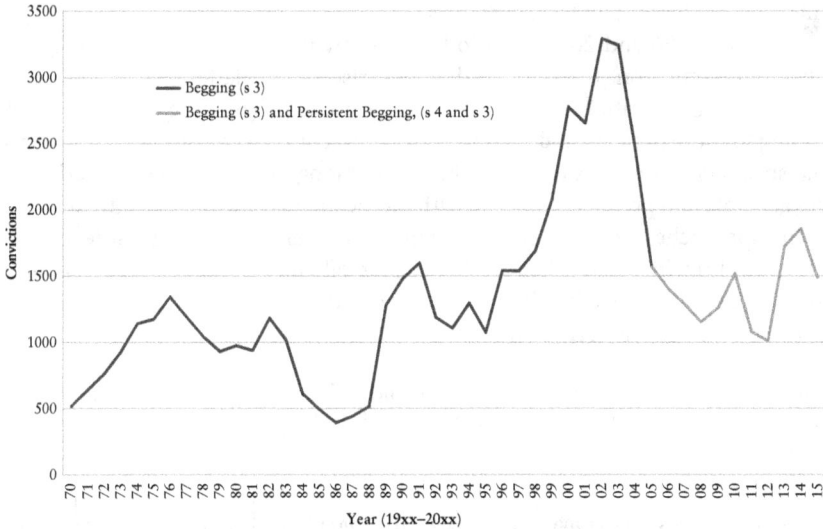

Source: Criminal Justice Statistics, England and Wales, 1970–1997, 1998–2004, Supplementary Tables. Ministry of Justice, Criminal Justice Statistics, England and Wales, 2005–2015.

It is difficult to discern, given the range of post-war changes and reforms (such as the National Assistance Act of 1948), when exactly the 1935 Act started to have teeth in terms of curtailing arrests and prosecutions for rough sleeping. This is particularly true given that the prosecution rates for begging followed a similar decline in the post-war years as that of rough sleeping – although they would spike upwards in the early 1970s. My guess is that it was not until the early 1970s that one saw a distinct decline that was directly linked to the more restrictive circumstances under which the rough-sleeping offence could be made out. From the mid 1970s, the rough-sleeping offence dwindled down to a trickle of convictions, and it was widely viewed to be unenforceable by the early 1980s.

Figure 17 portrays conviction rates for begging (1970–2004) and begging and persistent begging (2005–2015). Persistent begging is an unruly statistical figure. Criminal justice statistics released by the Ministry of Justice did not distinguish between the two begging offences when the persistent-begging offence was

---

[29] HMSO, *Working Party on Vagrancy and Street Offences Memorandum on 'Sleeping Out'.* 2.

available for enforcement in June 2004. I address this situation below. Before doing so, a number of modest and cautious observations can be made.

When the Working Party on Vagrancy and Street Offences began its deliberations in 1971, convictions for begging would almost treble to 1339 by the time they finished their work. Convictions would fall rapidly to the lowest point this century by the mid-eighties. The rapid increase between 1988 and 1990 was the impetus for the formation of EVA, a period when the Metropolitan Police carried out Operations Meyer and Taurus, which became the forerunners of the homeless units in Manchester and Charing Cross.

Between 1996 and 2003, a period which saw the rise of diverted giving and gift-crime regulation, there was a dramatic rise in convictions of 300 per cent. When academics criticised the RSU's Change a Life programme in 2000 as likely leading to more policing and Vagrancy Act prosecutions, Louise Casey responded that such a view was 'misleading and ... scare mongering'.[30] In fact their criticism was accurate and prescient: in 2000, with the 'death turn' introduced into diverted-giving approaches, convictions for begging had risen to their highest level since 1944. Starting in 2004, when both begging offences became trigger offences, convictions rapidly declined to settle at about the same levels that had alarmed EVA reformers in the early 1990s.

Table 2 Sentencing outcomes for offenders found guilty of both begging (s 3) and persistent begging (s 4 and s 3), Vagrancy Act 1824, at all courts, England and Wales, 2005–2015

Outcome	2005	2006	2007	2008	2009	2010	2011	2012	2013	2014	2015	Grand Total
Sentenced	1568	1405	1288	1151	1261	1518	1079	1010	1724	1857	1485	15,346
Absolute discharge	36	30	30	30	58	82	64	80	128	98	152	788 (5.1%)
Conditional discharge	361	317	341	305	335	432	294	252	443	436	369	3,885 (25.3%)
Fine	1,063	956	814	702	645	635	512	491	1,038	1,213	872	8,941 (58.3%)
Community sentence*	24	20	36	36	26	19	19	10	10	11	5	216 (1.4%)
Other**	84	82	67	78	197	350	190	177	105	99	87	1516 (9.9%)

Notes: Collected on a Principal Offence Basis. *Includes community orders (or predecessor), **Includes 'Otherwise Dealt With' offences. Source: Ministry of Justice, Criminal Justice Statistics, England and Wales, 2005–2015.

I now return to the question of the relationship between the persistent-begging offence and community sentences for drug treatment by examining

[30] Casey (2000) 2.

available data on conviction rates and court disposals. Table 2 illustrates the court disposals for begging and persistent begging for the period from 2005 to 2015. The sentences that involve community orders (as one of four types of community sentence) for drug treatment are minuscule: of the 15,346 people convicted of either begging offence, 1.4% were sentenced to drug treatment. Even without being able to differentiate the 'begging' and 'persistent begging' offences, one can come to the conclusion that being convicted of begging or persistent begging almost never results in a community order for drug treatment. Any claim that the reforms of 2003 have assisted 'persistent beggars' in getting badly needed drug treatment through community sentences is patently false. The most common form of sentence is the fine: on average 58 per cent of convictions resulted in a fine. The average fine in 2015 was £56, and between 2005 and 2015, the total fines given to people convicted of begging pocket change from the public amounted to £828,738.

In order to provide further clarity and detail to this conclusion, I was able to obtain limited datasets from the Ministry of Justice and the Crown Prosecution Service, where figures for the offence of persistent begging have been extracted from the total begging offences depicted in Table 2. The results are listed in Table 3.

Table 3 Sentencing outcomes for offenders found guilty of persistent begging (s 3) as a percentage of sentence outcomes for all begging offences (s 3), Vagrancy Act 1824, at all courts, England and Wales, 2011–2015

Outcome	2011	2012	2013	2014	2015
Sentenced	11% (121)	11% (113)	11% (186)	12% (220)	10.7% (160)
Absolute Discharge	9% (6)	29% (23)	32% (41)	32% (31)	34% (51)
Conditional Discharge	9.5% (32)	7% (18)	5% (22)	8% (35)	8% (28)
Fine	11% (57)	10.5% (59)	11% (112)	12% (140)	9% (75)
Community Sentence*	0.5% (1)	0% (0)	30% (3)	27% (3)	0% (0)
Other**	13% (25)	7% (13)	8% (8)	5% (11)	7% (6)

Notes: Collected on a Principal Offence Basis. *Includes community orders (or predecessor), **Includes 'Otherwise Dealt With' offences. Source: Justice Statistics Analytical Services, Ministry of Justice. 'Offenders found guilty and sentenced at all courts of offences of persistently begging in a public place (second or subsequent offence), England and Wales, 2011–2016'. FOI 180611017.

Of all convictions for begging between 2011 and 2015, only an average of 11 per cent for that period were for 'persistent begging', and the number of people sentenced with community orders was, again, practically non-existent. In addition, data on persistent-begging prosecutions for the period between 2005 and 2010 suggest that the likely rate of conviction for the first five years of the new offence did not vary much from 11 per cent.[31] This suggests that the offence was never very much used; even in the first few years it was introduced as a reform. In general terms, in the first 10 years that the new offence of persistent begging was enforced, it accounted for about 1 in 10 of overall begging convictions.

At first glance this seems surprising. Was it not a widespread assumption that almost all people begging were drug addicts who begged persistently? Would this not mean that the majority of begging charges would be laid for persistent begging? And further, would one not expect an increase in the use of the Act after the offence became operable in June 2004, not a decline? One can make the very general observation that the new offence was not used very often. Beyond this observation, on all of these questions, it is impossible to say what the answers are. As I indicated above, there are too many variables at play in relation to a relatively small number of offences to make any assertions beyond guesswork. However, there is one area that may shed some overall light on this peculiar offence: the nature of 'persistence'.

III. The Folly of 'Persistence'

The picture that has been assembled so far is that the new begging offence and accompanying reforms have almost no connection to securing mandatory drug treatment through community sentences. At this point the reader may, quite reasonably, ask: why exactly was the offence of persistent begging introduced at all? After all, the only difference between the two offences – they are both trigger offences and both have the same fine upon conviction – is that 'persistent begging' is begging that occurs after one has already been convicted of begging at least once. What purpose does the persistent-begging offence actually serve?

One possible answer lies in the observation that the notion of persistence has been intricately tied to an understanding of the 'true meaning' of the 1824 Act. Questions about the characteristics of 'persistence' in relation to the legitimacy of the Act are not new. In fact, as the Home Office has pointed out, persistence has been 'of concern, in various guises, for a century or more. In so far as the problem is identified with vagrancy, its history goes back to at least the 16th century'.[32] As I discuss in chapter five, the new offence of persistent begging needed no textual amendments to the Act; in fact the offence was already present in the sentencing grades. Anyone convicted once of begging is marked with the status of 'idle and disorderly person'. Anyone thus convicted again was marked as a 'rogue and vagabond'. The offence of persistent begging occurs when someone is begging after one conviction. The offence is by definition a status offence: it can occur only after one is deemed 'idle and disorderly'.

---

[31] Figures released to me by the Crown Prosecution Service for first attendance at a magistrates' court for the offence of 'persistent begging' from the period between 2005/06 and 2015/2016 suggest that the percentage of persistent-begging convictions from 2005 to 2010 would not deviate greatly from the yearly average of 11% from 2010 to 2015. Crown Prosecution Service, FOI, 7699.
[32] S Fairhead, *Persistent Petty Offenders*, iii.

Persistence, then, is intricately tied to the archaic purpose of the Act, that of policing status offences. I spend the last few pages of this concluding chapter by reviewing the notion of persistence, and in doing so, make clearer how the offence remains archaic in targeting specific kinds of people. I will start by noting that there are three distinct notions of persistence that are present in debates about reforming the vagrancy law, and they often overlap in confusing and unintended ways.

First is the notion of persistence that is measured solely in terms of the convictions. In this sense, a 'persistent begger' is a reoffender as measured by convictions. Suzan Fairhead pointed out the problems associated with this, most notably that the sheer visibility of homeless people makes them exposed to apprehension.

The second notion of persistence is broader than simply a concern with convictions, and has to do with the frequency with which the begging behaviour is carried out. For example, a person begging would offend if he was doing it at the same time every day in a particular spot. The frequency of his begging is the offence, not the character of the begging itself.

The third meaning has to do with the actual character or nature of the begging conduct itself. For example, a persistent beggar in terms of conduct would behave in an vexatious, importunate or obnoxious way. A typical example would be to follow someone down the street, calling out after a person for a donation. Conduct-based persistence is the sort of behaviour that can come close to other criminal offences that cause alarm or distress.

These three meanings of *persistence* (of conviction, frequency, or conduct) enable an analysis that not only demonstrates how redundant the new offence is but reveals how closely aligned it is to the archaic and discriminatory character of the 1824 Act. I have documented how the persistent-begging offence has in fact no relationship to drug treatment through community orders. A second rationale for the offence, as announced by Home Secretary David Blunkett in the 2003 white paper, is that it would protect people from 'aggressive behaviour'. The connection, however, is tenuous at best. The current persistent begging offence does not target the character or frequency of the begging conduct; it relies on a conviction notion of persistence. To encompass 'aggressive begging', the new offence would require an ingredient of conduct persistence.

So, for example, men sitting peacefully and begging – as in the Change a Life (Figure 14) or OxPAT (Figure 12) campaign poster – would be viewed as persistent beggars under the new offence if they had one or more convictions for begging. On the other hand, someone who is obnoxious and physically importunate would not be viewed as being a persistent beggar until they, like the peaceful beggars, already had a conviction.

The confusion over the three meanings of *persistence* I have outlined – which express a tension about what sort of behaviour begging is and if it should be criminalised at all – is visible in the two last major inquiries into the Act. A central theme of these inquiries was how the notion of persistence is linked to interpretations of the 'true meaning' of the 1824 Act. The 1976 Working Party on Vagrancy and Street Offences recommended that the current section 3 offence should be repealed and replaced by a new offence of 'begging whose essential element would be persistence'.[33] The report noted that the true purpose of the 1824 Act was to concern itself with begging being a 'mode of life' that was taken up, epitomised by the figure of a 'professional beggar'.[34] While conceding that begging 'is now a symptom of social inadequacy and social deprivation and often those who beg require rehabilitation',[35] the working party nevertheless took the view 'that the test of persistence is the most effective way to control behaviour which is a nuisance in streets and public places'.[36] This, according to the working party, enabled the 'desirable' approach that differentiated the 'professional beggar' from 'the kind of person who begged only in an emergency'.[37] In other words, the reform recommended by the working party, that of a frequency notion of persistence, is one that is congruent with policing a *type of person*, more specifically someone who 'does not work and has adopted the calling of a beggar'.

Like the 1976 report, the third report of the 1980/81 Home Affairs Committee argued that it was necessary to keep begging a criminal offence as a deterrent 'in keeping down the problem of begging to manageable levels'.[38] However, the committee declined to endorse the replacement offence of 'persistent begging' that the 1976 report had proposed, nor did it suggest alternative wordings for the offence. 'We do not believe,' the final report stated,

> that a qualification such as 'persistent' begging, which might in turn cause fresh diffi-
> culties of interpretation, would make much difference to the established practice of the
> police in deciding when to prosecute under the Act. In our opinion the only rational
> choice lies between abolishing these offences altogether and retaining them in essen-
> tially their present form.[39]

Unlike the Home Office and its 2003 reforms, the 1981 Home Affairs Committee seemed cognisant that trying to attach a persistence ingredient to the begging offence of begging would be highly problematic. Their position was an either/or one – either retain the original status offence of begging in section 3 or abolish it altogether. The evidence of a witness from the Campaign for the Homeless and Rootless (CHAR) to the 1981 Home Affairs Committee touched exactly upon this ambiguity and confusion of the frequency notion of persistence that the 1976 report recommended:

> [P]ersistent begging gives rise to tremendous legal problems because what is going to be
> 'persistent begging'? We are going to be faced with the same kinds of judicial decision
> on that as we faced with as to a suspected person. What makes a person a 'persistent

---

[33] HMSO Report of the Working Party on Vagrancy and Street Offences (1976) (London, HMSO) 4.
[34] ibid, 49.
[35] HMSO Working Party on Vagrancy (1974), 'A Working Party on Vagrancy and Street Offences working paper', (London, HMSO) 22.
[36] HMSO, 'Report of the Working Party', 5.
[37] HMSO, 'Working Party on Vagrancy', 22.
[38] HMSO (1981), *Third Report from the Home Affairs Committee, Session 1980–81: Vagrancy Offences*, ix.
[39] ibid.

beggar'? Is it someone who begs once every day, is it someone who begs ten times in a row one day and so forth? What we suggest is that when begging takes on an unsavoury feature it can be dealt with by the criminal law quite satisfactorily.[40]

It is significant, in arguing against the ingredient of persistence (and for the repeal of section 3), that the witness evoked the 'suspected person' or 'sus' offence in the Act, perhaps the most capricious and arbitrary Vagrancy Act power of the twentieth century, which was, in particular, linked to the racist policing of young black males.

The notion of persistence was raised again a year later, in the significant case of *R v Dalton*. As I discussed in chapter four, *Dalton* involved a gainfully employed electrician who, on his way to catch a train for which he already had a ticket, had begged something from the driver of a passing car. Drawing on *Pointon v Hill* and *Mathers v Penhold*, the court agreed with the defence that there was no case to answer because the defendant, who was employed, had 'not adopted the calling of a beggar', and that the defendant's action was not 'a habit or mode of life'.[41] The defendant in *Dalton* was viewed by the court as being the equivalent of what the 1976 report described as a case of one-time 'emergency begging' that did not fall within the true meaning of the 1824 Act. The case was significant in that it placed an evidential burden on the police: to make out the offence of begging, the evidence must show that the begging was carried out 'on more than one occasion'.

The *Dalton* case, like the 1976 report, relied on a frequency notion of persistence to confirm that the begging offence was about targeting a type of person: a person who will not work, who has taken on the 'calling' of a beggar, whose begging is a 'mode of life', a person who when convicted will be an 'idle and disorderly' person. The current offence of persistent begging, relying on a conviction notion of persistence, is an even more explicit expression that begging is not about conduct but about the character of the person. As a product of the gift-crime movement, the 'persistent beggar' is now tied to further moral offences: as a drug addict, a fraud pretending to be homeless, an extortioner of public feeling.

The inherently unjust nature of this crime of character remains the central argument for repeal of the begging offences. The capricious character of the begging offence was in particular a central argument of EVA in their repeal efforts. Lord Stallard spoke directly to this on the second reading (Lords) of the EVA-backed Crime of Vagrancy (Abolition) Bill 1990:

> In my opinion Section 3 and Section 4 of the 1824 Act should now be repealed for all the reasons I have just outlined and because the prosecution of a mode of life is entirely out of context in the 1990's. We have moved on. The mischief that legislation aims to correct should not be a person's way of life but the effect that a person's behaviour has on others.[42]

---

[40] S Fairhead, *Persistent Petty Offenders* (London, Home Office, 1981) 14–15.
[41] As established by *Pointon v Hill* 12 QB 306 (1884) and *Mathers v Penhold* 1 KB 513 (1914).
[42] *Hansard*, HL vol 357, cols 465–493, Crime of Vagrancy (Abolition) Bill (11 December 1990).

Have we moved on? Thirty years later, reforms to the vagrancy law against people begging have intensified policing, provided police with increased surveillance, made their criminal status more visible, and drawn them further into a punitive justice system. Driven by appeals to compassion and the right way to give to the poor, our present circumstances are disquieting, a reminder of how the centuries-old figure of the beggar continues to haunt the most basic questions about how we collectively care for one another.

IV. Closing Observations

When I first encountered the diverted-giving scheme in Winchester in 1995, I thought it was conceptually interesting and novel, an eruption of regulatory energy that would soon fade as a quirky provincial project. The idea that the Winchester experiment might evolve into a national movement that provided the conditions for a historic reform of vagrancy law would have seemed fantastic. After 20 years of watching these programmes, I remain struck by how strange they are in their simultaneously mundane and profound character. There is, after all, nothing more commonplace in everyday life than to participate in the giving and taking of gifts of all kinds. At the same time, gift-crime regulation dramatises a centuries-old story about what to do with the poor and raises uncomfortable questions about how one can be a 'good person' when confronted with a fellow human being who is suffering.

Gift-crime regulation resists any easy categorisation in terms of conforming to a theory of the gift. It seems more important, in any case, to understand how this mode of regulation has mobilised various ideals of gift giving *as a resource of regulation*. For example, early diverted-giving schemes clearly evoked a classic idea of exchange and reciprocity ('make every penny count') in terms of the appearance of getting 'something for something' for diverted money. However, the much later schemes, while not abandoning the pretence of reciprocity, were primarily focused on questions of authenticity – of divining the difference between real and fake homelessness. Gift-crime regulation presented the beggar as a counterfeit coin, a fake to be inspected for signs of legitimacy. As the money-man icon warns, to give to a beggar is to contribute to the circumstances of his death.

The question of authenticity, then, looms large at the end of this work. One of the most regrettable consequences of diverted giving is the semiotic confusion that it produces, one that calls into question the authenticity of any visible poverty. When Nottingham officials were asked why they used the poster image of sleeping bags, when their ads were about begging, the city replied that those begging often disguised themselves as rough-sleepers. This of course suggests that there are no 'real' or legitimate rough-sleepers, only those who fake homelessness in the hope of public sympathy and coin. While worries about disguise and theatricality have historically been a central aspect of vagrancy, one has to wonder if a distinct and overtly punitive mode of seeing the poor has emerged. This is not an abstract question: today the vagrancy crime of begging has been fortified as a status offence to target types of people who are *seen* to be disorderly.

In this book I have tried to understand the mechanics and consequences of gift-crime regulation. In doing so, another theme has been carried along, one that is less tangible but perhaps more important: how is it that the expression of one of the most beautiful acts of being human, of trying to relieve the suffering of a stranger, has been turned into a source of control and punishment?

What I have documented cannot be described as an overtly coherent or organized form of social control. Officials are usually ambivalent and ambiguous about what the purpose of diverted giving is, for example, beyond general claims about who is deserving of donations and who is deserving of police action. Officials are far more likely to contend with public apathy and lack of interest. It is more fitting to describe diverted-giving schemes as channels through which various types of regulatory resources and techniques can be accessed by actors and alliances at politically expedient times. Certainly the mechanics of gift giving provide a rich and detailed reserve of tropes and themes that can enforce a particular 'truth' about begging. That giving to someone begging is often viewed as open-ended and unpredictable – a 'stranger to the law' – only seems to make it a more coveted and attractive target of regulation.

My last point is that it would be a grave error to dismiss compassion and kindness as cheap and insincere sentimentality. I think one can, in the end, take some consolation in recognising that appeals to compassion do remain a central category of how poor and vulnerable people are treated. Public feeling, 'the humanity of the population', remains as much a force today, however unstable, as it was when it was stirred into action by the death of ex-guardsman Thomas Parker. The result in 1935 was a new law that still protects many rough-sleepers from arrest and prosecution. To what extent such reform is still possible today remains an open and even hopeful question.

REFERENCES

Primary Sources

Aberdeen City Council (2004) 'Street Begging Report', Report of the Community Services Committee, 14 September.

ASA (Advertising Standards Authority) (2004) Non-broadcast adjudication, Bristol City Council, 25 February.

—— (2006) Non-broadcast adjudication, Nottingham City Council t/a/Respect for Nottingham, 23 March.

ATCM (1997) *Year Book*, Macmillan.

Bath (1996a) Minutes of meeting, City Environmental Improvement Team, 3 September.

—— (1996b) 'Making It Count', update paper, City Environmental Improvement Team, 27 September.

—— (1996c) Minutes of meeting, City Environmental Improvement Team, 8 October.

—— (1996d) Minutes of meeting, City Environmental Improvement Team, 2 December.

—— (1998) 'Bath Busker's Badge Scheme: The Code of Practice', City of Bath and North East Somerset.

Big Issue Scotland (1997) Letter from Mel Young, director, *The Big Issue Scotland*, to Keith Geddes, Labour Group Leader, Edinburgh City Council, 30 July.

Blackpool (1995) 'Street Entertainment in Blackpool: A Code of Practice', Blackpool Town Centre Forum.

Brighton (1997) 'Busking in Brighton', Brighton Borough Council.

Bristol (2005) 'Bristol Crime and Drugs Strategy 2005–08' (Safer Bristol Partnership).

British Transport Police (1996a) Minutes of 'Meeting to Consider Children Begging on the Underground', at Westminster Social Services, 24 Greencoat Place, Victoria SW1.

—— (1996b) 'Travellers Survey: Children Being Used for Begging', Minutes of meeting at 55 The Broadway, London SW1, 2 September.

—— (1996c) 'Beggars Survey', 12 September.

—— (1996d) London Underground 'Pickpocket Target Profile'.

—— (1996e) 'Women/Girls Seen Begging on the Underground, 3rd, 6th and 12th September, 1996'.

—— (1996f) 'Children Begging on the Underground', Minutes of meeting held at 55 The Broadway, St James' Park Tube Station, London SW1, 5 December.

—— (1997) Internal memorandum, 27 June.

—— (1998a) Operation Report, 19 January.

—— (1998b) Operation Report, 12 March.

Cambridge (1997) 'Winchester Begging Scheme: Notes of Visit on 28th January 1997' [by assistant city centre manager].

Camden 'Killing with Kindness campaign continues' Press release Ref. 04/364.

Casey, L (2000a) Letter to S Fitzpatrick, 30 October.

Casey, L (2000b) 'Brother, Spare the Dime' *The Guardian* 10 October, 20.

Crisis, Response to *Living Places: Powers, Rights and Responsibilities*, consultation by the Department of the Environment, Food and Rural Affairs, 2002.

Edinburgh (1996) Motion by Conservative group to Policy and Resources Committee on proposed local by-law, Beggars in Edinburgh.

—— (1997a) Letter from Edward Bain, Council Solicitor, to Secretary, Scottish Office, Criminal Justice Division, 19 August.

—— (1997b) Letter from Edward Bain, Council Solicitor, to M Baxter, Home Department, Scottish Office, 15 December 1997.

—— (1997a) Economic Development Committee, Urban Regeneration Sub-committee (/C), item 13, 'Social Exclusion'.

—— (1997b) Economic Development Committee, Urban Regeneration Sub-committee (/D), Motion on 'Social Exclusion', item 8.7.

—— (1998a) 'Managing Edinburgh's City Centre', Strategic Policy 0092/SP/IF (1998).

—— (1998b) 'Begging and Homelessness', Appendix 6 to Strategic Policy 0092/SP/IF (1998).

—— (1998c) 'City Centre Inter-agency Stage 1', item 7.6, minutes of full City Council meeting, 28 May 1998.

—— (1998d) 'Proposed Bye-Law: Legal Issues', prepared by director of corporate services, 5EB03540, 21 May 1998.

—— (1998e) 'Crime and Incident Trends', app. 5 to strategic policy, 0092/SP/IF (1998).

Erewash (1997) 'Street Entertainers Code of Practice', Erewash Borough Council.

End the Vagrancy Act Campaign (EVA) Papers

EVA 1. Letter from Home Secretary David Waddington to Matthias Kelly and Mark Grindrod, 21 March 1990.

EVA 2. Letter from Home Office Minister of State John Patten to Michael Portillo, MP, on behalf of constituent Mrs Jepson, CL/91/12/36/1, 21 January 1991.

EVA 3. Letter from M de Pulford, C4 Division, Home Office, to Matthias Kelly and Mark Grindrod, m544, 20 November 1990.

EVA 4. Letter from Home Secretary David Waddington to Harry Fletcher, Assistant General, National Association of Probation Officers, 6 March 1990.

EVA 5. Letter from Home Office Minister of State John Patten to Llin Golding, MP, CRI/90 655/7/4, 1990.

EVA 6. Letter from Home Office Minister of State Robin Ferrers to Lord Jock Stallard, 20 December 1990.

EVA 7. Letter from Ruth Duckworth, Social and Pastoral Action, Westminster Diocese, to Matthias Kelly and Mark Grindrod, subject: 'End the Vagrancy Act: London Churches' Meeting with Police Commissioner 26/11/90', 5 November 1990.

EVA 8. Letter from Home Office Minister of State Robin Ferrers to Lord Alexander of Weedon, QC, 20 May 1991.

EVA 9. Letter from Richard Monk, Commander, Territorial Operations Department, Community Involvement and Crime, New Scotland Yard, to Walter Easey, Association of London Authorities, 12 February 1990.

EVA 10. Letter from Mark Grindrod and Matthias Kelly, EVA, to M de Pulford, Home Office, 28 November 1990.

EVA 11. Letter from Harry Fletcher, Assistant General Secretary, National Association of Probation Officers, to David Faulkner, Deputy Under-Secretary of State, Home Office, 13 March 1990.

EVA 12. CHAR (Housing Campaign for Single People) briefing paper.

EVA 13. Minutes of meeting of Working Party on Young Homeless Persons, Westminster City Hall, Central Westminster Police/Community Consultative Group, 28 February 1991.

EVA 14. Briefing paper No 5.

EVA 15. Letter from Adam Woolf, Information Assistant, CRISIS, to Lord Alexander of Weedon, 3 June 1991.

EVA 16. Minutes of meeting, 16 January 1990.

EVA 17. Letter from Baroness Hooper, Parliamentary Under-Secretary of State for Health (Lords), Department of Health, to Lord Carter, KH/6278p, 6 June 1990.

EVA 18. Minutes of meeting, 24 October 1989.

EVA 19. Minutes of meeting, 19 September 1989.

EVA 20. Letter from Lorna Reith, CHAR [on EVA letterhead], to Mr I McGregor, ACC Operations, British Transport Police, 7 August 1990.

EVA 21. Letter from Graham W Smith, Chief Probation Officer, Inner London Probation Service, to Matthias Kelly, 6 February 1990.

EVA 22. Letter from John Newbiggin, Office of the Leader of the Opposition [Neil Kinnock], to Lorna Reith, CHAR, 10 January 1991.

EVA 23. Letter from Peter Campbell, Housing Desk Officer, Conservative Research Department, to Matthias Kelly, 15 November 1990.

EVA 24. Letter to the editor, *The Independent*, from Ian Sparks, Director, Children's Society, 26 October.

EVA 25. 'Further Briefing' [9 pages].

EVA 26. 'Schedule of Alternatives' [3 pages].

Gloucester (1998) 'Approved Street Entertainers' Scheme'. City Environmental Services.

Greater Manchester Police (1998) 'Vagrancy Act 1824: General Powers of Arrest; Apprehended; Preserved', D2858 [in-house legal advice on arrest powers].

Halton (1997) 'Code of Practice for Street Entertainers', Environmental Health Services.

Hampshire Constabulary (1995) 'Useful Police Powers and By-Laws for Dealing with Offences in Winchester City Centre'.

Home Office (1972a) Memorandum from E1 Division to Secretary of the Working Party, 'Working Party on Vagrancy and Street Offences: Street Collections', CRI 655/3/9(71), 10 March.

—— (1972b) Memorandum from E1 Division to Secretary of the Working Party, 'Working Party on Vagrancy and Street Offences: Street Begging', CRI 655/3/9(71), 31 August.

—— (1972c) 'Working Party on Vagrancy and Street Offences: Charitable Collections. Note by E1 Division, Home Office', CRI 655/3/9(71), 10 March.

—— (1972d) Working Party on Vagrancy and Street Offences Memorandum on 'Sleeping Out' CRI 655/3/13/7 1972–1975 [Preserved Working Papers].

—— (1972e) Working Party on Vagrancy and Street Offences Memorandum on 'Begging' CRI 655/3/9/71 1971–1973 [Preserved Working Papers].

—— (1973) 'Alternative Paragraphs for Inclusion in Draft Consultative Document on the Vagrancy Acts: Charitable Collections', CRI 655/3/49 (71).

Horsham (1997) *Horsham Town Centre Activities*.

London (2013) 'Evaluation of the Anti-Begging Campaign April May/2013', app A of 'Rough Sleepers Quarterly Update', Community and Children's Services.

Lothian and Borders (1998) Letter from Robert F Lees, Regional Procurator Fiscal, to Edward Bain, Council Solicitor, Edinburgh City Council, RFL/DMLM/RPFF/18, 12 March.

Mendicity Society (1888) 'Specimens of Constables' Cases' in *Annual Report for the Year 1888*, John Johnson Collection, Bodleian Library.

—— (1889a) 'The Mendicity Society' *Charity* (June), John Johnson Collection, Bodleian Library.

—— (1889b) 'Seven Reasons for Supporting the Above Society', 3 June, John Johnson Collection, Bodleian Library.

Metropolitan Police Service [London] (1997) 'Homelessness: The Charing Cross Homeless Unit', by Sergeant, Charing Cross Homeless Unit, 6 June.

—— (1998a) 'Power of Arrest for Begging', in-house memorandum.

—— (1998b) 'What Is the Charing Cross Police Homeless Unit and What Services Can We Provide to the Homeless', by Sergeant, Charing Cross Homeless Unit.

—— (1998c) 'Power of Arrest', in-house memorandum.

New Philanthropy Capital (January 2008) 'Thames Reach, Analyst: Eleanor Stringer' (London).

Peterborough (1998) 'Busking in Peterborough: A Code of Conduct', Environmental Services Department.

Scotland (2009) Letter to City of Aberdeen from Fraser, Criminal Justice Directorate, Criminal Law and Licensing Division, January.

Scottish Executive (2006), Letter from Anna Cossar, Policy Advisor, Justice Department, Criminal Law Division, to Councillor Martin Grieg, Safer Aberdeen Task Group, 10 January.

Scottish Office (1996a) Letter from Minister of State James Douglas-Hamilton to Councillor JL Walls, City of Edinburgh, RB24086, 29 August.

—— (1996b) Letter from Rt Hon Michael Forsyth, Minister of State, to Councillor JL Walls, City of Edinburgh, 29 August.

—— (1997a) Letter from M Baxter, Home Department, to Edward Bain, Council Solicitor, Edinburgh City Council, HPK00102.028, 4 February 1997.

—— (1997b) Letter from M Baxter, Home Department, to Edward Bain, Council Solicitor, Edinburgh City Council, HPK0021097, 29 September.

Solihull (1998) 'Buskers Code of Practice'.

Staffordshire Police (Nigel Manning) (2000) 'Make-It-Count Scheme: Partnership Response to Begging in Stoke-on-Trent City Centre' *Problem Solving Quarterly: Newsletter of the Police Executive Research Forum* Vol 13, No 3.

Stoke-on-Trent (1999) 'Make it Count Project Summary/Revised Action Plan/Additional Background Briefing Notes' (Stoke-on-Trent City Centre Management).

Streetwork (Edinburgh) (1997) Letter from Tam Hendry, Co-ordinator, to Keith Geddes, Group Leader, Labour Group, City of Edinburgh Council, 31 July.

Taunton Deane (1997) 'Taunton Street Entertainers Code of Practice'.

Trinity Day Centre [Winchester] (1996a) Letter to petition organiser from Chief Executive, Winchester, 'Collecting Boxes: City Centre Begging', 19 March.

—— (1996b) Letter to Trinity Centre team leader from Estates Officer, 'Diverted Giving Campaign: Winchester City Centre', 20 March.

—— (1997) *Trinity Day Centre Annual Report, 1996–1997.*

—— (1998) Bank statements, Winchester City Centre Collection account, 10 February 1997 to 9 January 1998.

United Kingdom [UK] (1815) Parliamentary Papers Vol 5, *Report from the Select Committee on the State of Mendicity in the Metropolis.*

—— (1816) Parliamentary Papers Vol 5, *Select Committee on Mendicity in the Metropolis: Final Report.*

—— (1821) Parliamentary Papers Vol 4, *Report from the Select Committee on the Existing Laws Relating to Vagrants.*

Vision 21 (2000) *Time for Change: A Study of Street Drinking and Begging in Camden and Islington* (London, Vision 21).

Walls, L (1996), Letter to Rt Hon Michael Forsyth, Minister of State, Scottish Office, 24 July.

Westminster (2004) 'An integrated approach to reduce begging in Westminster', 25 November.

—— (2004) 'Your kindness could kill: Campaign Evaluation Report'.

—— (1996) Letter to police constable, British Transport Police, from Child Protection Co-ordinator, Westminster Social Services, with reference to 'Children Begging on the Underground', 6 November.

West Sussex (1997) 'Activities in Precinct'.

—— (1998) 'This Is Not a Permit' [letter of no objection].

Winchester (1996a) 'City Centre Begging' [flyer], Estates Office.

—— (1996b) 'City Centre Begging' [poster], Estates Office.

—— (1996c) Invoice from Tuskguard Ltd to Estates Officer and Marks and Spencer Security Manager, 'To design, supply and fit: 15 No Cylindrical Charity Boxes', invoice No 3413, 1 October.

—— (1996d) 'Winchester Buskers Code', Winchester City Council and Hampshire Constabulary, C\U\Az\Cbusk.cdr.08.96.

—— (1996e) Minutes of meeting of Diverted Giving Scheme Project [relaunch committee], May [nd], 22 May and 23 June, with attachments: 3 technical drawings of begging boxes and brackets with Tuskguard watermark; Diverted Giving Project Group membership list, May; 'Making it Count', Winchester Diverted Giving press release for relaunch, 25 July.

—— (1996f) 'Home Office Challenge 1996 CCTV Bid by Winchester City Council', City Engineer.

—— (1997a) 'Operation Diverted Giving: Aim', Estates Office.

—— (1997b) 'Operation Diverted Giving', Estates Office.

—— (1997c) Completed 'Make It Count' forms from several merchants, Estates Office.

—— (1998) Minutes of Winchester District Crime Prevention Group, 6 February 1995 to 2 February 1998.

Winchester Churches Nightshelter (1996b) Letter from principal of a private school to Manager, 20 August.

Winchester City Engineer, 'Home Office Challenge 1996 CCTV Bid', Winchester, 1996.

Young, M (1997), Letter to Keith Geddes, Labour Group Leader, Edinburgh City Council, 30 July.

Interviews and Personal Communications

Angal Limited. Letter from director, Angal Service to Fundraisers, with 'Angal: Make Ideas Work for Fundraisers' [package with marketing materials], 11 August 1998.

BAA [British Airports Authority]. Letter from public relations officer, BAA Heathrow, with 'Charity Boxes at Heathrow' [fact sheet], 20 February 1998.

Bath. Interviews with assistant city-centre manager, October 1998 and April 1999.

Big Issue. Interview with manager, *Big Issue in the North*, Manchester, December 1997.

Boots Company PLC. Interview with manager, Boots Drug Store, Winchester, June 1997.

British Red Cross. Letter from Regional Fundraising, with 'Collection Pack' containing 'Helpful Hints for Collectors', 5 March 1998.

British Transport Police, London Underground Area. Interviews with police constable, February and April 1998.

—— Letter from police inspector, Criminal Justice Unit, 27 May 1999.

Bromley. Letter from section leader, Environmental Services, with attachments concerning 'street entertainment', 19 November 1997.

Cambridge. Interview with assistant city-centre manager, October 1998.

Carlisle. Letter from chief executive, City of Carlisle, 11 February 1997.

Edinburgh. Letter from Susan Hart, assistant to Councillor Keith Geddes, Labour Group, 29 May 1998.

EVA [End the Vagrancy Act]. Interview with Matthias Kelly, co-founder, September 1998.

Greater Manchester Police. Interview with two police constables, Homeless Unit, August 1998.

Hampshire Constabulary [Winchester]. Interviews with police inspector, November 1996 and July 1997.

Lewisham. Letter from principal licensing officer, Lewisham Environmental Health, 1 September 1998.

London. Letter from chief trading standards officer, with sample letter to applicants (C17/2); 'Guidance Notes for Street Collections Police, Factories & (Miscellaneous Provisions) Act 1916 s.5.'; 'Specimen Collectors Authority'; list of fundraising activities and sources; and opinion 'Re: Sale of "Big Issue" Magazine', 6 November 1997.

London Underground Limited. Interviews with personal security manager, January 1998 and April 1999.

Marks & Spencer. Interview with manager, Winchester store, June 1997.

McDonald's Corporation. Interview with owner/operator of McDonald's restaurant, Winchester, June 1997.

Metropolitan Police Service [London]. Letter from secretary, Street Collections Advisory Committee, with sample letter to applicants and 'Street Collections Within the Metropolitan Police District', GN82/97/MISC4/42, 21 November 1997.

—— Interview with sergeant, Charing Cross Homeless Unit, August 1998.

MSS (Multiple Sclerosis Society). Letter from marketing assistant with various ephemera; excerpt from *teaMSpirit* (January 1997, 10); Branch Fundraising Guidelines No 4, 'House to House Collections'; Branch Fundraising Guidelines No 3, 'Static Collection Boxes' (December 1996); and Branch Fundraising Guidelines, No 1, 'Flag Day Collections', 4 February 1998.

NSPCC (National Society for the Prevention of Cruelty to Children). Letter from administrator, Regional Appeals, with volunteer handbook, ch 2, 'Fundraising: House to House Collections' and 'Flag Days: Street Collections', 20 February 1998.

National Trust. Letter from Supporter Fundraising co-ordinator, 5 February 1998.

Oxfam. Letter from Supporters' Information team officer, with *The Oxfam Annual Review, 1996–97*, 16 January 1998.

Oxford University. Interview with Ted Roberts, university marshal, August 1998.

—— Email from university marshal, 29 April 1999.

Portsmouth. Letter from corporate projects manager, with attachments on 'Street Entertainment Permit', 28 August 1997.

Restormel. Letter from chief executive, Borough of Restormel, 14 February 1997.

Royal British Legion. Letter from head of Poppy Appeals, 322/1/A.1/R.B, 22 January 1998.

RNIB (Royal National Institute for the Blind). Letter from fundraising development officer, with 'Royal National Institute for the Blind Information Sheet' (October 1997), 16 January 1998.

RNLI (Royal National Lifeboat Institution). Letter from regional manager with minutes of RNLI City of London Branch annual general meeting (28 May 1997), 2 February 1998.

Royal Society for the Prevention of Cruelty to Animals. Letter from Enquiries Service, with collection boxes fact sheets and *Inside News* 27 (Winter 1997), 21 January 1997.

Sainsbury's. Interview with manager, Sainsbury's store, Winchester, July 1997.

SCOPE. Letter from marketing researcher with 'Introducing Fund-Raiser Services' handout, 5 February 1998.

WH Smith PLC. Interview with manager, WH Smith store, Winchester, June 1997.

Southampton. Letter from head of Legal Services, 11 November 1997.

South Ribble. Letter from chief executive, South Ribble Borough Council, 17 February 1997.

Taunton. Interview with Taunton City Centre manager, October 1998.

Trinity Day Centre [Winchester]. Interviews with team leader June 1997, July 1997 and January 1998.

Tuskguard Limited. Letter from managing director with reference 'Donation Boxes', enclosing marketing materials including 'Premises Protection' graphic, 13 August 1998.

Walls, JL, Letter from Councillor JL Walls, City of Edinburgh, 7 November 1997.

Winchester. Interview with deputy mayor, June 1997.

—— Interviews with estates officer, June and August 1997.

—— Interview with trading officer, June 1997.

—— Interview with tourism director, June 1997.

—— Interview with environmental health officer, July 1997.

—— Interview with licensing officer, July 1997.

—— Interview with manager, Tourism Services, July 1997.

—— Interview with manager, Victoria House, January 1998.

Winchester Cathedral. Interview with receiver general, July 1997.

Winchester Chamber of Commerce. Interview with vice-president and chair, June 1997.

Winchester Churches Nightshelter. Interviews with manager, July 1997 and January 1998.

Yeovil. Letter from town clerk, enclosing 'Helping Hands Scheme', 28 January 1998.

Secondary Sources

Acton, T (1994) 'Modernisation, Moral Panics and the Gypsies', *Sociology Review* 4.

Adler, M, Bromley, C and Rosie, M (2000) 'Begging as a Challenge to the Welfare State' in R Jowell et al (eds), *British Social Attitudes Survey: The Seventeenth Report* (London, Sage) 209–37.

Adriaenssens, S and Hendrickx, J (2011) 'Street-level Informal Economic Activities: Estimating the Yield of Begging in Brussels' *Urban Studies* 48(1), 23–40.

Angal Limited (1993) 'The Legal Requirements and Commonsense Practice Relating to the Use of Collecting Boxes Generally', *Angal Service to Fundraisers* (December).

Archard, P (1979) *Vagrancy, Alcoholism and Social Control* (London, Macmillan).

Ashworth, A, Gardner, J, Morgan, R, Smith, ATH, von Hirsch, A and Wasis, M (1998) 'Neighbouring on the Oppressive: The Government's "Anti-Social Behaviour Order" Proposals' *Criminal Justice* 16, 7–14.

Aydelotte, F (1913; 1976) *Elizabethan Rogues and Vagabonds* (New York, Barnes and Noble).

Barry, JV (1958) *Alexander Maconochie of Norfolk Island* (Melbourne, Oxford University Press).

Bassler, J (1991) *God and Mammon: Asking for Money in the New Testament* (Nashville, Abington Press).

Beck, U (1992) *Risk Society: Towards a New Modernity* (London, Sage).

Becker, HS (1998) *Tricks of the Trade: How to Think about Your Research While You're Doing It* (Chicago, University of Chicago Press).

Beech, P (1983) 'Charlotte Guillard: A Sixteenth-Century Business Woman' *Renaissance Quarterly* 36, 345–67.

Beier, AL (1983) *The Problem of the Poor in Tudor and Early Stuart England, 1500–1650* (London, Methuen).

—— (1985) *Masterless Men: The Vagrancy Problem in England, 1560–1640* (London, Methuen).

Berking, H (1999) *Sociology of Giving* (London, Sage).

Bernasconi, R (1992) 'The Poor Box and the Changing Face of Charity in Early Modern Europe' *Acta Institutionis Philosphiae et Aestheticae* 10, 33–54.

Beveridge, W (1948) *Voluntary Action: A Report on Methods of Social Advance* (London, George Allen & Unwin).

Big Issue (1997a) 'Tony Blair' *The Big Issue* 214 (6–12 January).

—— (1997b) 'Britain's Best PM?' *The Big Issue* 218 (3–9 February).

—— (1997c) 'The Big Issue: Helping the Homeless Help Themselves'.

—— (1997d) 'Selling the Big Issue the Easy Way'.

—— (1998). 'The Big Issue Code of Conduct'.

Bird, J (2002) *Retreat from the Streets* (London, Politeia).

Bourdieu, P (1987) 'The Force of Law: Toward a Sociology of the Juridical Field' *Hastings Law Journal* 38, 814–53.

—— (1997) 'Marginalia: Some Additional Notes on the Gift' in Alan D Schrift (ed), *The Logic of the Gift: Towards an Ethic of Generosity* (New York, Routledge).

Bristol (2004) 'Advertising Standards Decision Attacked as Very Dangerous', press release, 25 February.

Broadcasting Support Services (2002) *Change A Life End of Campaign Report* Compiled by Pete Edwards and Karen Elliott (Broadcasting Support Services, London).

Bulwer, J (1644; 1974) *Chirologia: or the Natural Language of the Hand* and *Chironomia: or the Art of Manual Rhetoric*, ed JW Cleary (Carbondale, Southern Illinois University).

Burnett, K (1986) 'Creating Successful Advertising' in K Burnett (ed), *Advertising by Charities* (London, Directory of Social Change).

—— (1992) *Relationship Fundraising: A Donor Approach to the Business of Raising Money* (London, White Lion Press).

—— (1996) *Friends for Life: Relationship Funding in Practice* (London, White Lion Press).

Burns, T (1992) *Erving Goffman* (London, Routledge).

Bushaway, B (1982) *Custom by Rite: Custom, Ceremony and Community in England, 1700–1800* (London, Junction Books).

Callon, M and Law, J (1989) 'On the Construction of Socio-Technical Networks: Content and Context Revisited' *Knowledge and Society: Studies in the Sociology of Science Past and Present* Vol 8, 57–83, 59.

Carroll, WC (1996) *Fat King, Lean Beggar: Representations of Poverty in the Age of Shakespeare* (Ithaca, Cornell University Press).

—— (1996b) 'The Crisis of the Sign: Vagrancy and Authority in the English Renaissance' *Semiotic* 108, 381–88.

Carvel, J (1990) 'Fourfold Rise in Arrest of Homeless under Vagrancy Law', *The Guardian*, 14 May, 1.

Cathay Pacific (1998) 'Cathay Pacific and UNICEF announce $3.6 Million Change for Good Result', press release (9 March).

Chadwick, E (1842; 1965) *Report on the Sanitary Condition of the Labouring Population of Gt. Britain* (Edinburgh, Edinburgh University Press).

Chalmers, T (1900) *Chalmers on Charity*, ed N Masterman (Westminster, Archibald Constable).

Chambliss, WJ (1964) 'A Sociological Analysis of the Law of Vagrancy' *Social Problems* 12, 67–77.

Charity Organisation Society (1891) '*The Science of Charity*', an Address Delivered by the Archbishop of Canterbury at the Annual Meeting of the London Charity Organisation Society, April 23, 1891, Occasional Paper 19 (Bodleian Library, John Johnson Collection).

Cheal, D (1988) *The Gift Economy* (New York, Routledge).

City Traders Group [Winchester] (1996) 'Winchester News' (December).

Clayson, C (1996) 'Street Wise' *Justice of the Peace and Local Government Law* (3 August), 573–75.

Clements, L, and Campbell, S (1997) 'The Criminal Justice and Public Order Act and Its Implications for Travellers' in T Acton (ed), *Gypsy Politics and Traveller Identity* (Hertfordshire, University of Hertfordshire Press).

Cohen, N (1990) 'Vagrancy Act Dismays Reformers', *The Independent*, 26 October, 5.

Colquhoun, P (1800) *A Treatise on the Police of the Metropolis, etc*, 6th edn (London, J Mawman).

—— (1806) *A Treatise on Indigence, Exhibiting a General View of National Resources for Productive Labour* (London, J Hatchard).

Corre, N (1984) 'A Proposal for Reform of the Law of Begging' *Criminal Law Review*, 750–53.

Corrigan, P, and Sayer, D (1985) *The Great Arch: English State Formation as Cultural Revolution* (Oxford, Basil Blackwell).

Cromarty, H, and Strickland, P (2018) 'Rough Sleepers and Anti-Social Behaviour (England)' House of Commons Briefing Paper Number 07836. 27 February 2018 (UK Parliament).

Cromarty, H, and McGuiness, T (2016) 'Rough Sleepers and Anti-Social Behaviour (England)' House of Commons Briefing Paper Number 07836. 13 December 2016 (UK Parliament).

Cunningham, H (1980) *Leisure in the Industrial Revolution* (London, Croom Helm).

Curtis, B (1995) 'Taking the State Back Out: Rose and Miller on Political Power' *British Journal of Sociology* 46, 575–89.

Danczuk, S (2000) 'Walk on by: Begging, street drinking and the giving age' (London, Crisis).

Davis, M (1990) *City of Quartz: Excavating the Future in Los Angeles* (London, Vintage).

Dawson, AJ (1923) *Britain's Lifeboats: The Story of a Century of Heroics* (London, Hodder and Stoughton).

Dean, H (2000) *Social Policy Review* 12, H Dean, R Sykes and R Woods (eds), (Newcastle, Social Policy Association).

Deane, M (1991) *The Constitution of Poverty: Towards a Genealogy of Liberal Governance* (London, Routledge).

DETR (Department of Environment, Transport and Regions) (Rough Sleepers Unit) (2000), *The Facts of Change A Life* (London, DETR).

DEFRA (Department for Environment, Food and Rural Affairs) (2002), *Living Places – Powers, Rights and Responsibilities: A Review of the Legislation Framework* (London, DEFRA).

Derrida, J (1992) *Given Time. 1. Counterfeit Money*. Translated by P Kamuf (Chicago, University of Chicago Press).

Douglas, M (1990) 'Foreword: No Free Gifts' in M Mauss, *The Gift: The Form and Reason for Exchange in Archaic Societies* (London, Routledge).

Downes, D (1998) 'Toughing It Out: From Labour Opposition to Labour Government' *Policy Studies* 19, 191–99.

Dumoulin, D, Orchard, B, Turner, S and Glew, C (2016) 'Stop the Scandal: an investigation into mental health and rough sleeping' (London, St Mungo's).

Durkheim, E (1915; 1947) *The Elementary Forms of the Religious Life: A Study in Religious Sociology* (Glencoe, IL, Free Press).

Eagleton, T (1990) *The Ideology of the Aesthetic* (Oxford, Blackwell).

Emerson, RE (1844; 1997) 'Gifts' in AD Schrift (ed), *The Logic of the Gift: Towards an Ethic of Generosity* (New York, Routledge).

End the Vagrancy Act Campaign (1991) Press release, 24 June (EVA 15).

Erskine, A and McIntosh I (1999) 'Why begging offends: historical perspectives and continuities in Begging Questions: Street-level economic activity and social policy failure. ed H.Dean (Bristol: The Policy Press).

Evening News (Edinburgh), 'Begging Battle Victory in Sight', *Evening News*, 29 August 1997, 1.

—— 'City Study into the Obvious Beggars Belief', *Evening News*, 22 September 1997, 2.

Fairhead, S (1981) *Persistent Petty Offenders* (London, Home Office).

Falkus, ME (1982) 'The Early Development of the British Gas Industry, 1790–1815' *Economic History Review* 35(2), 229–31.

Fido, J (1977) 'The Charity Organisation Society and Casework in London, 1869–1900' in AP Donajgrodzki (ed), *Social Control in Nineteenth Century Britain* (London, Croom Helm).

Fielding, J (1753) *An Account of the Origin and Effects of a Police Set on Foot* (London).

Finer, SE (1972) 'The Transmission of Benthamite Ideas, 1820–1850' in G Sutherland (ed), *Studies in the Growth of Nineteenth Century Government* (London, Routledge and Kegan Paul).

Fitzpatrick, S, and Jones, A (2005) 'Pursuing Social Justice or Social Cohesion? Coercion in Street Homelessness Policies in England' *Journal of Social Policy* 34(3), 389–406.

Fitzpatrick, S, and Kennedy, C (2000) 'The links between begging, rough sleeping and The Big Issue in Glasgow and Edinburgh' (York, Joseph Rowntree Foundation).

—— (2001) 'The Links between Begging and Rough Sleeping: A Question of Legitimacy?' *Housing Studies* 16(5), 549–68.

—— (2001) 'Begging, Rough Sleeping and Social Exclusion: Implications for Social Policy' *Urban Studies* 38(11), 2001–2016.

Flinn, MW (1965) 'Introduction' in *Report on the Sanitary Condition of the Labouring Population of Great Britain* (Edinburgh, Edinburgh University Press).

Foote, C (1956) 'Vagrancy-Type Law and Its Administration', *University of Pennsylvania Law Review* 104, 603–50.

Ford, R (1995) 'Rid Our Streets of the Beggars and Addicts, Says Straw', *The Times and Sunday Times*, 6 September, 2 (compact disc).

Foucault, M (1977) *Discipline and Punish* (London, Allan Lane).

—— (1980) *Power/Knowledge: Select Interviews and Other Writings*, ed C Gordon (Brighton, Harvest Press).

—— (1982) 'The Subject and Power' in H Dreyfus and P Rabinow (eds), *Foucault: Beyond Structuralism and Hermeneutics* (Chicago, University of Chicago Press).

—— (1985) *The Care of the Self* Vol 3, *The History of Sexuality* (New York, Pantheon).

—— (1988) 'Technologies of the Self' in LH Martin (ed), *Technologies of the Self: A Seminar with Michel Foucault* (Amherst, University of Massachusetts Press).

—— (1991) 'Governmentality' [1978] in G Burchell, C Gordon and P Miller (eds), *The Foucault Effect: Studies in Governmentality* (Hemel Hempstead, Harvester Wheatshead).

—— (1994a) 'Security, Territory and Population' in P Rabinow (ed), *Michel Foucault: Ethics* Vol 1 (London, Allen Lane).

—— (1994b) 'The Masked Philosopher' in P Rabinow (ed), *Michel Foucault: Ethics* Vol 1 (London, Allen Lane).

Garfinkel, H (1967) *Studies in Ethnomethodology* (Englewood Cliffs, NJ, Prentice-Hall).

Garland, D (1985) *Punishment and Welfare: A History of Penal Strategies* (London, Gower).

—— (1996) 'The Limits of the Sovereign State: Strategies of Crime Control in Contemporary Society' *British Journal of Criminology* 36 (4), 445–71.

—— (1997) '"Govermentality" and the Problem of Crime: Foucault, Criminology, Sociology', *Theoretical Criminology* 1(2), 173–214.

—— (2018) *Punishment and Welfare: A History of Penal Strategies* (New Orleans, Quid Pro).

George, MD (1966) *London Life in the Eighteenth Century* (Harmondsworth, Penguin).

Gillan, A (1999) 'Charity Rethink on Homeless' *Guardian Weekly*, 18–24 November, 8.

Ginzburg, C (1990) *Myths, Emblems, Clues*, trans J and AC Tedeschi (London, Hutchinson Radius).

Girouard, M (1985) *Cities and People: A Social and Architectural History* (New Haven, Yale University Press).

Goffman, E (1961a) *Encounters: Two Studies in the Sociology of Interaction* (Indianapolis, Bobbs-Merrill).

—— (1961b) *Asylums: On the Characteristics of Total Institutions* (Harmondsworth, Penguin).

—— (1963a) *Behaviour in Public Places: Notes on the Social Organization of Gatherings* (New York, Macmillan).

—— (1963b) *Stigma: Notes on the Management of Spoiled Identity* (Englewood Cliffs, NJ, Prentice Hall.

—— (1971) *Relations in Public: Microstudies of the Public Order* (New York, Basic Books).

—— (1972) *Interaction Ritual* (Harmondsworth, Penguin).

Gomien, D, David, H and Leo Z (1996) *Law and Practice of the European Convention on Human Rights and the European Social Charter* (Strasbourg, Council of Europe).

Gordon, C (1991) 'Government Rationality: An Introduction' in G Burchell, C Gordon and P Miller (eds), *The Foucault Effect: Studies in Governmentality* (Hemel Hempstead, Harvester Wheatshead).

Gouldner, AW (1973a) 'The Norm of Reciprocity' in *For Sociology: Renewal and Critique in Sociology Today* (London, Allen Lane).

—— (1973b) 'The Importance of Something for Nothing' in *For Sociology: Renewal and Critique in Sociology Today* (London, Allen Lane, 1973).

Graham, V (1995) 'Street Unit Helps Homeless and Targets Problem Beggars' *Police Review*, 2 June, 13.

Gramsci, A (1971) *Selections from the Prison Notebooks* (London, Lawrence and Wishard).

Greater Manchester Police (1995) 'Police Scheme to Help Homeless' news release PR/170, 8 December.

—— (1997) 'City Centre Homeless and Begging Initiative, May 1995 to January 1997' with Appendix 1, 'Statistics Summary' and Appendix 2, 'Graphs and Charts'.

Guardian Weekly (1999) 'A Tsar in the Soup', 19–24 November, 14.

Hacking, I (1998) 'Canguilhem amid the Cyborgs' *Economy and Society* 27(2/3), 202–16.

Handler, J (1992) 'Discretion: Power, Trust, Quiescence' in K Hawkins (ed), *The Uses of Discretion* (Oxford, Clarendon Press).

Haraway, DJ (1991) *Simians, Cyborgs and Women* (London, Free Association Books).

Harrison, B (1966) 'Philanthropy and the Victorians' *Victorian Studies* 9(4), 353–74.

Healy, J (1988) *The Grass Arena* (London, Faber and Faber).

Hendry, S, 'We've Got as Much Right as You to Sit on Streets: Beggars Hit Back at News Plan' *Evening News*, 10 September 1997, 6.

Higgins, M (1985) *From Slavery to Vagrancy in Brazil* (New Brunswick, NJ, Rutgers University Press).

Hill, T (1999) *Underground* (London, Faber).

Hilton, B (1988) *The Age of Atonement* (Oxford, Clarendon Press).

Hermer, J (1997) 'Keeping Oshawa Beautiful: Policing the Loiterer in Public Nuisance By-law 72–94' *Canadian Journal of Law and Society* 12(1), 172–92.

Hermer, J and Hunt, A (1996) 'Official Graffiti of the Everyday' *Law and Society Review* 30(3), 455–80.

Hermer, J and MacGregor, D (2007) 'Urban Renaissance and the Contested Legality of Begging in Scotland' in Atkinson, R and Helms, G (eds), *Securing an Urban Renaissance: Crime, Community and British Urban Policy* (Bristol, The Policy Press).

Heywood, JS (1959) *Children in Care: The Development of the Service for the Deprived Child* (London, Routledge and Kegan Paul).

Hitchcock, T (2005) 'Begging on the Streets of Eighteenth-Century London' *Journal of British Studies* 44, 478–498.

HMSO (Her Majesty's Stationery Office) (1974) *Working Party on Vagrancy and Street Offences* (London, HMSO).

—— (1976) *Report of the Working Party on Vagrancy and Street Offences* (London, HMSO).

—— (1981) *Third Report from the Home Affairs Committee, Session 1980–81: Vagrancy Offences* (London, HMSO).

—— (1991a) *The Children Act: Guidance and Regulations*, Vol 1, *Court Orders* (London, HMSO).

—— (1991b) *The Children Act: Guidance and Regulations*, Vol 3, *Family Placements* (London, HMSO).

—— (1991c) *Working Together under the Children Act 1989: A Guide to Arrangements for Inter-agency Co-operation for the Protection of Children from Abuse* (London, HMSO).

—— (1995) *Child Protection: Message from Research* (London, HMSO).

—— (1998) *Rough Sleeping: Report by the Social Exclusion Unit, July 1998*, CM 4008 (London, HMSO).

—— (2003) 'Respect and Responsibility: Taking a Stand Against Anti-Social Behaviour' (London, HMSO).

Holme, C, 'Councillors "Outed" over Beggars', *The Herald*, 11 September 1997, 5.

Home Office (1985) *Police and Criminal Evidence Act 1984*, circular 88/1985, 18 December.

—— (1998a) *A Community Crime Reduction Partnership: The Retail Contribution* (London, Home Office Communication Directorate).

—— (1998b) *Guidance on Statutory Crime and Disorder Partnerships* (London, Home Office Communication Directorate).

—— (1999) *The Crime and Disorder Act: Guidance – Anti-Social Behaviour Orders*.

—— (2004) *Drugs Use and Begging: A Practice Guide* (London, Home Office).

Homeless Link (2016) 'Responses to begging: Case studies of local responses' (London, Homeless Link).

Hough, M, Edmunds, M, Turnbull, PJ and May, T (1999) 'Doing Justice to Treatment: Referring offenders to drug services' (London, Home Office).

Housden, LG (1955) *The Prevention of Cruelty to Children* (London, Jonathan Cape).

Hunt, A (1993) *Explorations in Law and Society* (New York, Routledge).

Hunt, A and Wickham, G (1994) *Foucault and Law: Towards a Sociology of Law as Governance* (London, Pluto).

Hyde, L (1979) *The Gift: Imagination and the Erotic Life of Property* (New York, Random House).

Ignatieff, M (1978) *A Just Measure of Pain: The Penitentiary in the Industrial Revolution, 1750–1850* (London, Macmillan).

—— (1994) *The Needs of Strangers* (London, Vintage).

Ikin, AE (1933) *Children and Young Persons Act, 1933* (Toronto, Sir Isaac Pitmans & Sons).

Ivins, WM (1973) *On the Rationalization of Sight* (New York, Plenum).

Ivison, D (1998) 'The Technical and the Political: Discourses of Race, Reasons of State' *Social and Legal Studies* 7(4), 561–66.

Jaffe, A (1990) 'Detecting the Beggar: Arthur Conan Doyle, Henry Mayhew, and "The Man with the Twisted Lip"' *Representations* (Summer), 96–117.

Johnsen, S, and Fitzpatrick, S (2008) 'The Use of Enforcement to Combat Begging and Street Drinking in England: A High Risk Strategy?' *European Journal of Homelessness* 2, 191–204.

—— (2010) 'Revanchist Sanitisation or Coercive Care? The Use of Enforcement to Combat Begging, Street Drinking and Rough Sleeping in England' *Urban Studies* 47(8), 1703–1723.

Jones, D (1982) *Crime, Protest, Community and Police in Nineteenth Century Britain* (London, Routledge Kegan and Paul).

Jones, GS (1971) *Outcast London* (Oxford, Clarendon Press).

Jowett, S, Banks, G, Brown, A and Goodall, G (2001) *Looking for Change: The Role and Impact of Begging on the Lives of People Who Beg* (London, RSU).

Kahn, R and Cannell, C (1957) *The Dynamics of Interviewing* (New York, John Wiley).

Kelling, GL and Coles, CM (1998) *Fixing Broken Windows: Restoring Order and Reducing Crime in Our Community* (New York, Free Press).

Kelly, S (1996) 'Police Launch New Guide to Help the City's Homeless Population' *Big Issue*, 19 December, 6.

Kennedy, C, and Fitzpatrick, S (2000) 'Begging, homelessness and social exclusion: implications for housing and social policies', Housing in the 21st Century: Fragmentation and Reorientation, Gävle, June (European Network for Housing Research Conference).

Knemeyer, FL (1980) 'Polizei' *Economy and Society* 9(2), 172–96.

Lacey, N (1998) *Unspeakable Subjects: Feminist Essays in Legal and Social Theory* (Oxford, Hart Publishing).

Laing, P (1997) 'Beggars Send Their Demands by Fax: Hi-Tech Battle against Ban Bid', *Daily Record*, 8 September, 17.

Latour, B (1986) 'Visualization and Cognition: Thinking with Eyes and Hands' *Knowledge and Society: Studies in the Sociology of Culture Past and Present* 6, 1–40.

—— (1987) *Science in Action: How to Follow Scientists and Engineers through Society* (Milton Keynes, Open University Press).

Law, J and Whittaker, J (1988) 'On the Art of Representation: Notes on the Politics of Visualisation' in G Fyfe and J Law (eds), *Picturing Power: Visual Depictions and Social Relations* (London, Routledge).

Liberal Democrats (1990) *Federal Conference Report*, Blackpool, 16–20 September.

Lister, D (1997) 'Beggars "Ruining Edinburgh"' *The Independent*, 12 August, 3.

Lister, S, Seddon, T, Wincup, E, Barrett, S and Traynor, P (2008) 'Street policing of problem drug users' (Joseph Rowntree Foundation).

Lofland, L (1973) *A World of Strangers: Order and Interaction in Urban Public Space* (New York, Basic Books).

Loveday, B (1999) 'Tough on Crime or Tough on the Causes of Crime? An Evaluation of Labour's Crime and Disorder Legislation' *Crime Prevention and Community Safety: An International Journal* 1, 7–24.

Loveland, I (1995) *Housing Homeless Persons* (Oxford, Clarendon Press).

Luther, M (1962) 'Ordinance of a Common Chest' in Jaroslav Pelikan HJ, Grimm HJ, Lehman HT and Oswold HC (eds), *Luther's Works*, Vol 45 (Philadelphia, Muhlenberg).

Lynch, DC and Lundquist, L (1996) *Digital Money: The New Era of Internet Commerce* (New York, John Wiley and Sons).

Maconochie, A (1846) *Crime and Punishment: The Mark System, Framed to Mix Persuasion with Punishment, and Make Their Effect Improving, Yet Their Operation Severe* (London, J Hatchard and Son).

—— (1855) *The Mark System of Prison Discipline* (London, Thomas Harrison).

Macara, CW (1922) *Getting the World to Work* (Manchester, Sherratt and Hughes).

MacKinnon, M (1987) 'English Poor Law Policy and the Crusade against Outrelief' *Journal of Economic History* 47(3), 603–25.

Marshall, D (1926) *The English Poor in the Eighteenth Century* (London, George Routledge and Sons).

Marshall, C and Rossman, G (1995) *Designing Qualitative Research* (London, Sage).

Marxism Today (1998) Special Issue (November/December).

Mauss, M (1990) *The Gift: The Form and Reason for Exchange in Archaic Societies*. Translated by WD Halls (London, Routledge).

Mayhew, H (1967 [1861–62]) *London Labour and the London Poor: A Cyclopaedia of the Condition and Earnings of Those That Will Work, Those That Cannot Work, and Those That Will Not Work* (London, Cass).

McBeth, J (1997), 'Capital's Beggars Needy or Greedy?' *The Scotsman*, 1997, 22.

MCCI [Manchester Chamber of Commerce and Industry] (1995) 'Special Unit to Tackle Problem of Begging on Manchester's Streets', press release, 23 May.

McMullan, JL (1998) 'The Arresting Eye: Discourse, Surveillance and Disciplinary Administration in Early English Police Thinking' *Social and Legal Studies* 7(1), 97–128.

Melville Lee, WL (1901) *A History of Police in England* (London, Methuen).

Millington, A (1996) 'Beggared in the Name of Charity' *The Observer*, 17 March.

Mitchell, D (1997) 'The Annihilation of Space by Law: The Roots and Implications of Anti-homeless Laws in the United States' *Antipode* 29(3), 303–36.

—— (1998a) 'Anti-homeless Laws and Public Space I: Begging and the First Amendment' *Urban Geography* 19(1), 6–11.

—— (1998b) 'Anti-homeless Laws and Public Space II: Further Constitutional Issues' *Urban Geography* 19(2), 98–104.

Mitchell, WJT (1994) *Picture Theory: Essays on Verbal and Visual Representation* (Chicago, University of Chicago Press).

More, T (1895 [1518]) *The Utopia of Sir Thomas More*, trans and ed JH Lupton (Oxford, Clarendon Press).

Morris, M (1986) 'Why Advertise?' in Burnett, K (ed), *Advertising by Charities* (London, Directory of Social Change).

Morrison, N, 'City of Edinburgh Byelaw' *Evening News*, 29 August 1997, 2.

Mowat, CL (1961) *The Charity Organisation Society, 1869–1913* (London, Methuen).

Murdoch, L (2003) *Begging 'imposters', street theatre and the shadow economy of the Victorian city*, unpublished paper presented at the North American Victorian Studies Association (NAVSA) Conference, Bloomingdale, IN.

Napier, A (1997) 'Stopping Beggars, Helping Homeless' *Hampshire Chronicle*, 28 January, 1.

NAPO [National Association of Probation Officers] (1990) 'Dramatic Rise in Vagrancy Prosecutions', press release, 14 May.

Neil, A, 'Scapegoats for Squalor' *The Scotsman*, 28 June 1997, A16.

Nieman, A, press release, 25 February 2004.

Nietzsche, FW (1909) *Beyond Good and Evil: Prelude to a Philosophy of the Future* (Edinburgh, TN Foulis).

O'Connor, P (1963) *Britain in the Sixties: Vagrancy, Ethos and Actuality* (London, Penguin).

O'Farrell, J (1999) *Things Can Only Get Better: Eighteen Miserable Years in the Life of a Labour Supporter, 1979–1997* (London, Black Swan).

O'Malley, P (1991) 'Legal Networks and Domestic Security' *Studies in Law, Politics and Society* 11, 171–90.

Owen, D (1965) *English Philanthropy, 1660–1960* (London, Oxford University Press).

Oxford University Gazette (1998) 'New Move to Help City's Homeless', 17 December, 512.

Poe, EA (1983) *The Unabridged Edgar Allan Poe* (Philadelphia, Running Press).

Pugliatti, P (2003) *Beggary and Theatre in Early Modern England* (Farnham, Ashgate).

Public Health England (2018) 'Evidence review: Adults complex needs (with a particular focus on street begging and street sleeping' (PHE Publications, London).

Pullan, B (1971) *Rich and Poor in Renaissance Venice* (Oxford, Blackwell).

Ramsey, B (1982) 'Almsgiving in the Latin Church: The Late Fourth and Early Fifth Centuries', *Theological Studies* 43(2), 226–59.

Randall, G (1994) 'Single Homelessness in Manchester: A Report for Crisis', 6 May.

Ribton-Turner, CJ (1887) *A History of Vagrants and Vagrancy and Beggars and Begging* (London, Chapman and Hall).

Roberts, MJD (1988) 'Public and Private in Early Nineteenth-Century London: The Vagrant Act of 1822 and Its Enforcement' *Social History* 13(3), 273–94.

—— (1991) 'Reshaping the Gift Relationship: The London Mendicity Society and the Suppression of Begging in England, 1818–1869' *International Review of Social History* 36, 201–31.

Rojek, C (1992) '"The Eye of Power": Moral Regulation and the Professionalization of Leisure Management from the 1830s to the 1950s' *Society and Leisure* 15(1), 355–73.

Rose, L (1988) *Rogues and Vagabonds: Vagrancy Underworld in Britain, 1815–1985* (London, Routledge).

Rose, N (1998) *Governing Freedom* (Cambridge, Cambridge University Press).

Rose, N and Valverde, M (1998) 'Governed by Law?' *Social and Legal Studies* 7(4), 541–51.

Ryan, M (1999) 'Penal Policy Making Towards the Millennium: Elites and Populists, New Labour and the New Criminology' *International Journal of the Sociology of Law* 27, 1–22.

Sabine, EL (1933) 'Butchering in Mediaeval London' *Speculum* 8(3), 335–53.

—— (1937) 'City Cleaning in Mediaeval London' *Speculum* 12(1), 19–43.

Sack, J (1998) *Street Music and Musicians: The Physical and Aural Nature of Performance*, thesis, Faculty of Anthropology and Geography, University of Oxford.

Sahlins, M (1997) 'The Spirit of the Gift' in AD Schrift (ed), *The Logic of the Gift: Towards an Ethic of Generosity* (New York, Routledge).

Salter, FR (1926) *Some Early Tracts on Poor Relief* (London, Methuen).

Sanders, B and Albanese, F (2017) 'An examination of the scale and impact of enforcement interventions on street homeless people in England and Wales' (London, Crisis).

Scott, R (1969) *The Making of Blind Men* (New York, Russell Sage Foundation).

The Scotsman (1997a) 'Zero Tolerance for Council Failures', editorial, 10 September, 11.

—— (1997b) 'Councillors Who Back Motion', 10 September, 3.

Schrift, AD (1997) *The Logic of the Gift: Towards an Ethic of Generosity* (New York, Routledge).

—— (1997) 'Introduction: Why Gift?' in AD Schrift (ed), *The Logic of the Gift: Towards an Ethic of Generosity* (New York, Routledge).

Simmel, G (1971) 'The Metropolis and Mental Life' in DN Levine (ed), *Georg Simmel: On Individuality and Social Forms* (Chicago, University of Chicago Press).

Skolnick, J (1999) 'Urban Crime Control Theory' *Theoretical Criminology* 3(2), 231–38.

Smith, DE (1990) *Texts, Facts and Femininity: Exploring the Relations of Ruling* (London, Routledge).

Smith, JT (1817) *Vagabondia; or, Anecdotes of Mendicant Wanderers Through the Streets of London* (London, np).

—— (1839) *The Cries of London: Exhibiting Several of the Itinerant Traders of Antient and Modern Times* (London, John Bowyer Nichols and Son).

Smith, N (1996) *The New Urban Frontier* (London, Routledge).

Strathern, M (1997) 'Partners and Consumers: Making Relations Visible' in AD Schrift (ed), *The Logic of the Gift: Towards an Ethic of Generosity* (New York, Routledge).

Strier, R (1979) 'Herbert and Tears' *ELH: A Journal of English Literary History* 46(2), 221–47.

Thevénot, L (1984) 'Rules and Implements: Investment in Forms' *Social Science Information* 23(1), 1–45.

Taylor, B (1991) *Vagrant Writing: Social and Semiotic Disorders in the English Renaissance* (Toronto, University of Toronto Press).

Thomas, B (2018) Homelessness kills: An analysis of the mortality of homeless people in early twenty-first century England (London, Crisis).

Thornton, KD (2018) 'Power Politics and the Representation of Poverty: The Nottingham Community Protection #Givesmart Campaign' *Visual Culture in Britain* 19(2), 237–54.

Titmuss, RM (1970) *The Gift Relationship: From Human Blood to Social Policy* (London, George Allen and Unwin).

Valverde, M (1994) *Studies in Moral Regulation* (Toronto, Centre of Criminology, University of Toronto).

Vardi, L (1993) 'Constructing the Harvest: Gleaners, Farmers, and Officials in Early Modern France' *American Historical Review* 98(5), 1424–47.

Vasgar, J and Scott, K (2000), 'Crime Risk of Anti-begging Policy' *The Guardian*, 31 October.

Vine, B (1991) *King Solomon's Carpet* (London, Viking).

Wahlstedt, E (2013) 'Evaluation study for the Oxford Begging Initiative' (Oxford City Council).

Ward, B (1990) 'Panhandlers to Take Plastic in Charge-It Charity Scheme' *Ottawa Citizen*, 31 March.

Wasik, M and Taylor, R (1991) *Blackstone's Guide to the Criminal Justice Act, 1991* (London, Blackstone).

Watts, B, Fitzpatrick, S and Johnsen, S (2018) 'Controlling Homeless People? Power, Interventionism and Legitimacy' *Journal of Social Policy* 47(2), 235–52.

Whitfield, N (2013) 'Who is my stranger? Origins of the gift in wartime London, 1939–45' *Journal of the Royal Anthropological Institute* 19(S1), 95–117.

Williams, R (1985) *The Country and the City* (London, Hogarth Press).

Wilson, W (2018) 'Rough sleeping (England)' House of Commons Briefing Paper Number 02007, 23 February (UK Parliament).

Winchester Churches Nightshelter (1996) Annual Report 1995–1996.

—— (1997) Annual Report 1996–1997.

Wohl, AS (1983) *Endangered Lives: Public Health in Victorian Britain* (London, Methuen).

Working Party on Vagrancy (1974) 'A Working Party on Vagrancy and Street Offences working paper' (HMSO).

WWW [World Wildlife Fund] (1997) 'Fact Card: A–Z of Fundraising'.

Zelizer, VA (1994) *The Social Meaning of Money* (New York, Basic Books).

INDEX

www.ingramcontent.com/pod-product-compliance
Lightning Source LLC
Chambersburg PA
CBHW050438280326
41932CB00013BA/2167